WONDER WOMAN

THE TRUE AMAZON

WON
WOM

THE TRUE A

DER
AN
MAZON

JILL THOMPSON
Writer and Artist

JASON ARTHUR
Letterer

Wonder Woman created by
William Moulton Marston

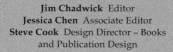

Jim Chadwick Editor
Jessica Chen Associate Editor
Steve Cook Design Director – Books
and Publication Design

Bob Harras Senior VP – Editor-in-Chief, DC Comics

WONDER WOMAN: THE TRUE AMAZON. Published by DC Comics. Copyright © 2016 DC Comics.
All Rights Reserved. All characters, their distinctive likenesses and related elements featured in this
publication are trademarks of DC Comics. The stories, characters and incidents featured in this publication
are entirely fictional. DC Comics does not read or accept unsolicited submissions of ideas,
stories or artwork.

DC Comics, 2900 West Alameda Ave., Burbank, CA 91505
Printed by RR Donnelley, Salem, VA, USA. 8/26/16. First Printing.
HC ISBN: 978-1-4012-4901-4

Library of Congress Cataloging-in-Publication Data is available.

INTRODUCTION
BY MARIKO TAMAKI

How do you introduce someone like Wonder Woman?

No small task.

I thought maybe I should write this introduction while simultaneously doing something kind of… extraordinary. Maybe because I spend a lot of time thinking about superheroes, and this makes my life seem kind of…lazy.

Like, what am I doing right now, really?

Sitting in my kitchen.

You know who rarely sits around in her kitchen listening to music and typing? Wonder Woman.

But it's not easy writing on a laptop while astride a great winged beast, wielding a long sword in battle, or while diving into a raging waterfall.

Laptops and waterfalls don't really mix.

And the truth is, my job as a writer isn't to be amazing, it's to think about people who are amazing, people who are heroic.

Take Wonder Woman, for example.

I've been thinking about Wonder Woman a lot lately, maybe because, like I said, I've been thinking about super-people in general, and Wonder Woman was my first superhero.

As a kid, Wonder Woman was the only hero I wanted to be for Halloween. Because Wonder Woman was, in my mind, the original goddess, an all-powerful warrior fighting for truth and justice whom every 9-year-old girl or boy should aspire to be for Halloween. (And I would have if mother hadn't been dead set on making me a Christmas tree costume instead.)

Of course, wanting to BE Wonder Woman didn't necessarily mean I knew all that much about her. Wonder Woman is kind of hard to get to know. She's an Amazon, and they tend to keep to themselves on their island. She's pretty busy saving the day most of the time, so she doesn't really have time to hang out. In her earlier manifestation, she transported herself in the strangest, most subtle aircraft ever invented: the invisible plane.

I think it's hard to get to know superheroes like Wonder Woman, because they spend so much time doing extraordinary things. It's hard to watch someone jump over a building and care if that person likes pizza, or the color green, or cats.

Who cares?! They just jumped over a building!
All the same, I think it's important to get to know our heroes. Because our heroes are saving the day, they're fighting the good fight; our heroes are the ones saving our society, maybe it would be nice to know how they fit into it.

I think if we do want to know our heroes, we need to know about more than just their daring adventures. We understand our heroes, the hearts of our heroes, when artists like Jill Thompson show us something about the hero that is more than just saving the day. Thompson gets to the core of Wonder Woman by showing us where Wonder Woman came from.

Because, hey, guess what? Wonder Woman wasn't always a woman. Just like you used to be a scrappy little kid yelling at your mom about how a Christmas tree isn't a real Halloween costume, Wonder Woman was a girl named Diana, a feisty, kind of bratty, albeit very powerful little kid, created by the gods.

Before she was Wonder Woman, Diana was a charmer and a great champion, a conqueror of seemingly unconquerable creatures, a retriever of seemingly irretrievable treasure, and she was a person who was not always the most fun to hang out with.

And, over time, as you'll see in this story, she changed.

Because people who can fly and crush diamonds with their pinky fingers are subject to the forces of change.

Even if the Diana you're about to meet does not seem like the Wonder Woman you know, she is still the Wonder Woman we love and aspire to be, on Halloween and otherwise, and hers is a legend we can all learn from. Hers is a legend about a society of powerful women who created, for good and for bad, a heroine for the ages. And it was an interesting journey, that which created our Wonder Woman.

Thompson's story is gorgeous and inspiring and heartfelt, a story about battles and gods, mothers and daughters, and friends. Thompson's characters are a cast I'm glad I got the pleasure to know.

And so, without further ado, may I introduce, our hero, Wonder Woman.

Mariko Tamaki's work includes the novels (You) Set Me on Fire *and* Saving Montgomery Sole, *comics* Skim *and* This One Summer, *co-created with Jillian Tamaki.* This One Summer *received Doug Wright and Eisner Awards in 2015, as well as Caldecott and Printz Honors. Mariko is currently working on the* Tomb Raider *series for Dark Horse comics, with Phillip Sevy. She has also written for radio, theater and film, including her own short film* Happy 16th Birthday, Kevin.

DEDICATION

For Terry Austin, Bill Reinhold and P. Craig Russell. Thank you for your kindness and encouragement and the lessons you taught me. They changed my life and made this work possible!

And a huge thank-you to Karen Berger, who gave me my first job at DC Comics, pencilling Wonder Woman. There were very few women working as artists on major books back then. Thanks for giving me the ball. I ran with it. Look how well it's turned out!

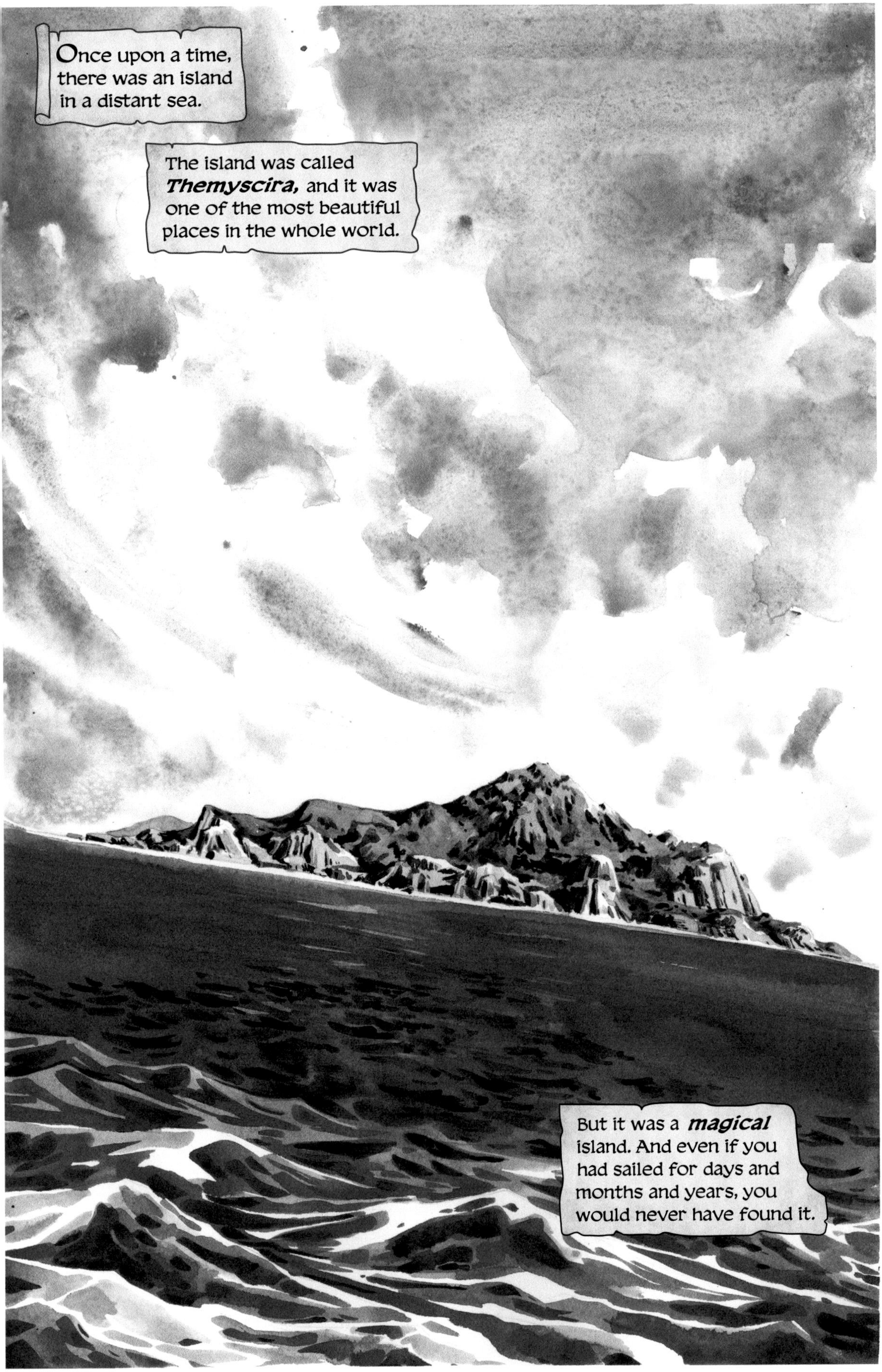
Once upon a time, there was an island in a distant sea.
The island was called *Themyscira,* and it was one of the most beautiful places in the whole world.
But it was a *magical* island. And even if you had sailed for days and months and years, you would never have found it.

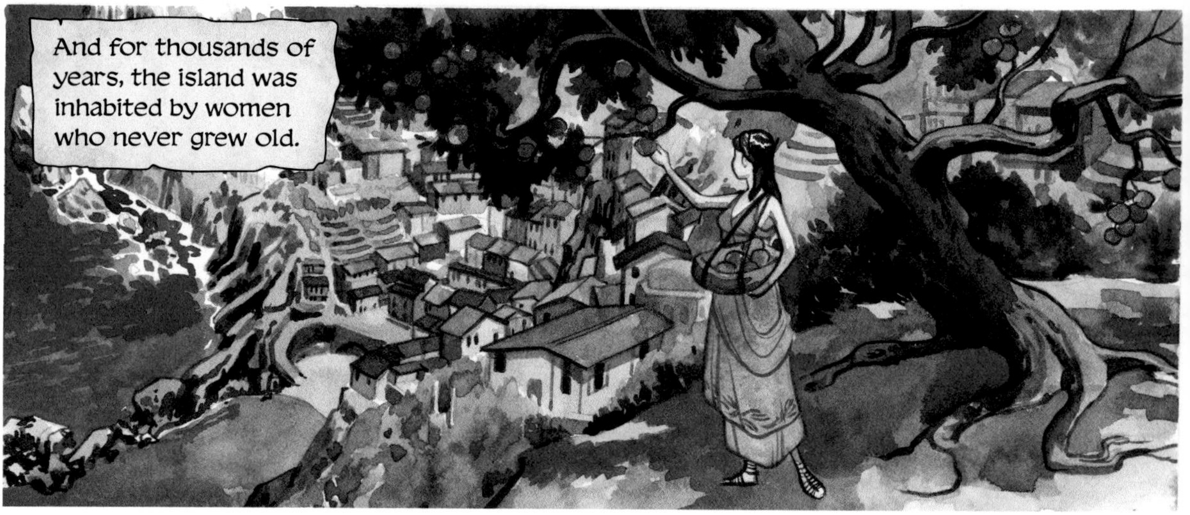
And for thousands of years, the island was inhabited by women who never grew old.

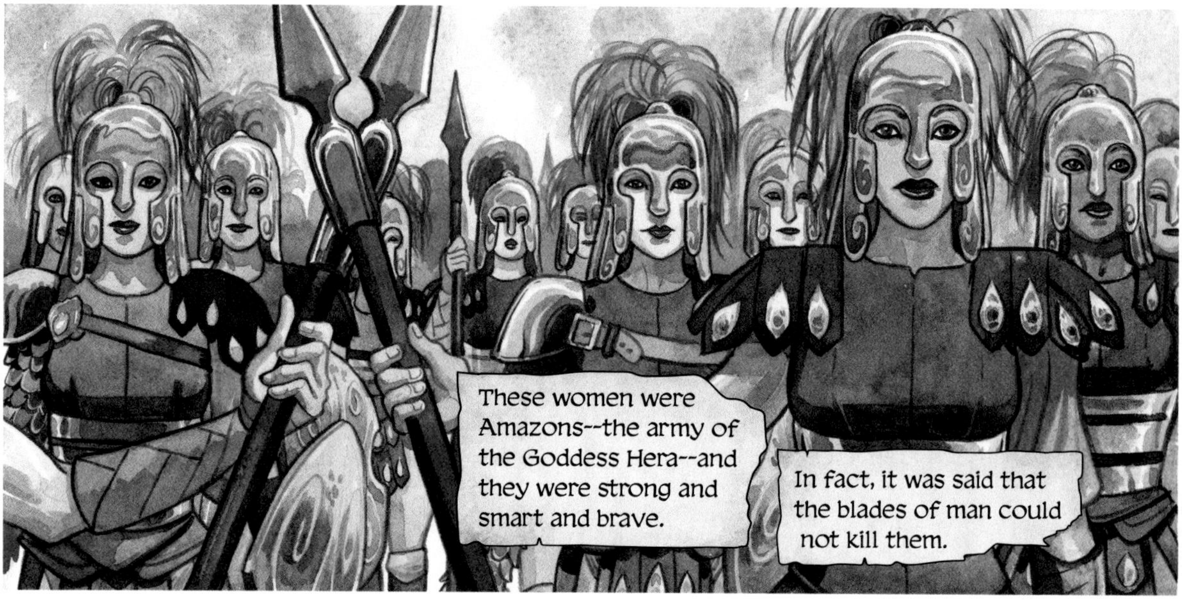
These women were Amazons--the army of the Goddess Hera--and they were strong and smart and brave.
In fact, it was said that the blades of man could not kill them.

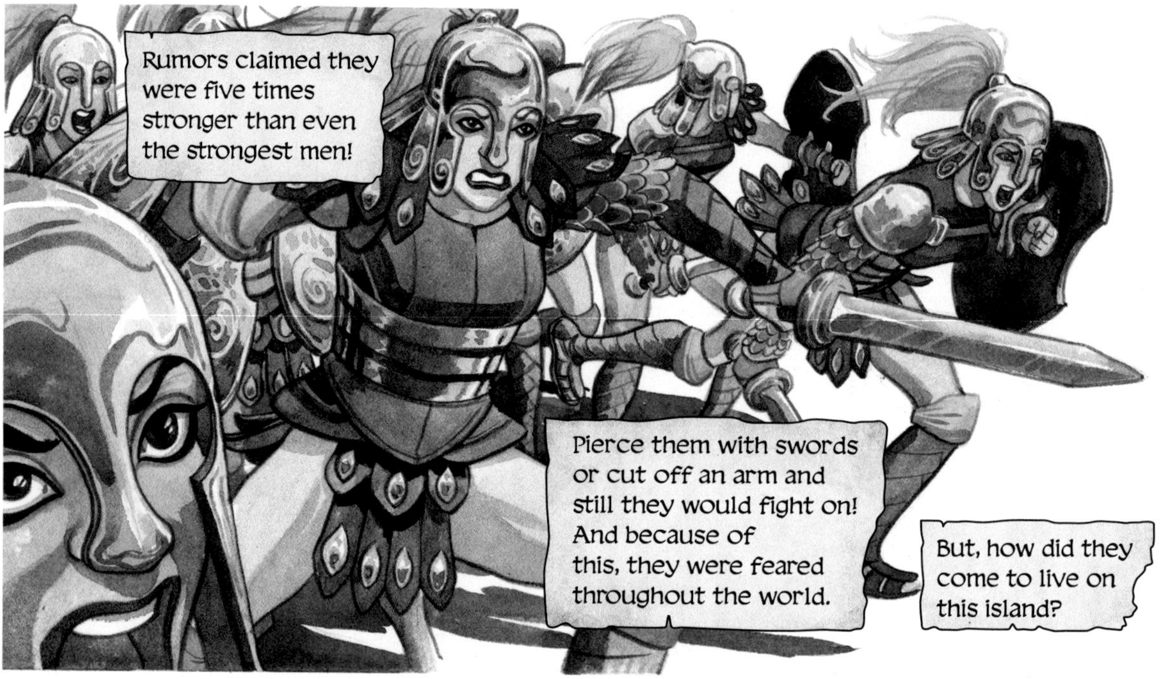
Rumors claimed they were five times stronger than even the strongest men!
Pierce them with swords or cut off an arm and still they would fight on! And because of this, they were feared throughout the world.
But, how did they come to live on this island?

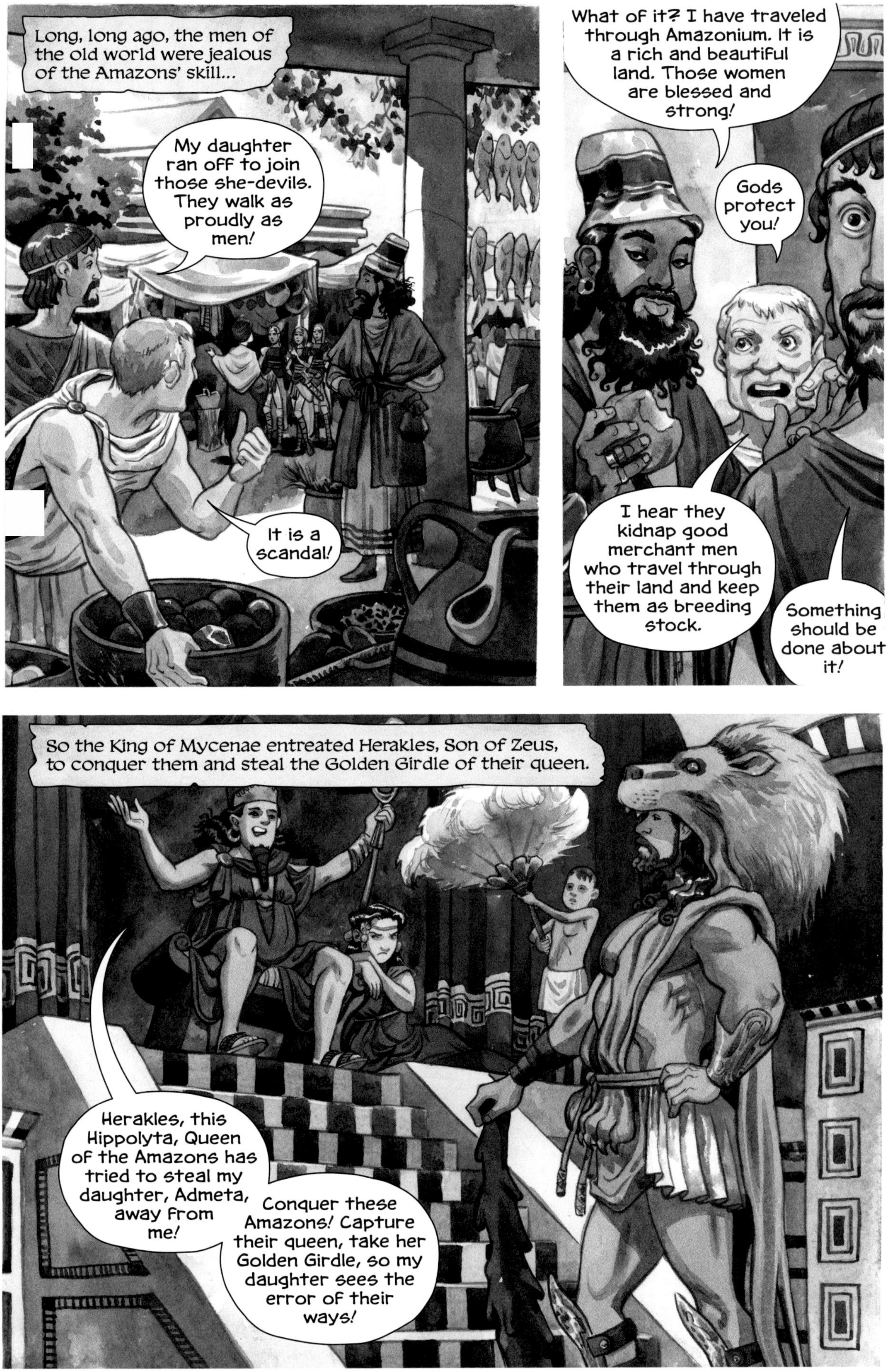

Long, long ago, the men of the old world were jealous of the Amazons' skill...
My daughter ran off to join those she-devils. They walk as proudly as men!
It is a scandal!
What of it? I have traveled through Amazonium. It is a rich and beautiful land. Those women are blessed and strong!
Gods protect you!
I hear they kidnap good merchant men who travel through their land and keep them as breeding stock.
Something should be done about it!
So the King of Mycenae entreated Herakles, Son of Zeus, to conquer them and steal the Golden Girdle of their queen.
Herakles, this Hippolyta, Queen of the Amazons has tried to steal my daughter, Admeta, away from me!
Conquer these Amazons! Capture their queen, take her Golden Girdle, so my daughter sees the error of their ways!

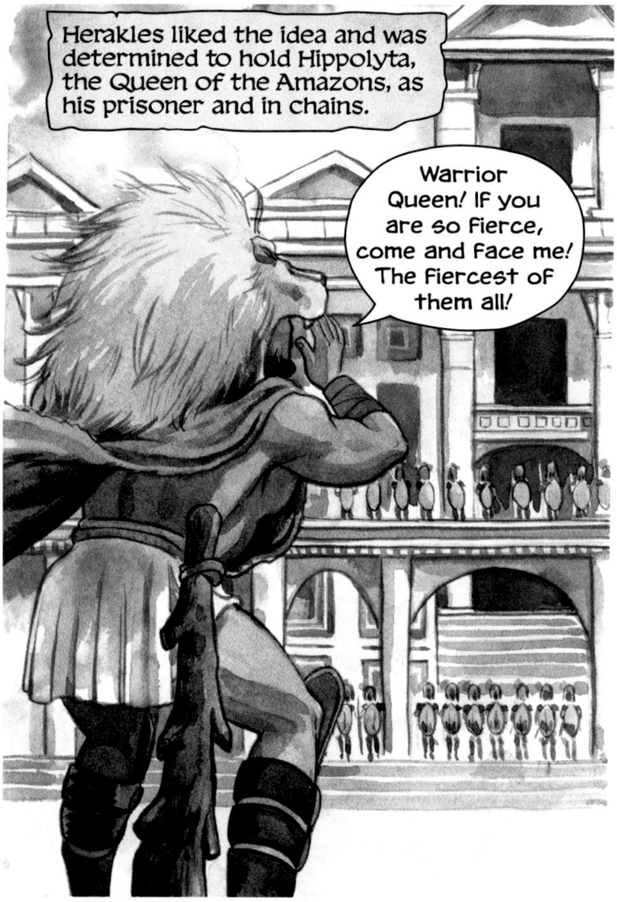
Herakles liked the idea and was determined to hold Hippolyta, the Queen of the Amazons, as his prisoner and in chains.
Warrior Queen! If you are so fierce, come and face me! The fiercest of them all!

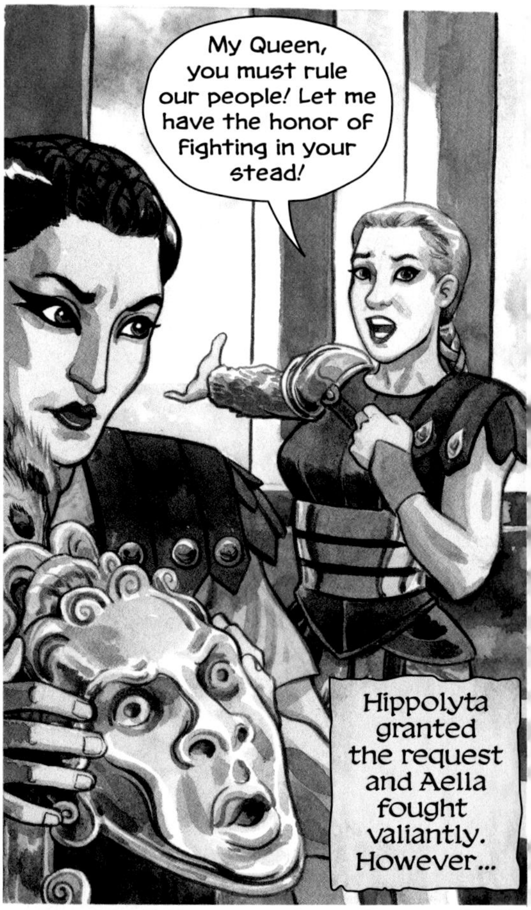
My Queen, you must rule our people! Let me have the honor of fighting in your stead!
Hippolyta granted the request and Aella fought valiantly. However...

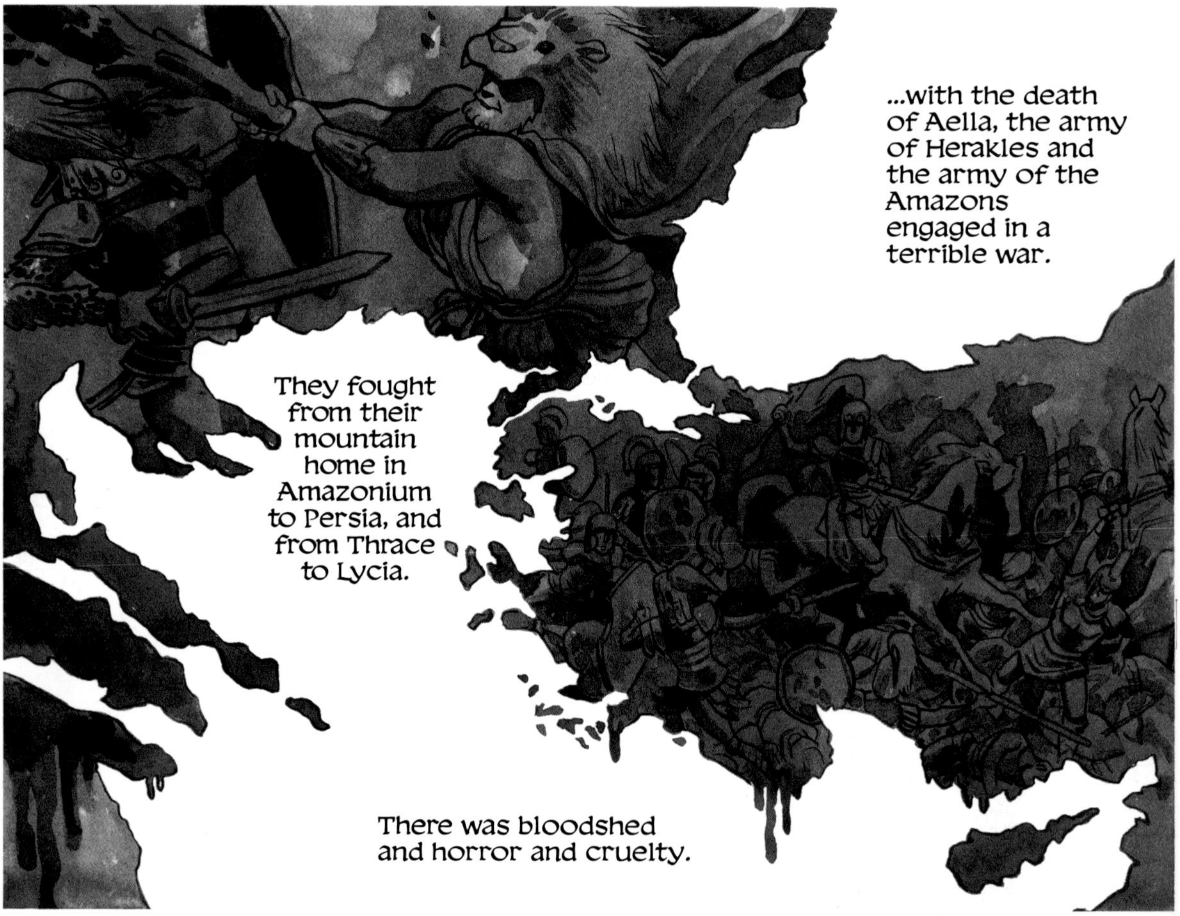
...with the death of Aella, the army of Herakles and the army of the Amazons engaged in a terrible war.
They fought from their mountain home in Amazonium to Persia, and from Thrace to Lycia.
There was bloodshed and horror and cruelty.

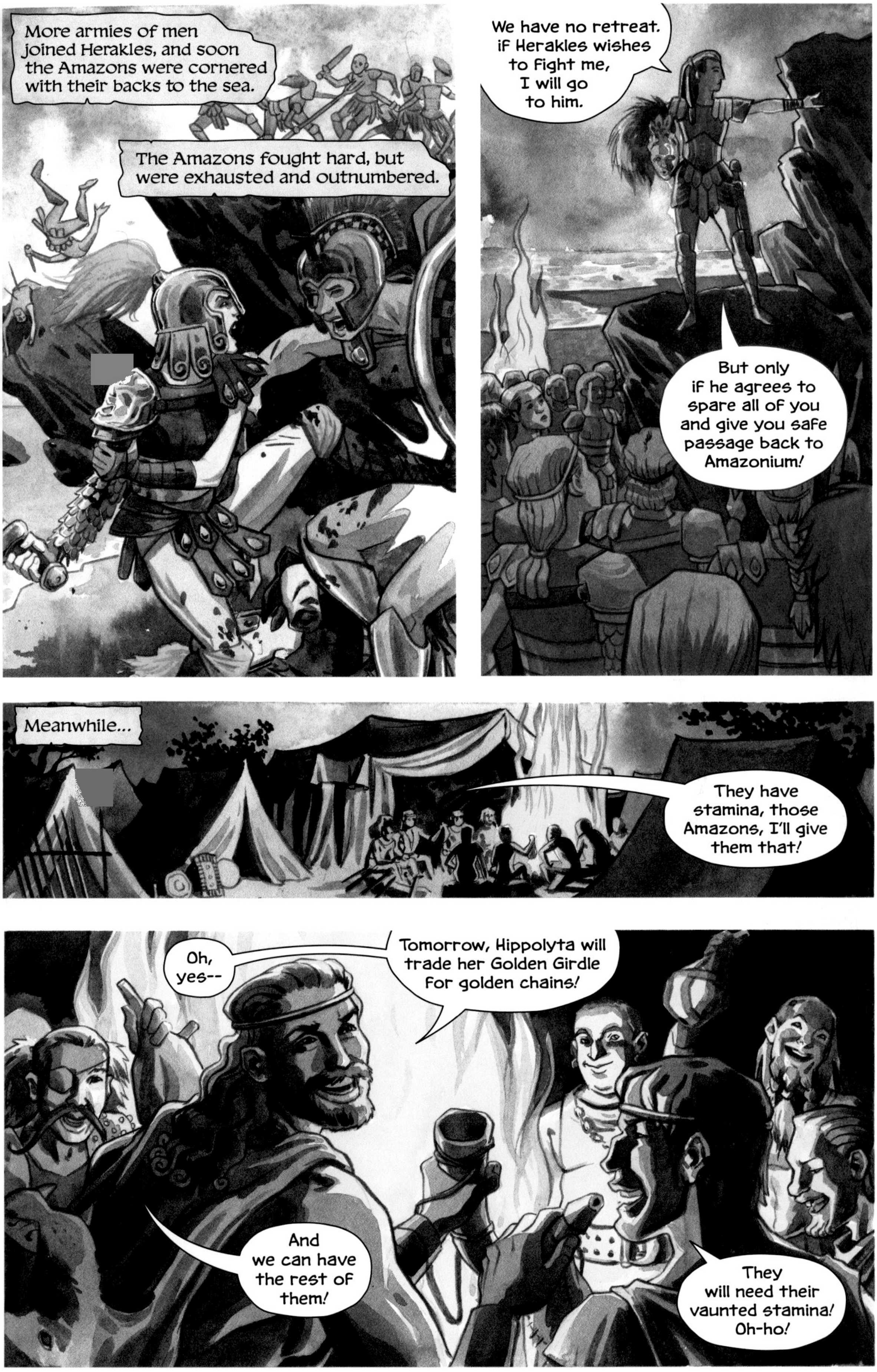
More armies of men joined Herakles, and soon the Amazons were cornered with their backs to the sea.
The Amazons fought hard, but were exhausted and outnumbered.
We have no retreat. if Herakles wishes to fight me, I will go to him.
But only if he agrees to spare all of you and give you safe passage back to Amazonium!
Meanwhile...
They have stamina, those Amazons, I'll give them that!
Oh, yes--
Tomorrow, Hippolyta will trade her Golden Girdle for golden chains!
And we can have the rest of them!
They will need their vaunted stamina! Oh-ho!

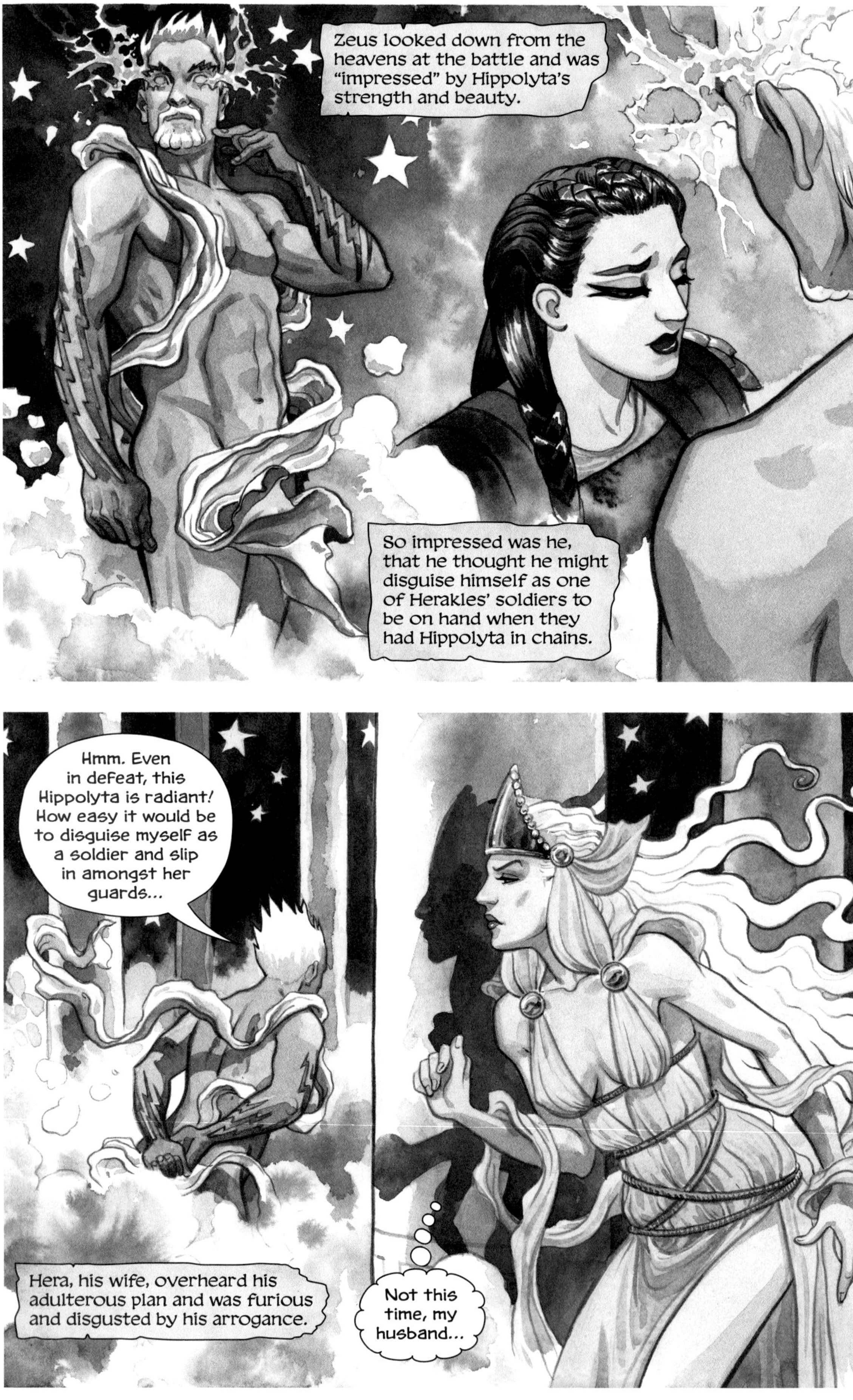
Zeus looked down from the heavens at the battle and was "impressed" by Hippolyta's strength and beauty.
So impressed was he, that he thought he might disguise himself as one of Herakles' soldiers to be on hand when they had Hippolyta in chains.
Hmm. Even in defeat, this Hippolyta is radiant! How easy it would be to disguise myself as a soldier and slip in amongst her guards...
Hera, his wife, overheard his adulterous plan and was furious and disgusted by his arrogance.
Not this time, my husband...

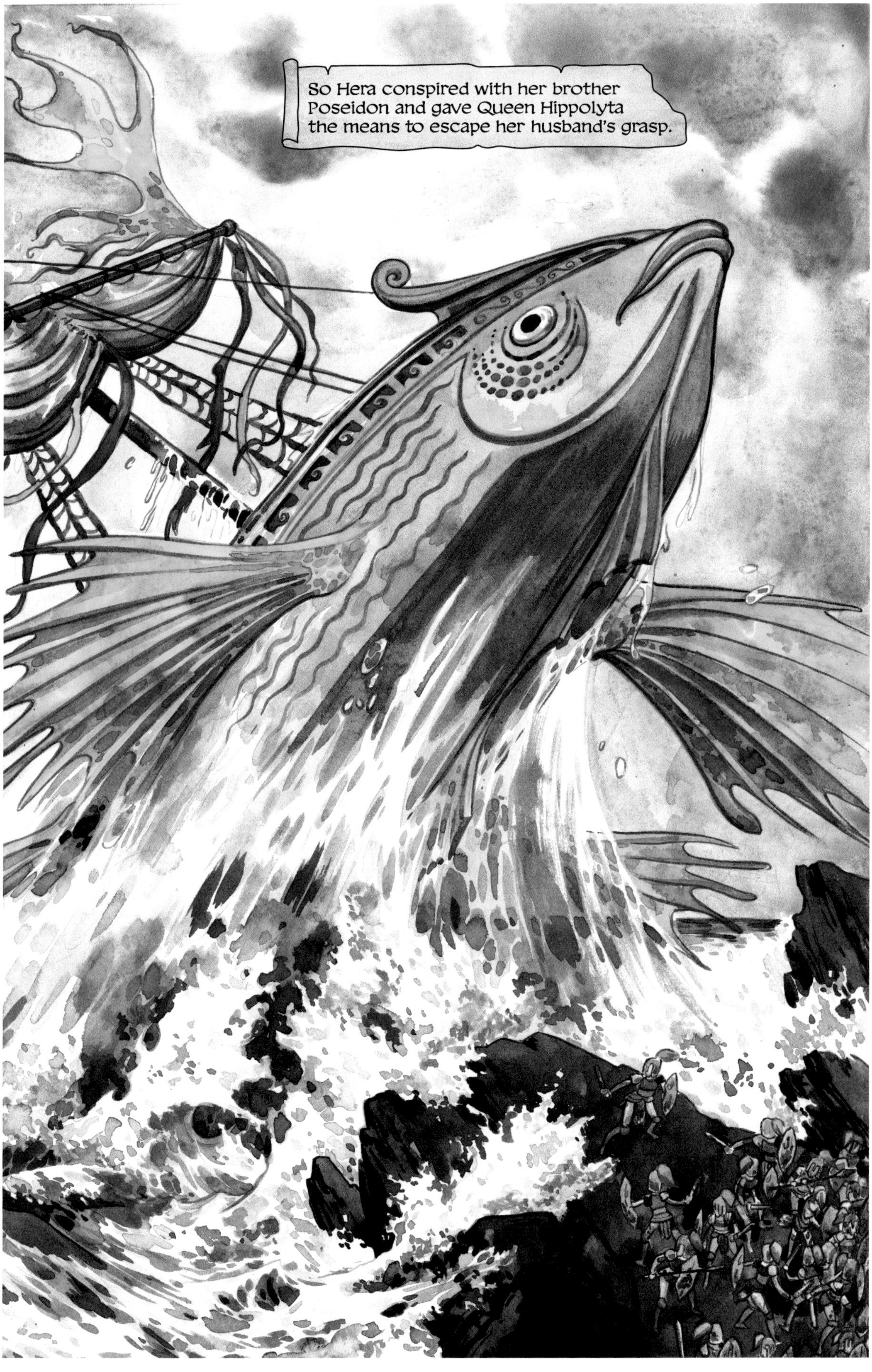
So Hera conspired with her brother Poseidon and gave Queen Hippolyta the means to escape her husband's grasp.

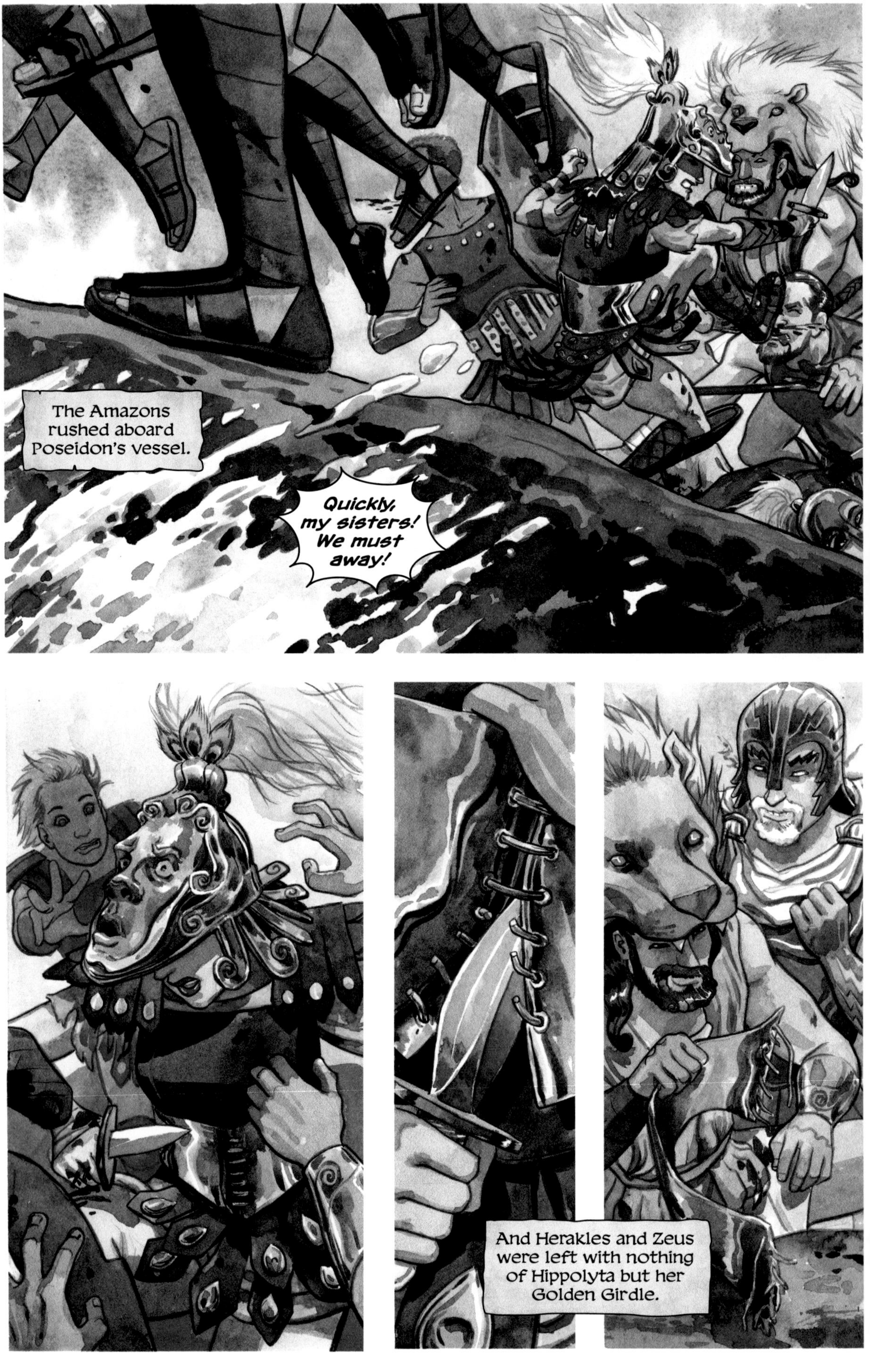
The Amazons rushed aboard Poseidon's vessel.
Quickly, my sisters! We must away!
And Herakles and Zeus were left with nothing of Hippolyta but her Golden Girdle.

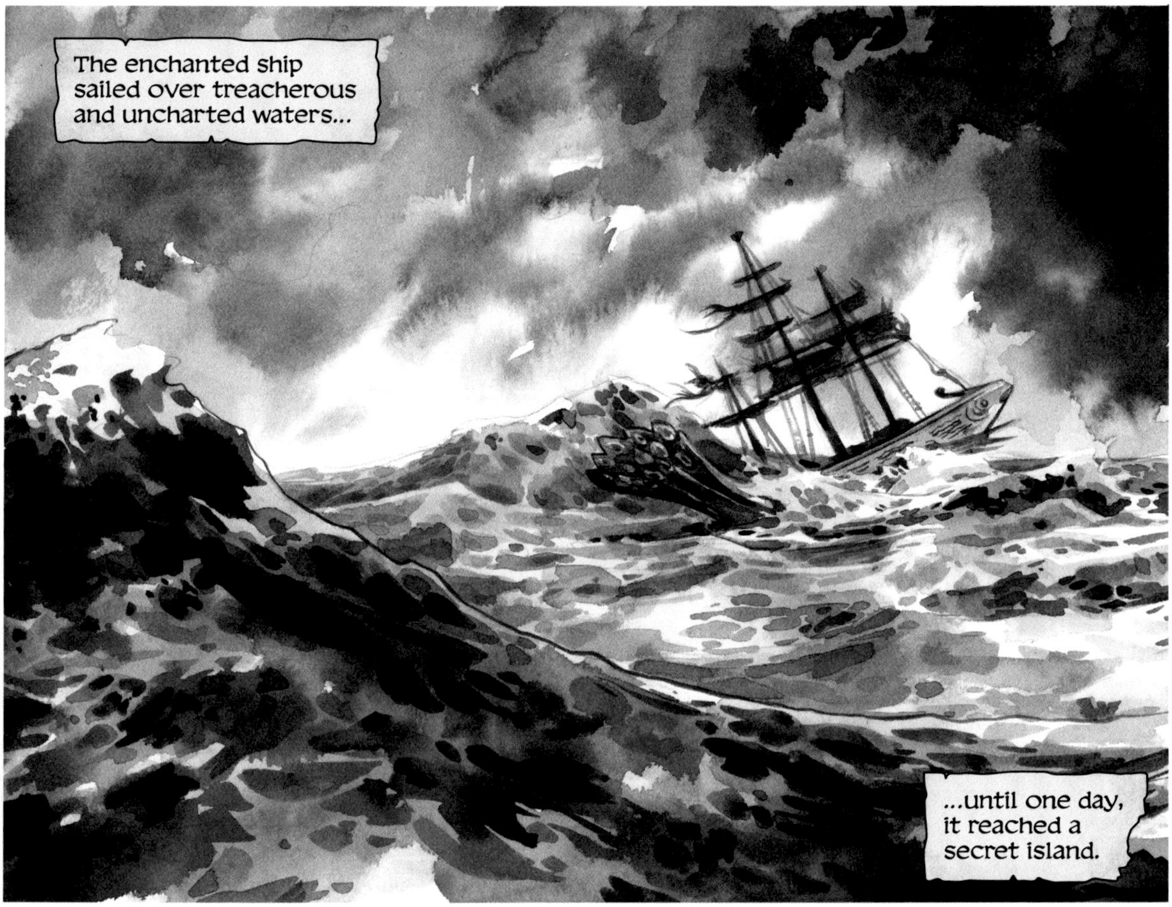
The enchanted ship sailed over treacherous and uncharted waters...
...until one day, it reached a secret island.

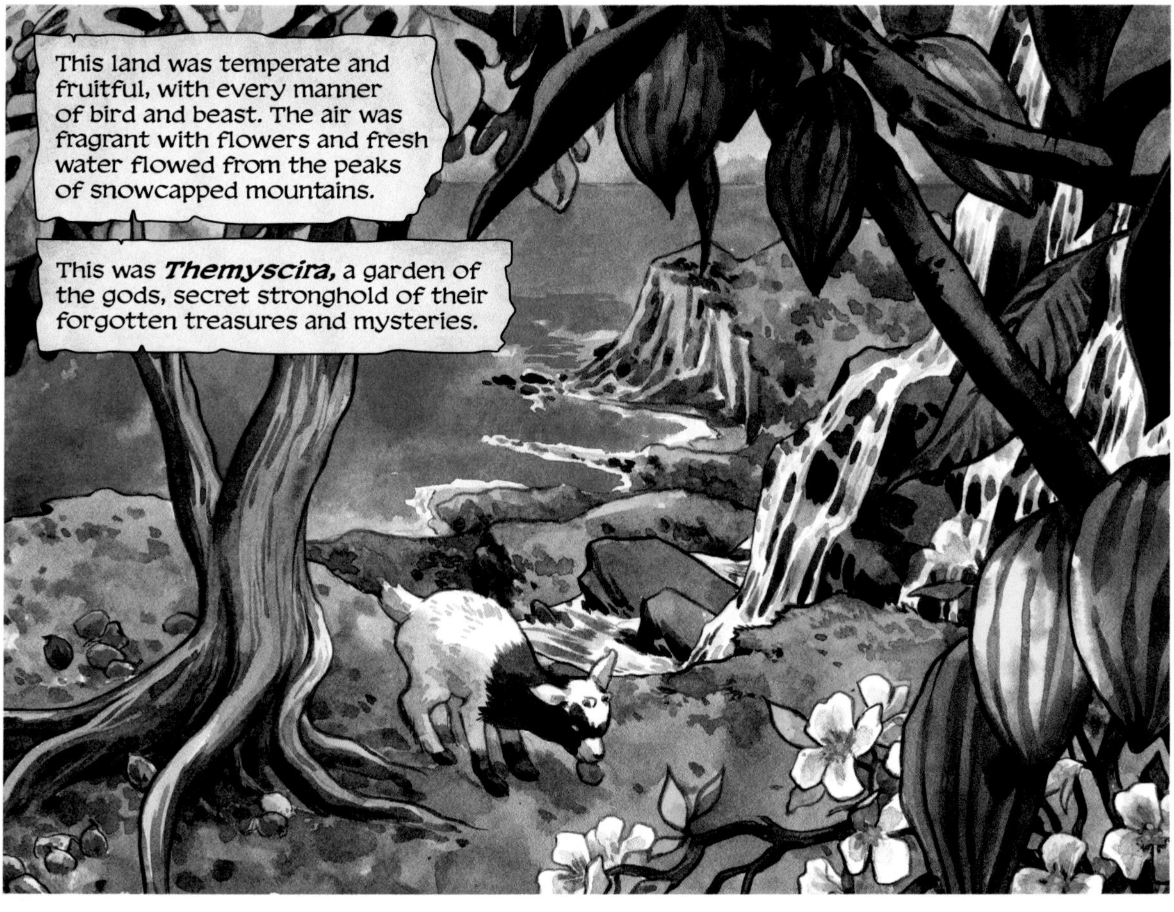
This land was temperate and fruitful, with every manner of bird and beast. The air was fragrant with flowers and fresh water flowed from the peaks of snowcapped mountains.
This was *Themyscira,* a garden of the gods, secret stronghold of their forgotten treasures and mysteries.

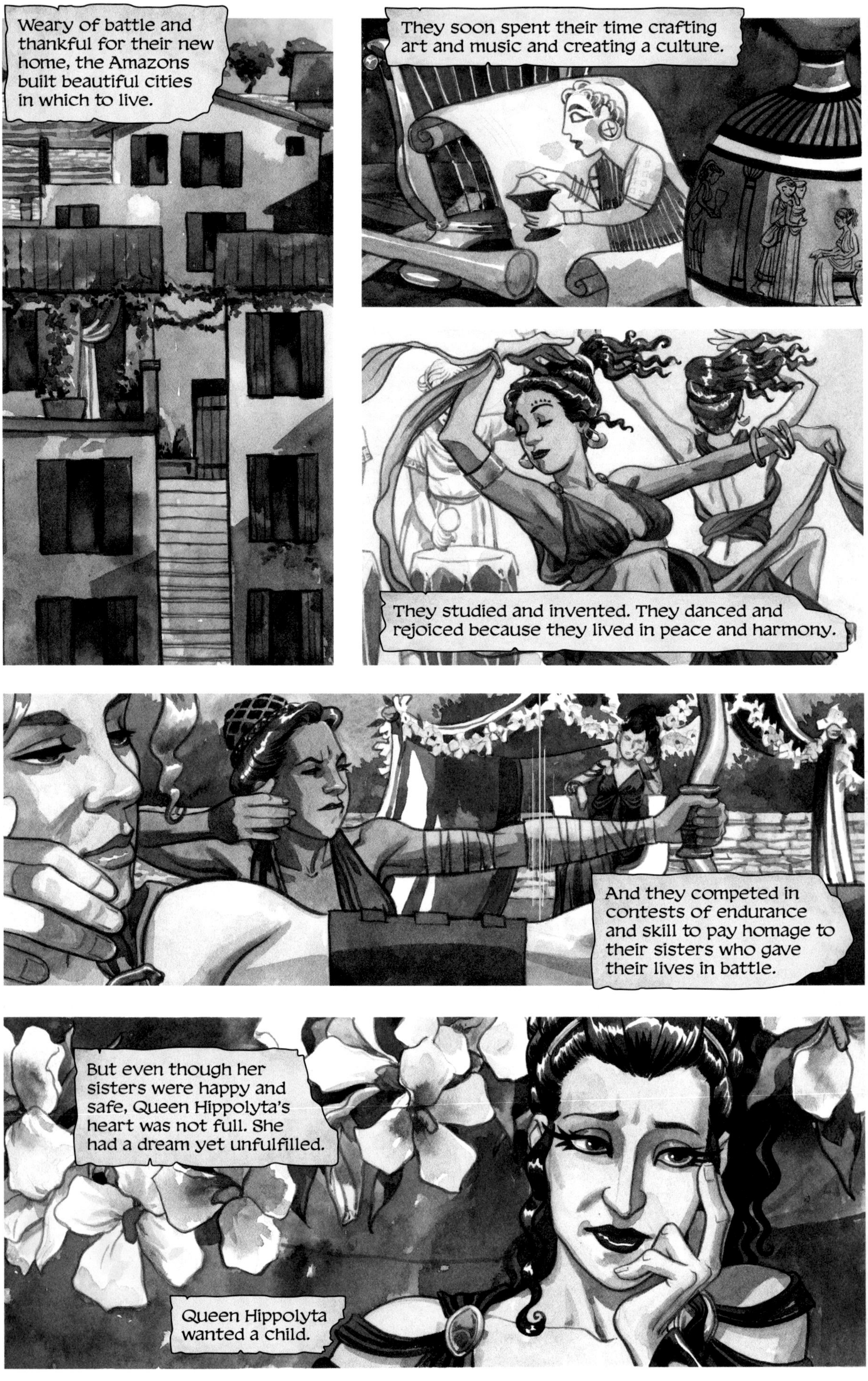
Weary of battle and thankful for their new home, the Amazons built beautiful cities in which to live.
They soon spent their time crafting art and music and creating a culture.
They studied and invented. They danced and rejoiced because they lived in peace and harmony.
And they competed in contests of endurance and skill to pay homage to their sisters who gave their lives in battle.
But even though her sisters were happy and safe, Queen Hippolyta's heart was not full. She had a dream yet unfulfilled.
Queen Hippolyta wanted a child.

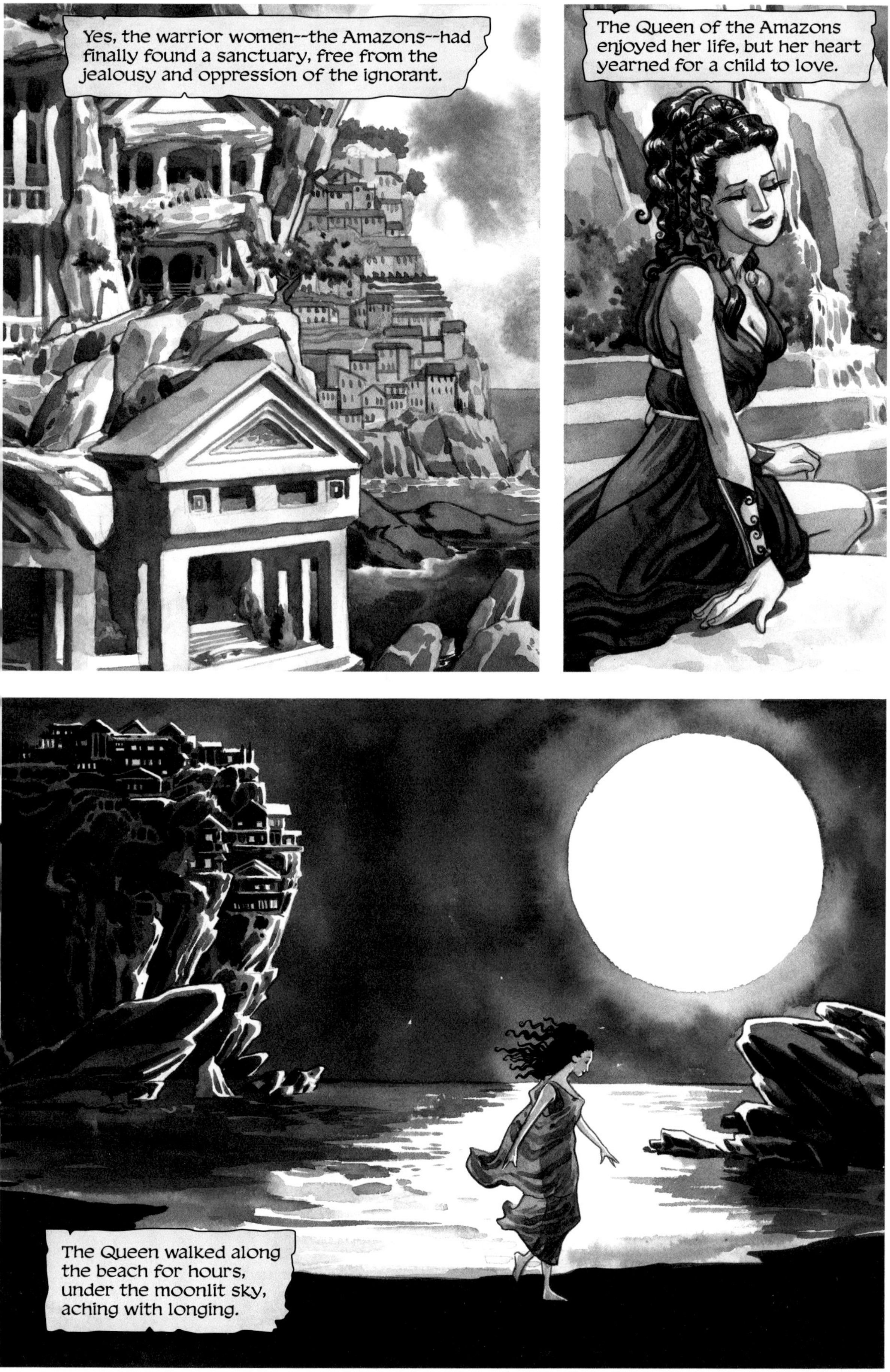
Yes, the warrior women--the Amazons--had finally found a sanctuary, free from the jealousy and oppression of the ignorant.
The Queen of the Amazons enjoyed her life, but her heart yearned for a child to love.
The Queen walked along the beach for hours, under the moonlit sky, aching with longing.

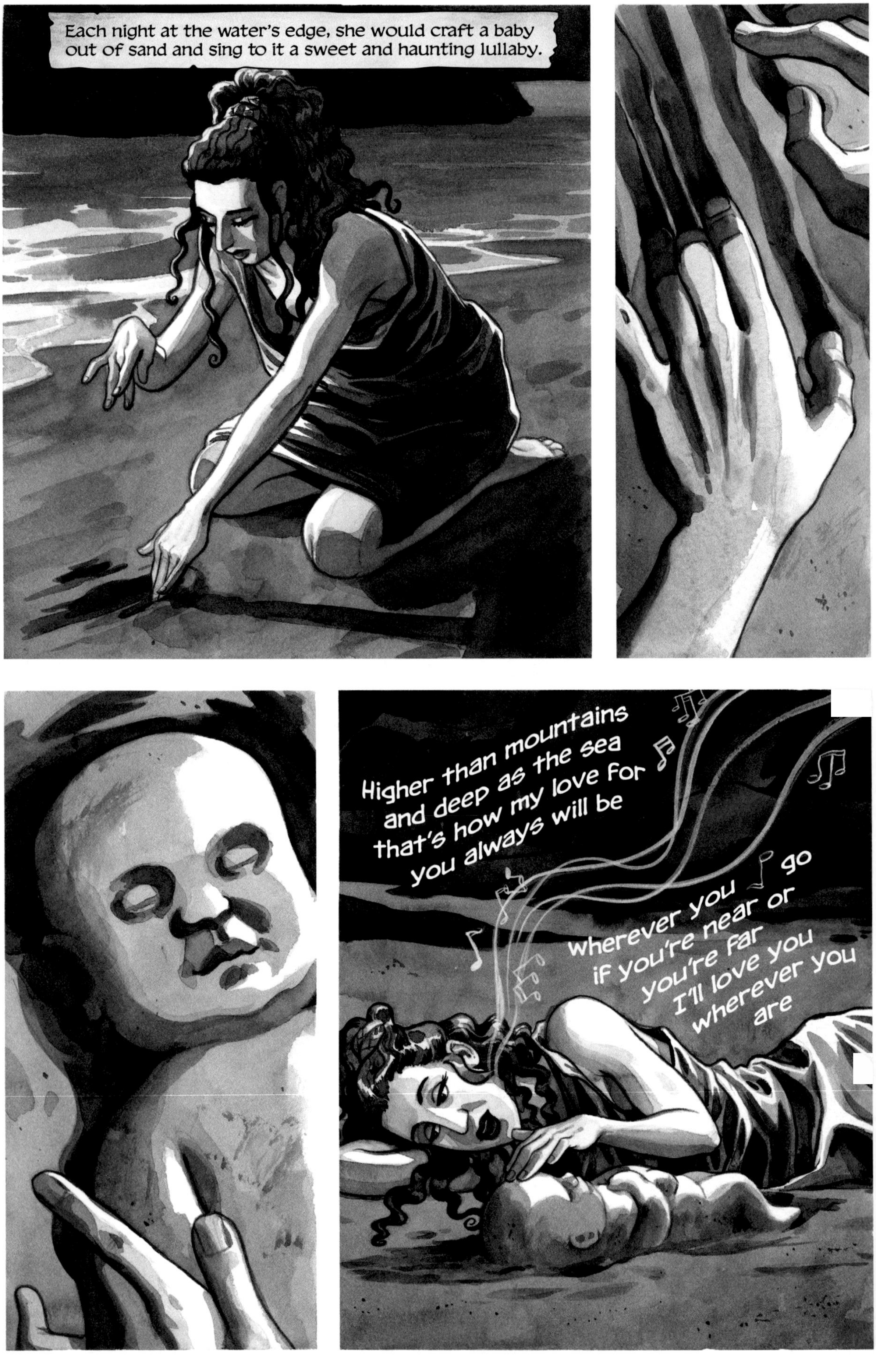
Each night at the water's edge, she would craft a baby out of sand and sing to it a sweet and haunting lullaby.
Higher than mountains and deep as the sea that's how my love for you always will be
wherever you go if you're near or you're far I'll love you wherever you are

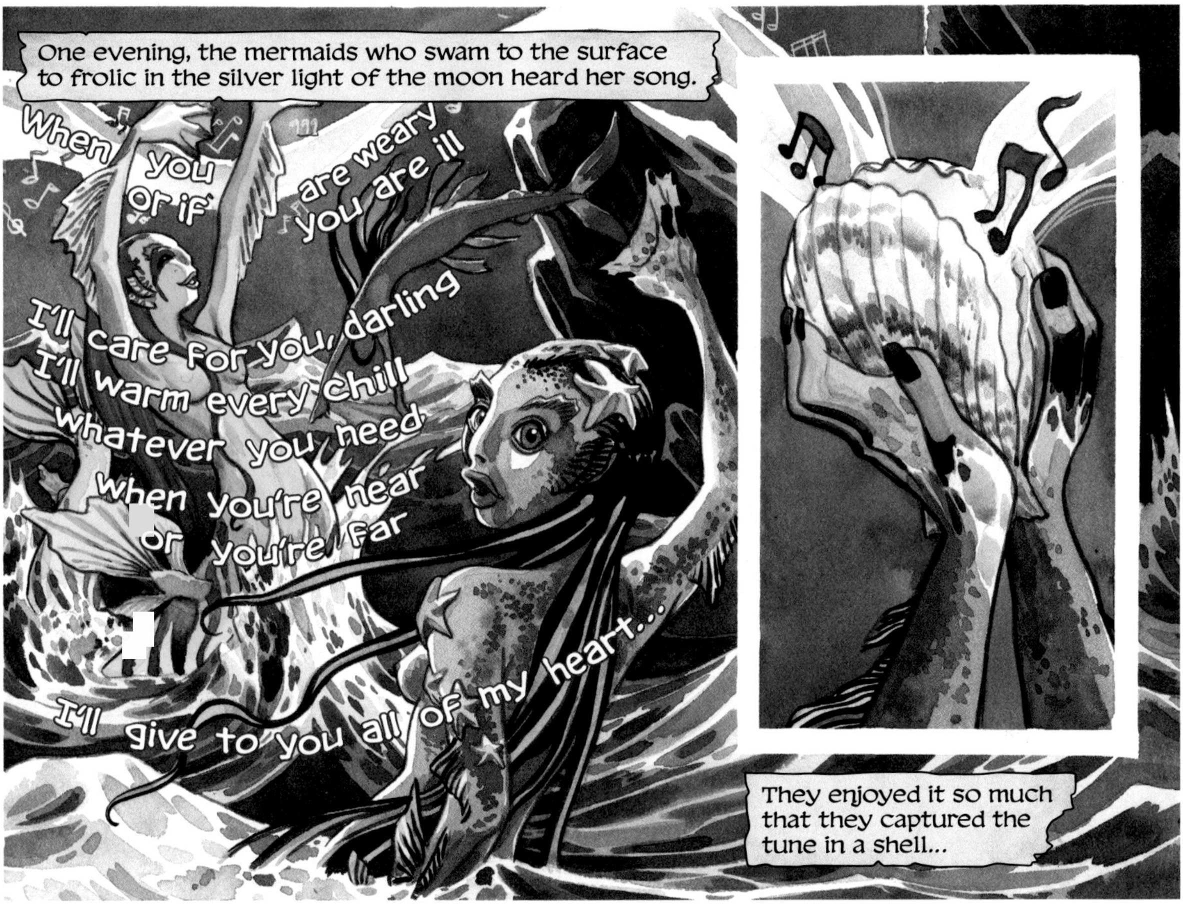
One evening, the mermaids who swam to the surface to frolic in the silver light of the moon heard her song.
When you are weary or if you are ill
I'll care for you, darling
I'll warm every chill
whatever you need
when you're near or you're far
I'll give to you all of my heart...
They enjoyed it so much that they captured the tune in a shell...

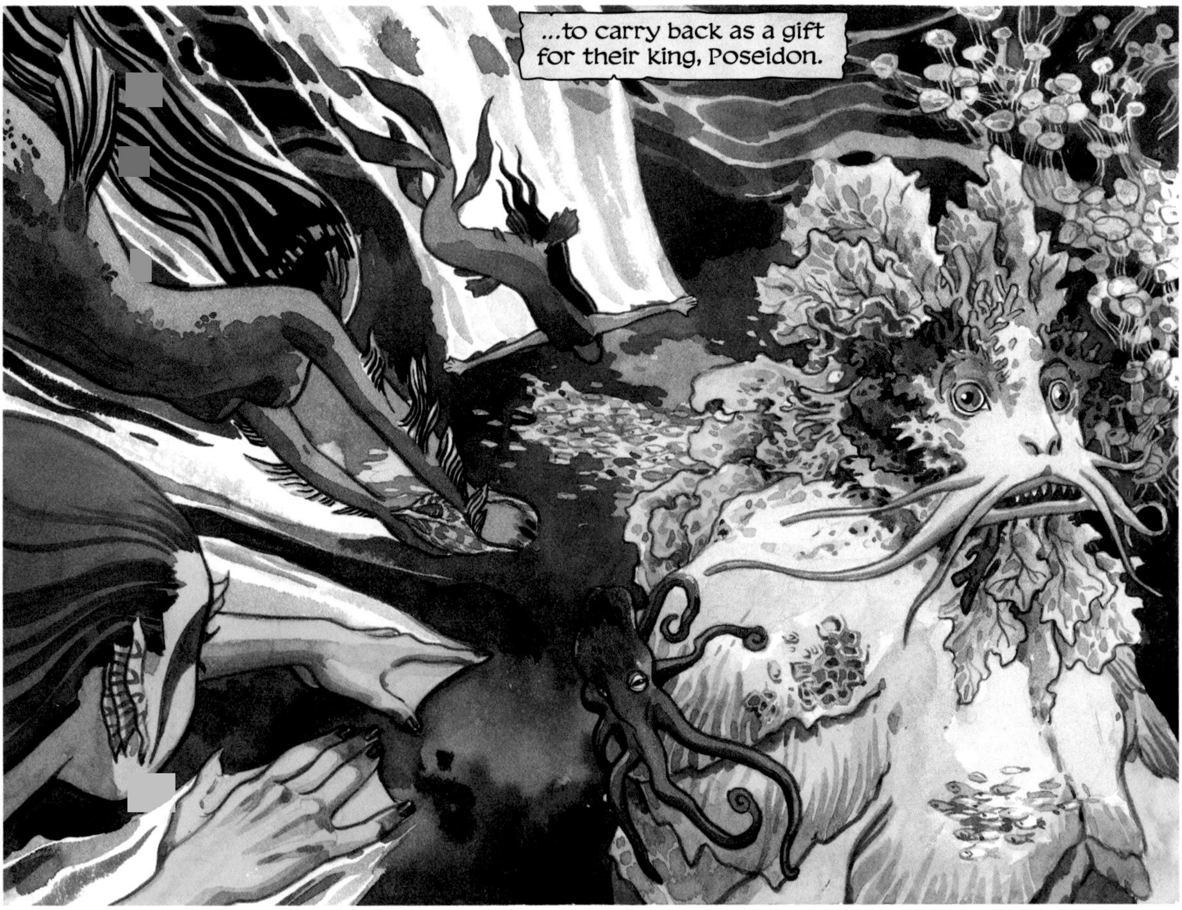
...to carry back as a gift for their king, Poseidon.

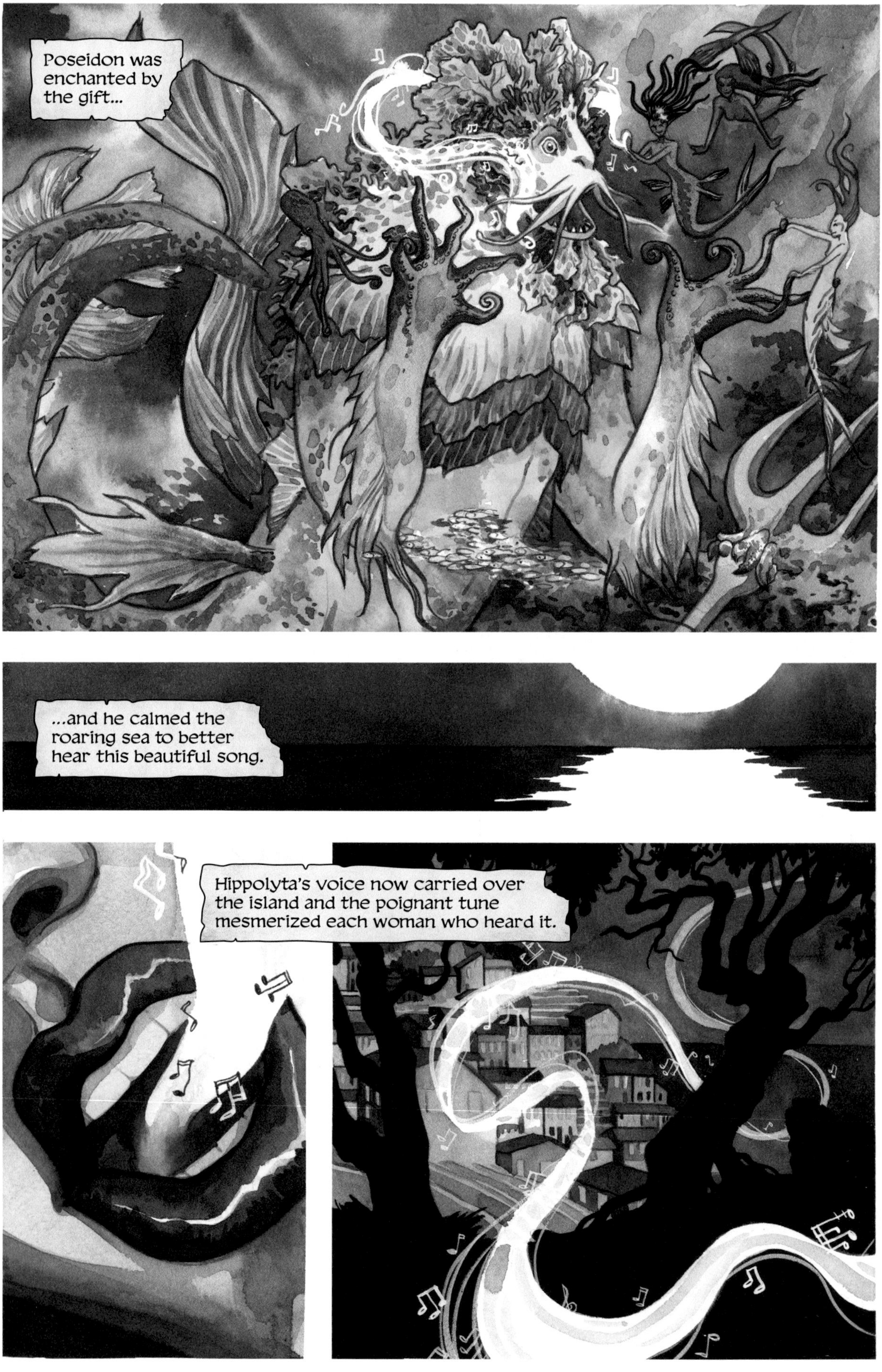
Poseidon was enchanted by the gift...
...and he calmed the roaring sea to better hear this beautiful song.
Hippolyta's voice now carried over the island and the poignant tune mesmerized each woman who heard it.

Soon, all the Amazons on Themyscira were singing the song.

Higher than mountains and deep as the sea that's how my love for you always will be...

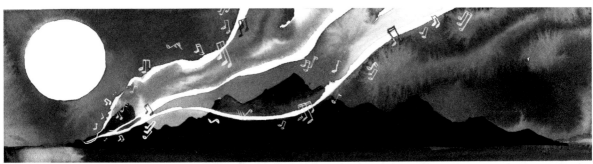

This chorus was carried up, over the whole island...

...and on the winds to the clouds of Mount Olympus!

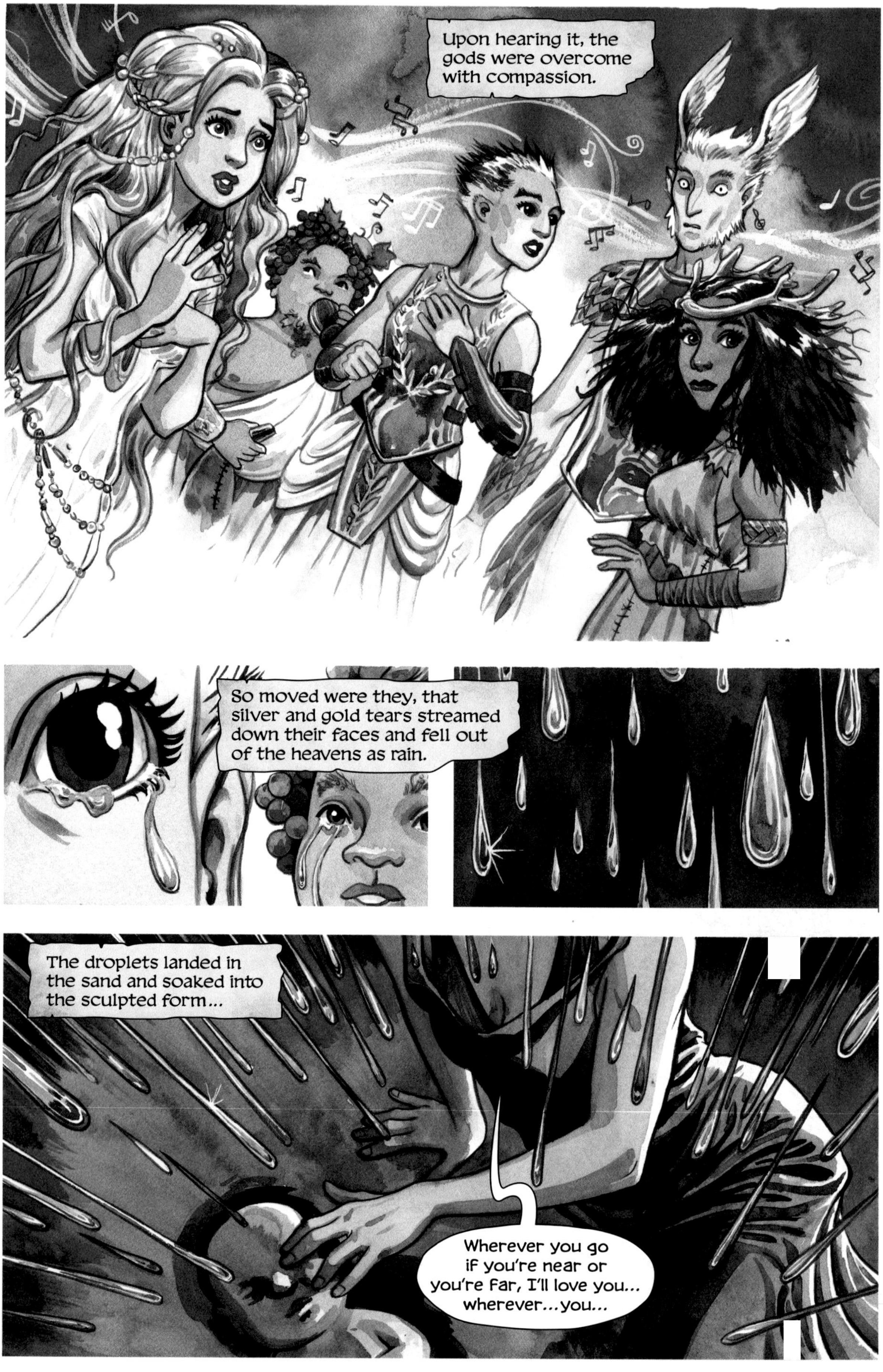
Upon hearing it, the gods were overcome with compassion.
So moved were they, that silver and gold tears streamed down their faces and fell out of the heavens as rain.
The droplets landed in the sand and soaked into the sculpted form...
Wherever you go if you're near or you're far, I'll love you... wherever... you...

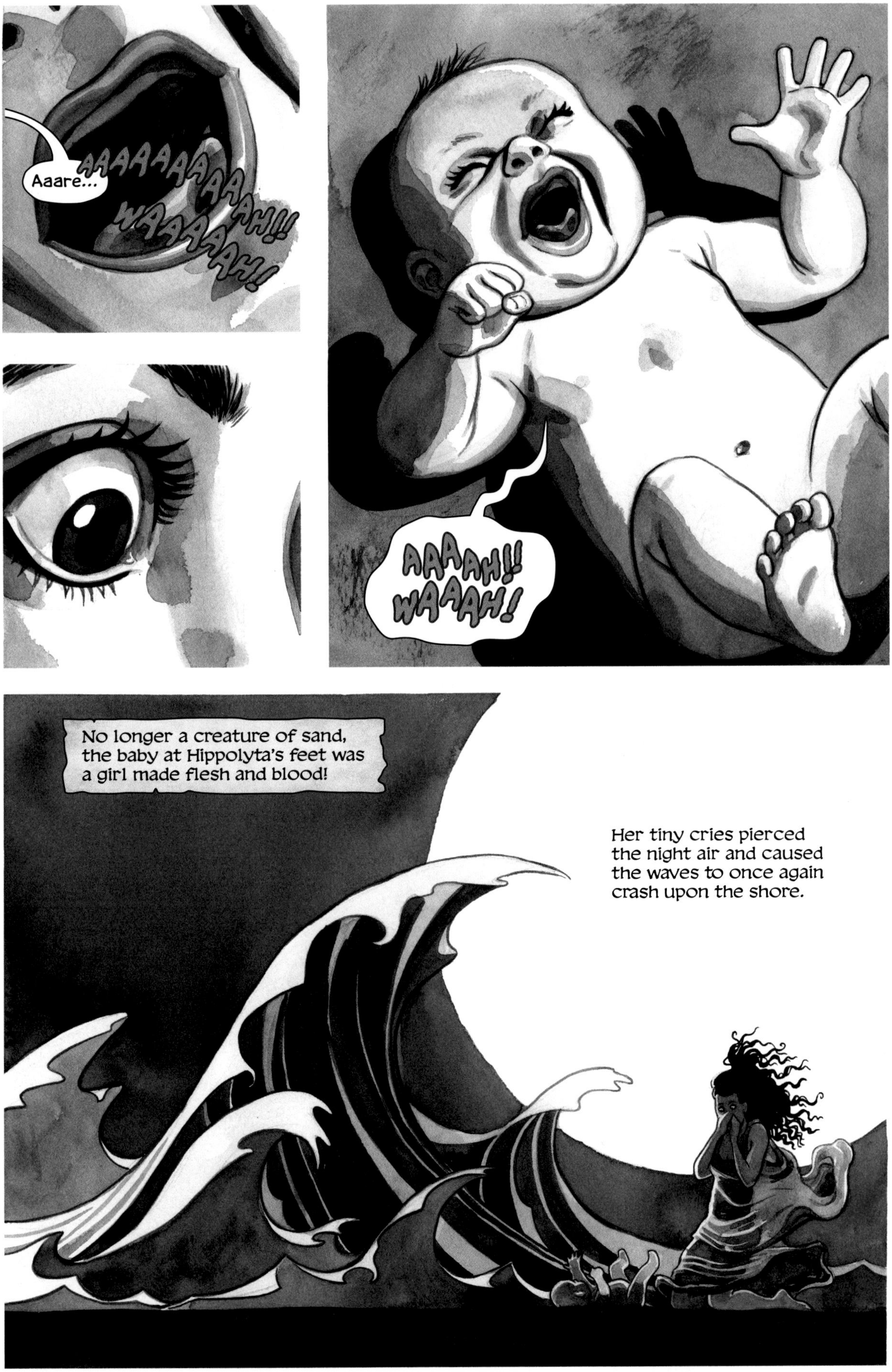
Aaare...
AAAAAAAAAAAAH!!! WAAAAAAH!
AAAAH!! WAAAH!
No longer a creature of sand, the baby at Hippolyta's feet was a girl made flesh and blood!
Her tiny cries pierced the night air and caused the waves to once again crash upon the shore.

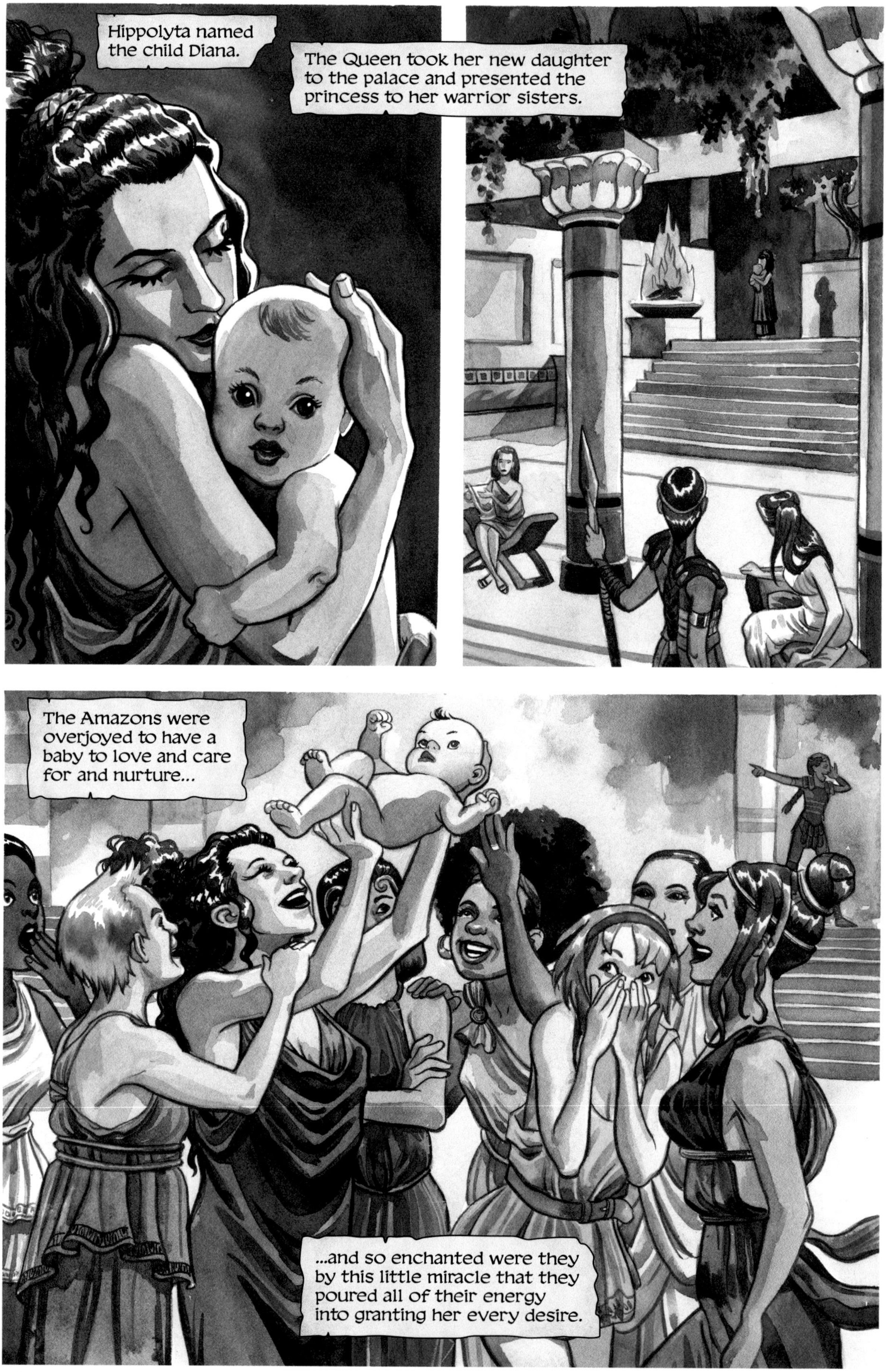
Hippolyta named the child Diana.
The Queen took her new daughter to the palace and presented the princess to her warrior sisters.
The Amazons were overjoyed to have a baby to love and care for and nurture...
...and so enchanted were they by this little miracle that they poured all of their energy into granting her every desire.

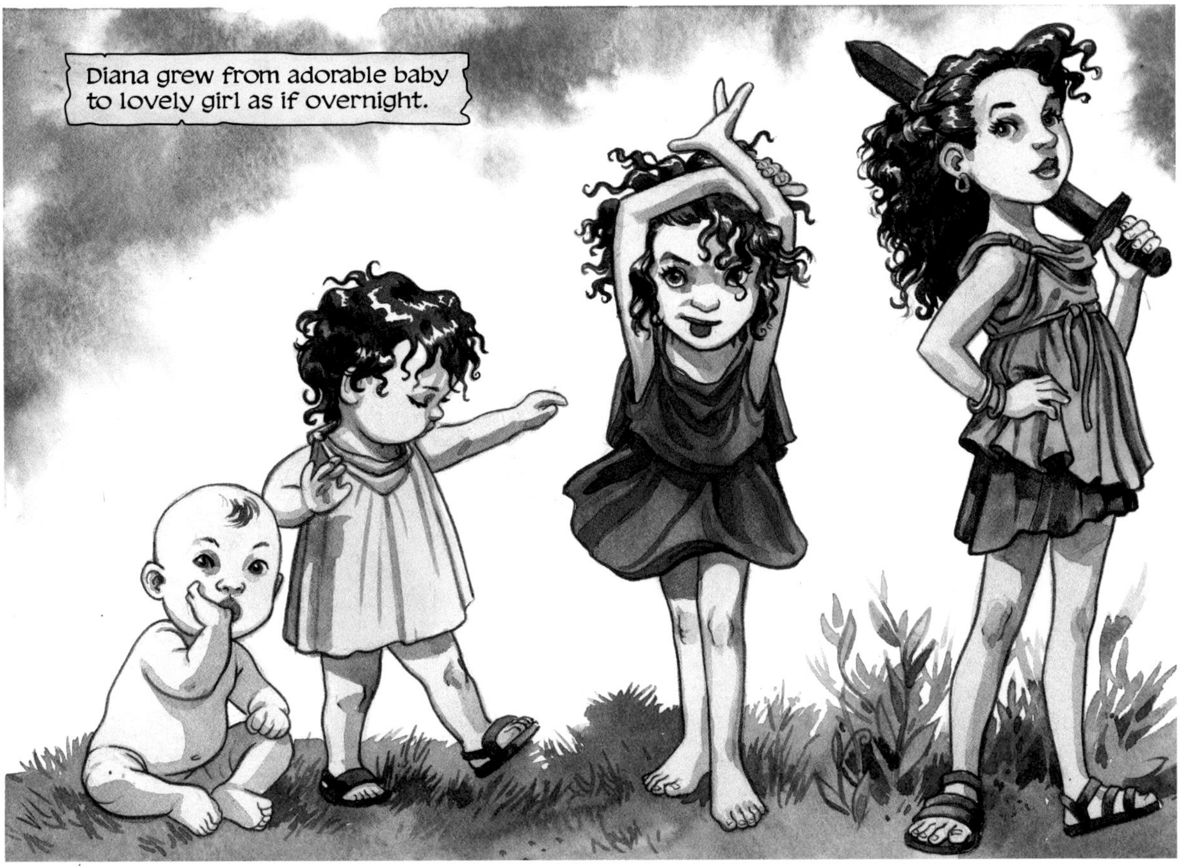
Diana grew from adorable baby to lovely girl as if overnight.

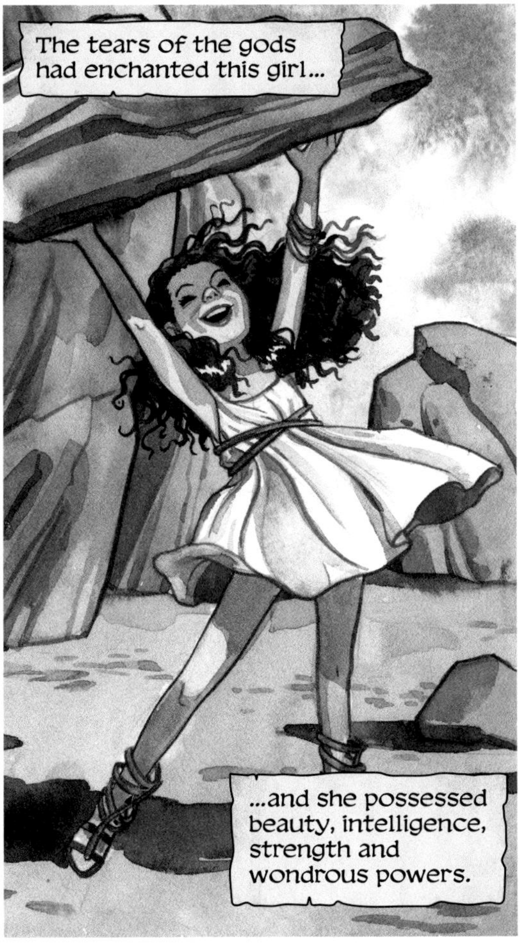
The tears of the gods had enchanted this girl...
...and she possessed beauty, intelligence, strength and wondrous powers.

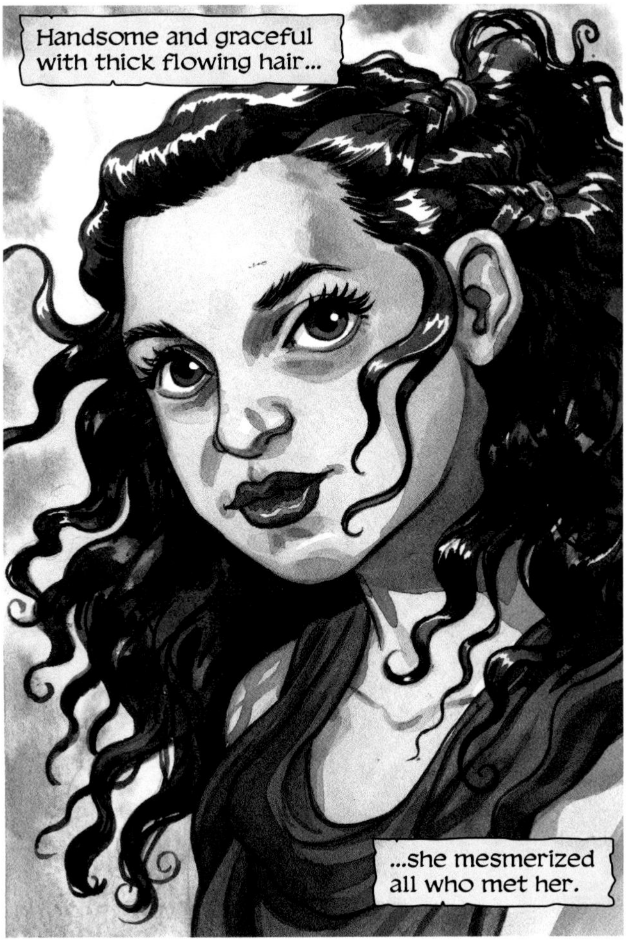
Handsome and graceful with thick flowing hair...
...she mesmerized all who met her.

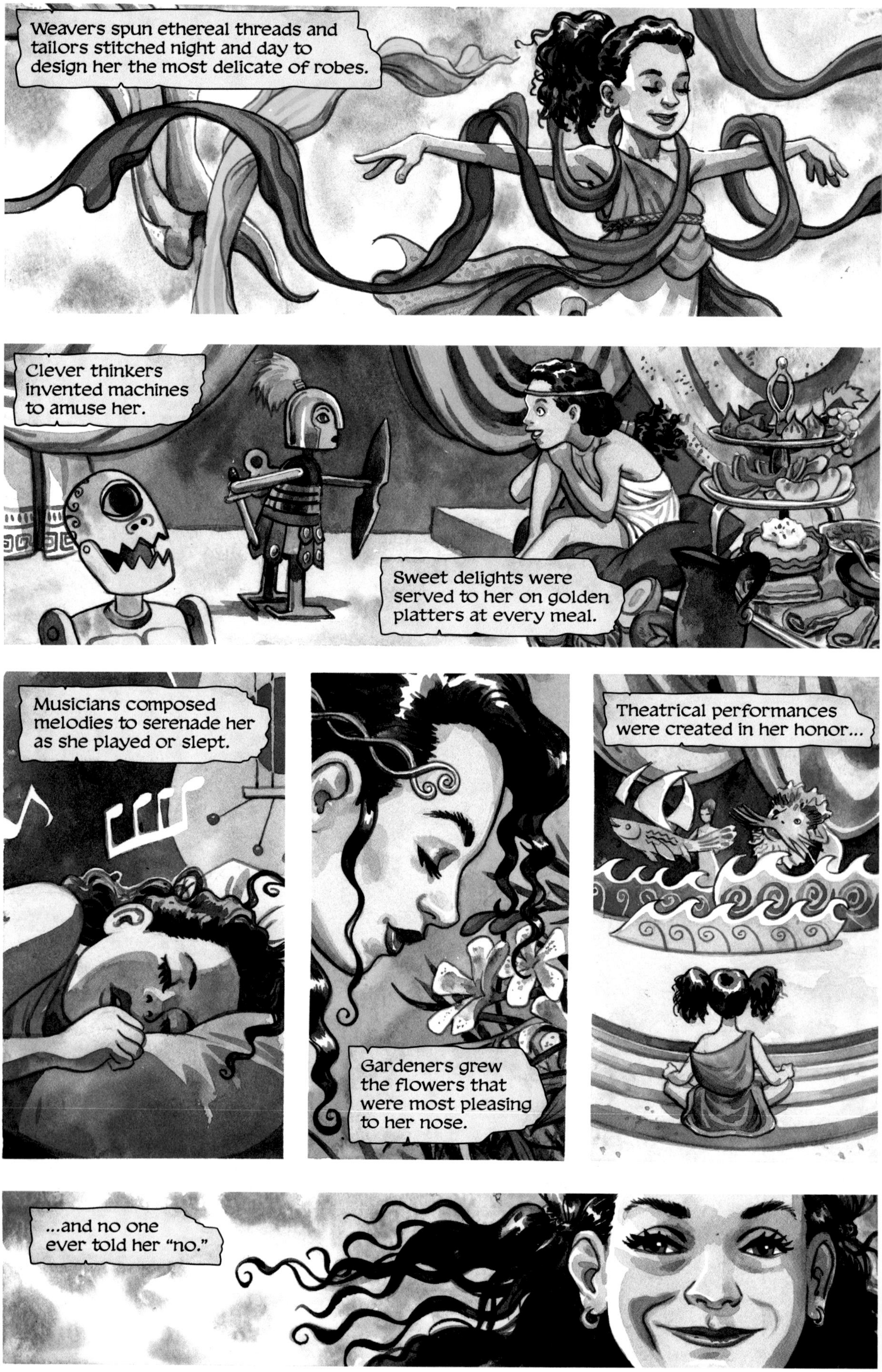
Weavers spun ethereal threads and tailors stitched night and day to design her the most delicate of robes.
Clever thinkers invented machines to amuse her.
Sweet delights were served to her on golden platters at every meal.
Musicians composed melodies to serenade her as she played or slept.
Gardeners grew the flowers that were most pleasing to her nose.
Theatrical performances were created in her honor...
...and no one ever told her "no."

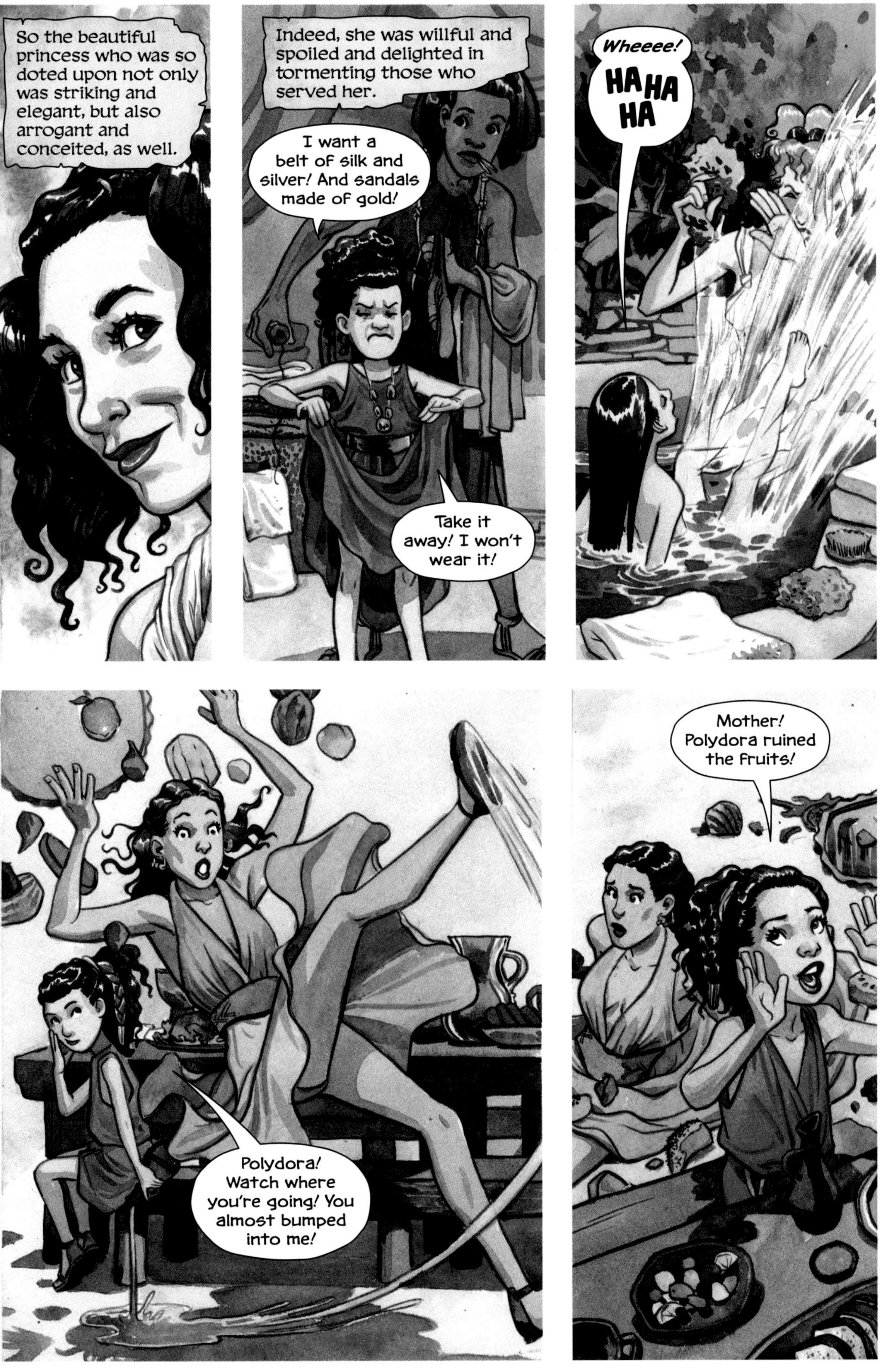
So the beautiful princess who was so doted upon not only was striking and elegant, but also arrogant and conceited, as well.
Indeed, she was willful and spoiled and delighted in tormenting those who served her.
I want a belt of silk and silver! And sandals made of gold!
Take it away! I won't wear it!
Wheeee!
HA HA HA
Polydora! Watch where you're going! You almost bumped into me!
Mother! Polydora ruined the fruits!

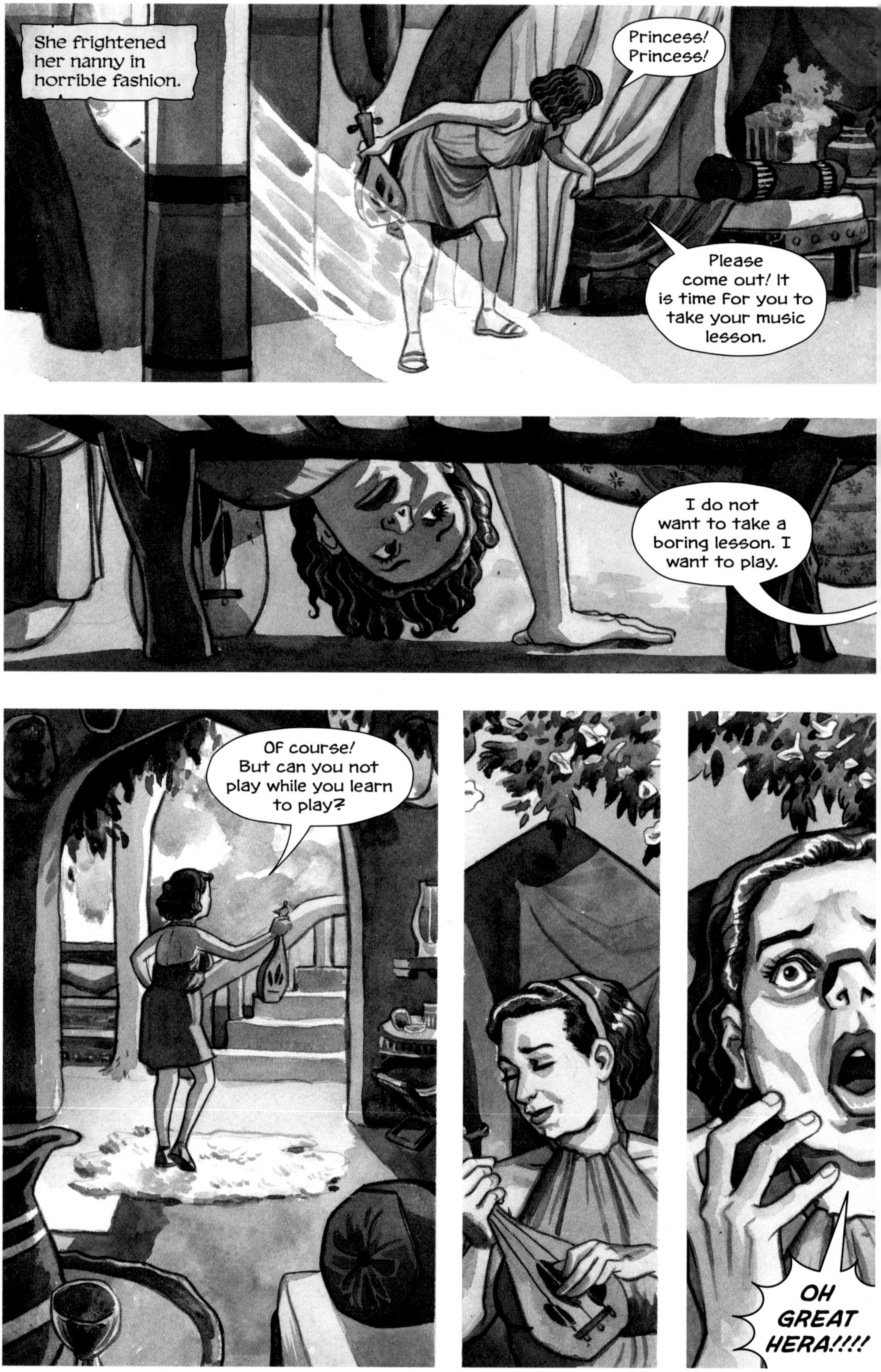

She frightened her nanny in horrible fashion.
Princess! Princess!
Please come out! It is time for you to take your music lesson.
I do not want to take a boring lesson. I want to play.
Of course! But can you not play while you learn to play?
OH GREAT HERA!!!!

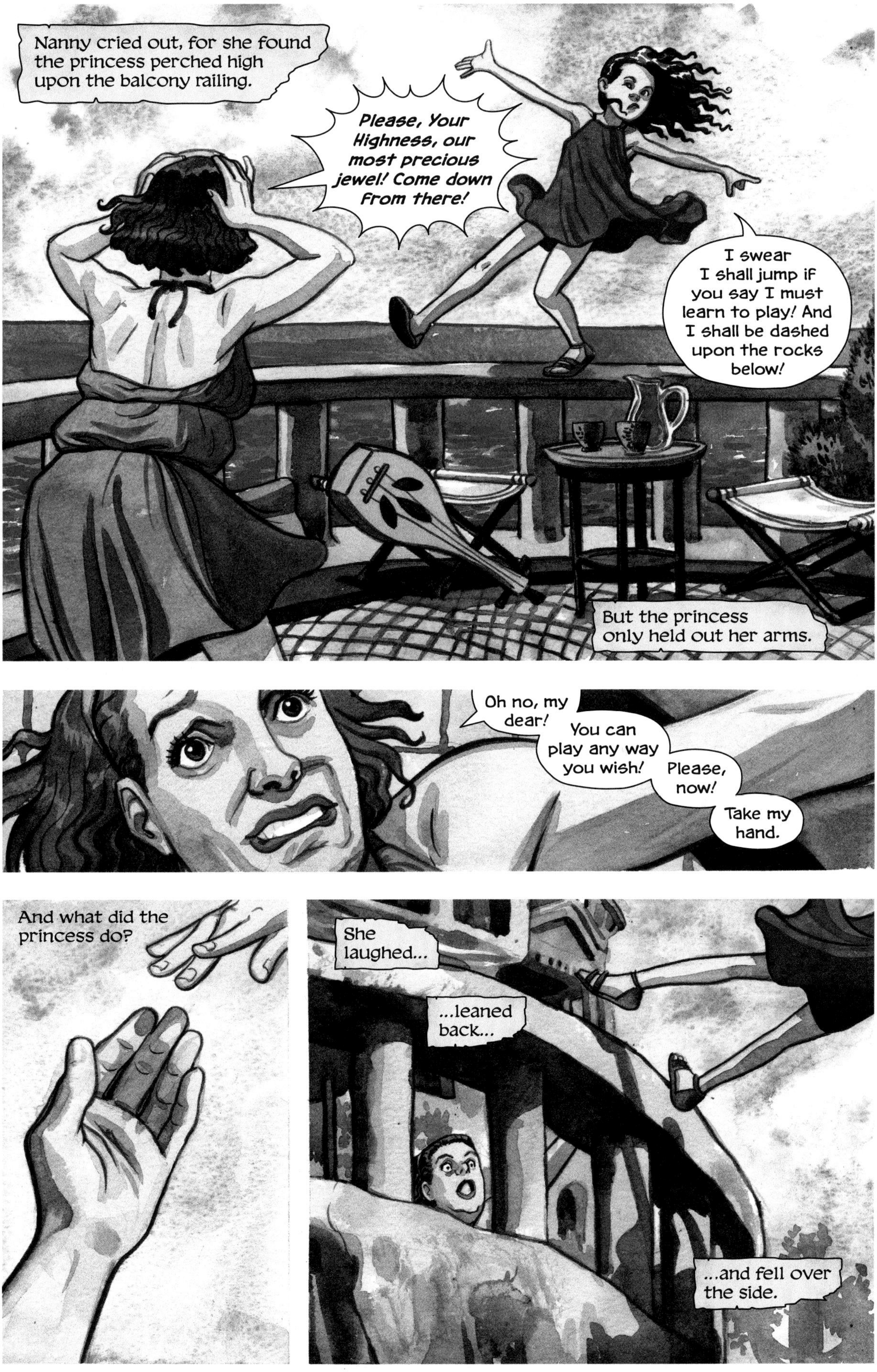

Nanny cried out, for she found the princess perched high upon the balcony railing.
Please, Your Highness, our most precious jewel! Come down from there!
I swear I shall jump if you say I must learn to play! And I shall be dashed upon the rocks below!
But the princess only held out her arms.
Oh no, my dear!
You can play any way you wish!
Please, now!
Take my hand.
And what did the princess do?
She laughed...
...leaned back...
...and fell over the side.

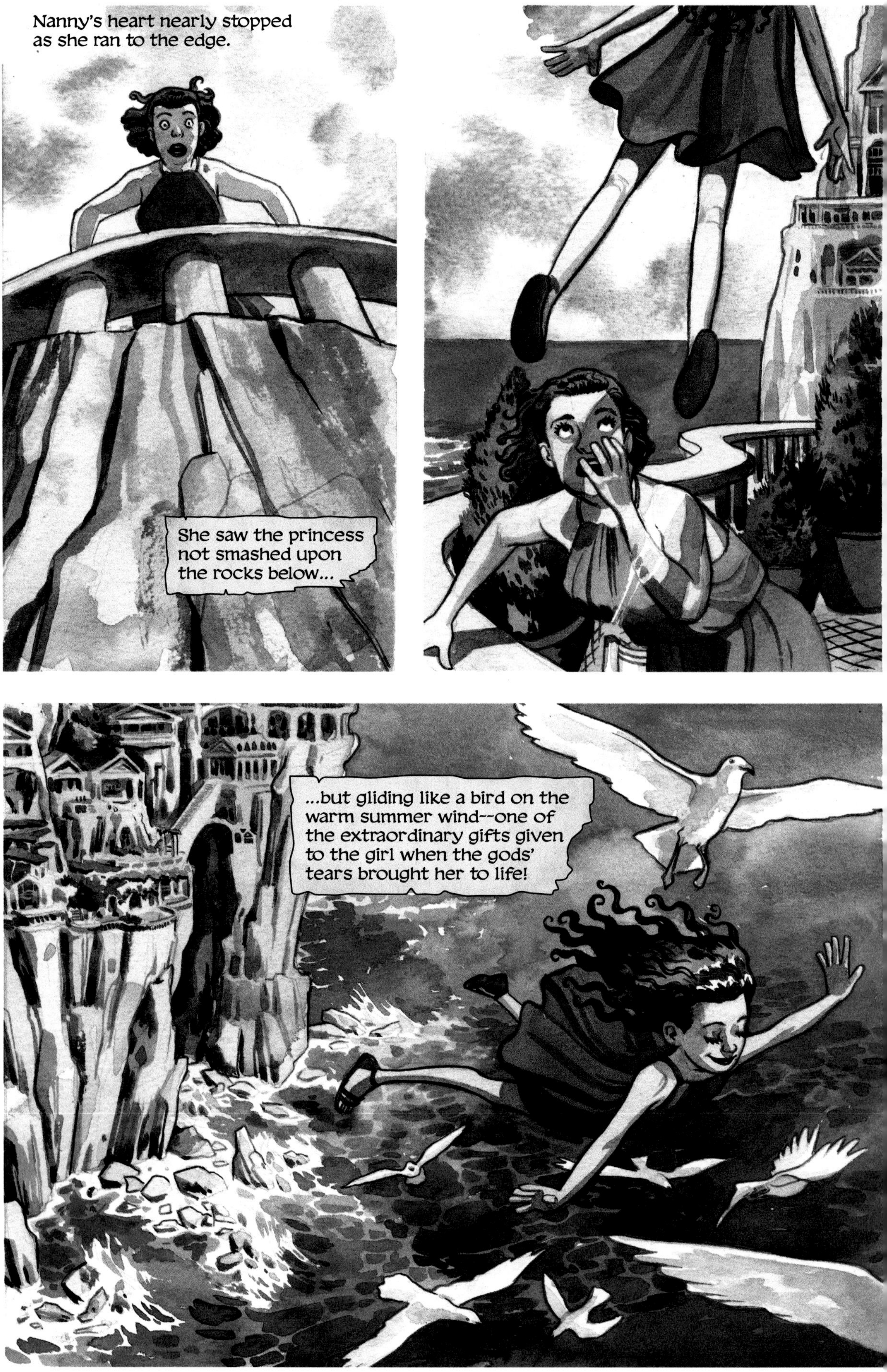
Nanny's heart nearly stopped as she ran to the edge.
She saw the princess not smashed upon the rocks below...
...but gliding like a bird on the warm summer wind--one of the extraordinary gifts given to the girl when the gods' tears brought her to life!

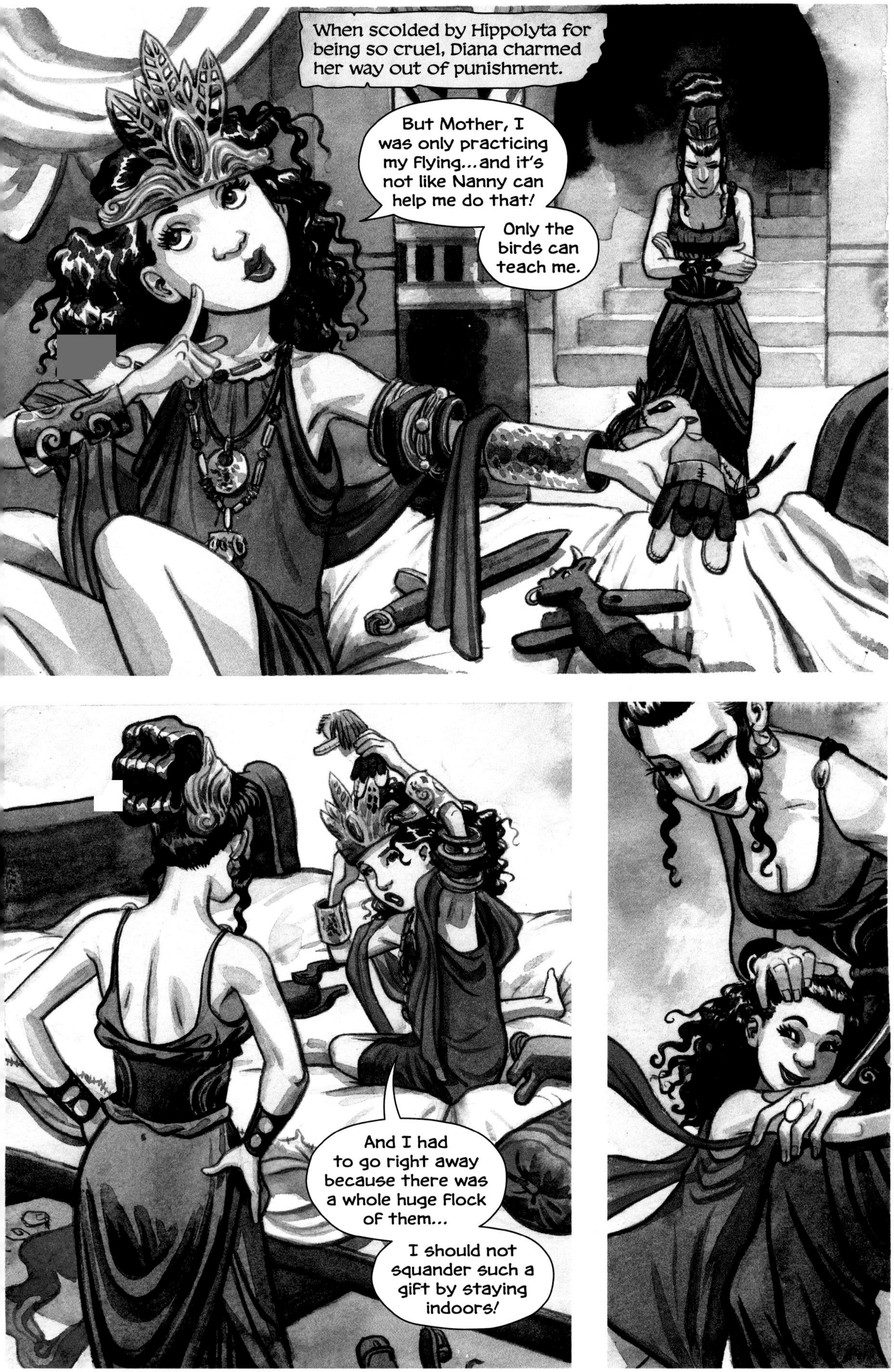
When scolded by Hippolyta for being so cruel, Diana charmed her way out of punishment.
But Mother, I was only practicing my flying...and it's not like Nanny can help me do that!
Only the birds can teach me.
And I had to go right away because there was a whole huge flock of them...
I should not squander such a gift by staying indoors!

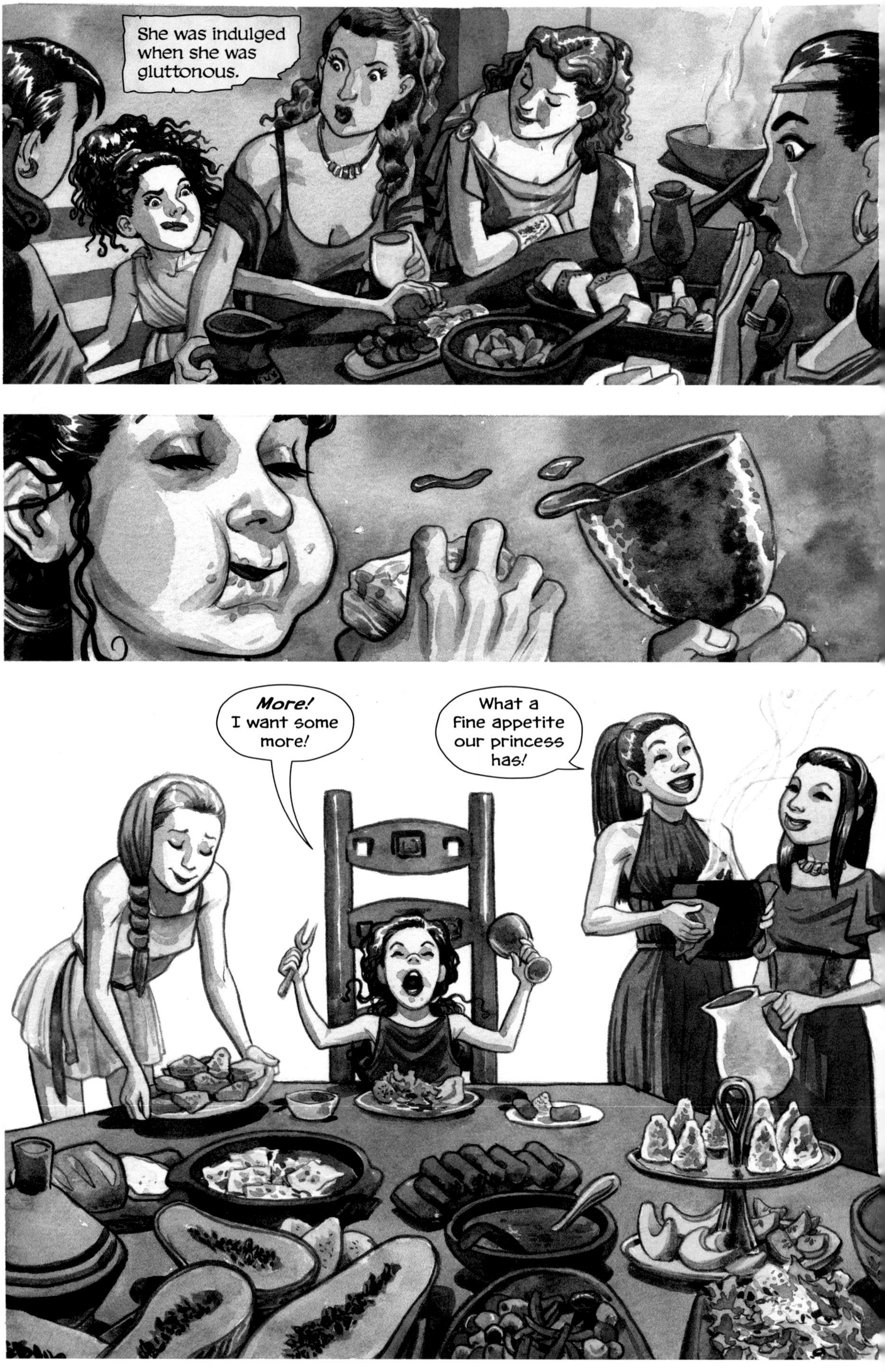

She was indulged when she was gluttonous.
More! I want some more!
What a fine appetite our princess has!

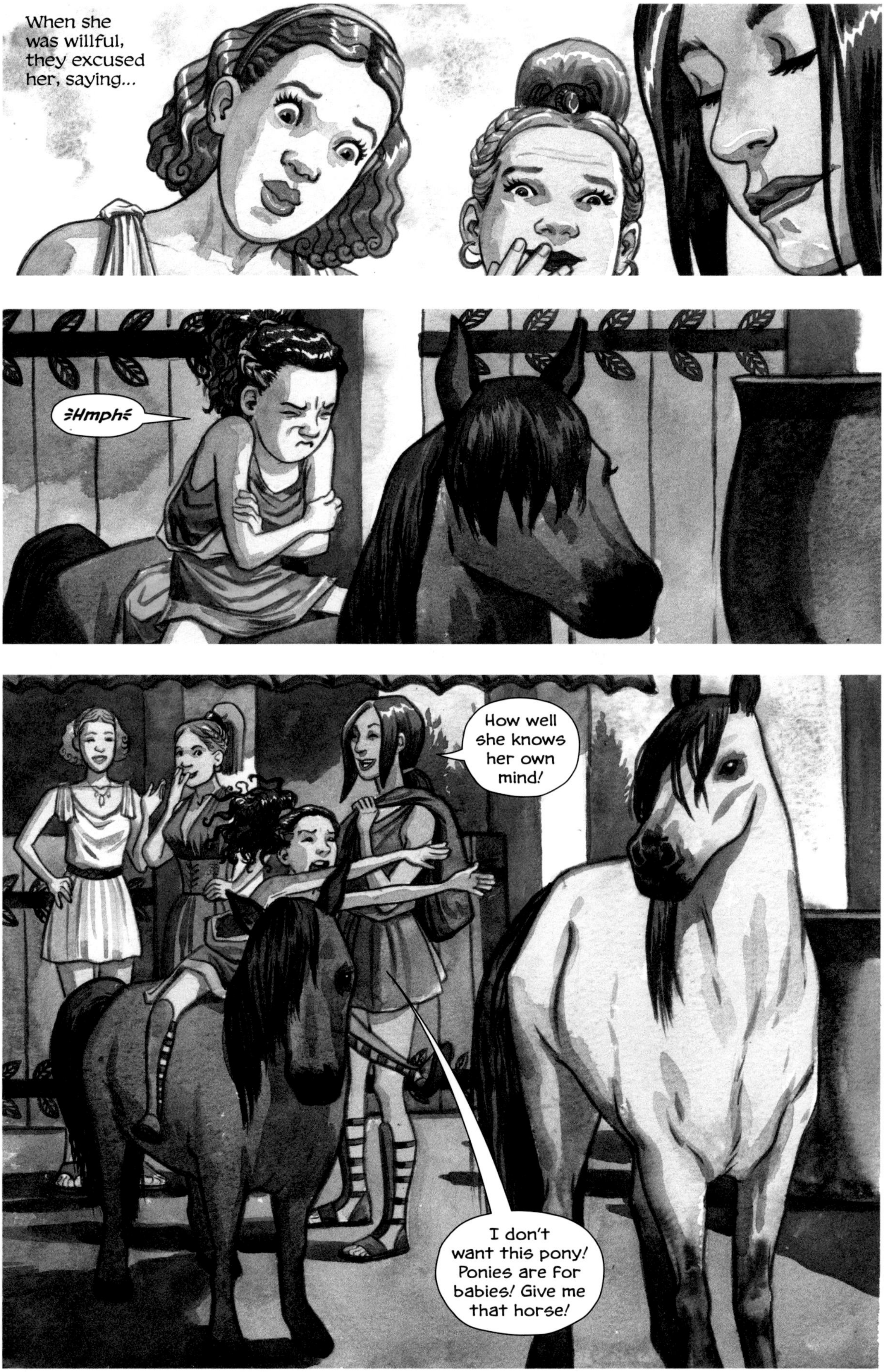
When she was willful, they excused her, saying...
Hmph
How well she knows her own mind!
I don't want this pony! Ponies are for babies! Give me that horse!

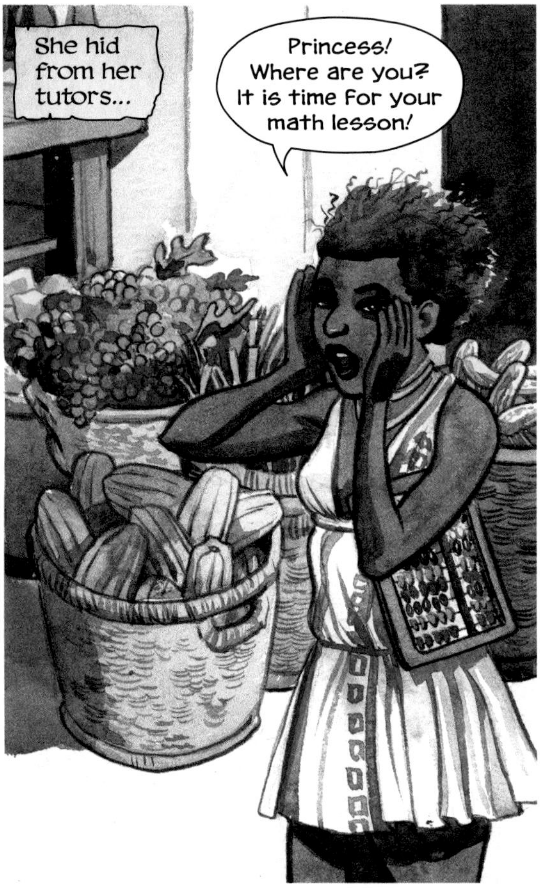
She hid from her tutors...
Princess! Where are you? It is time for your math lesson!

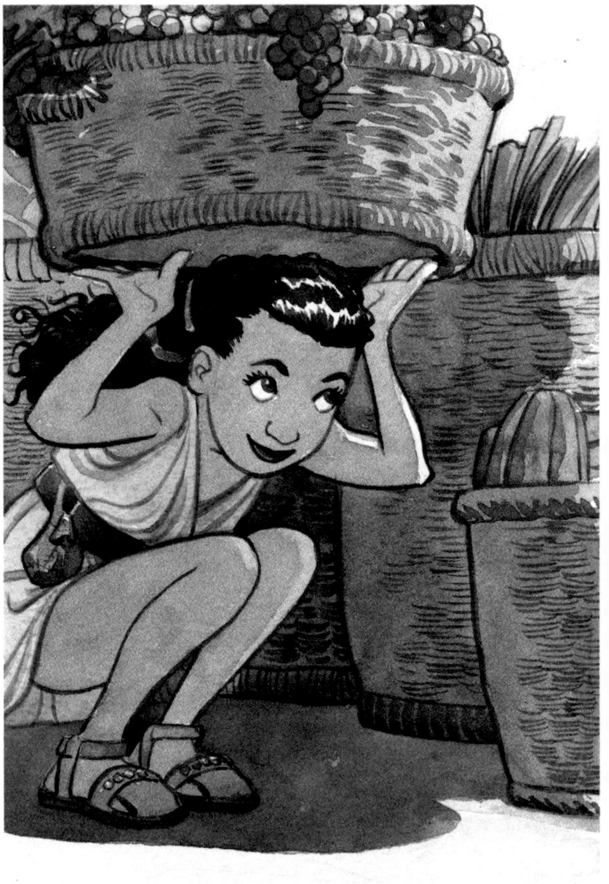

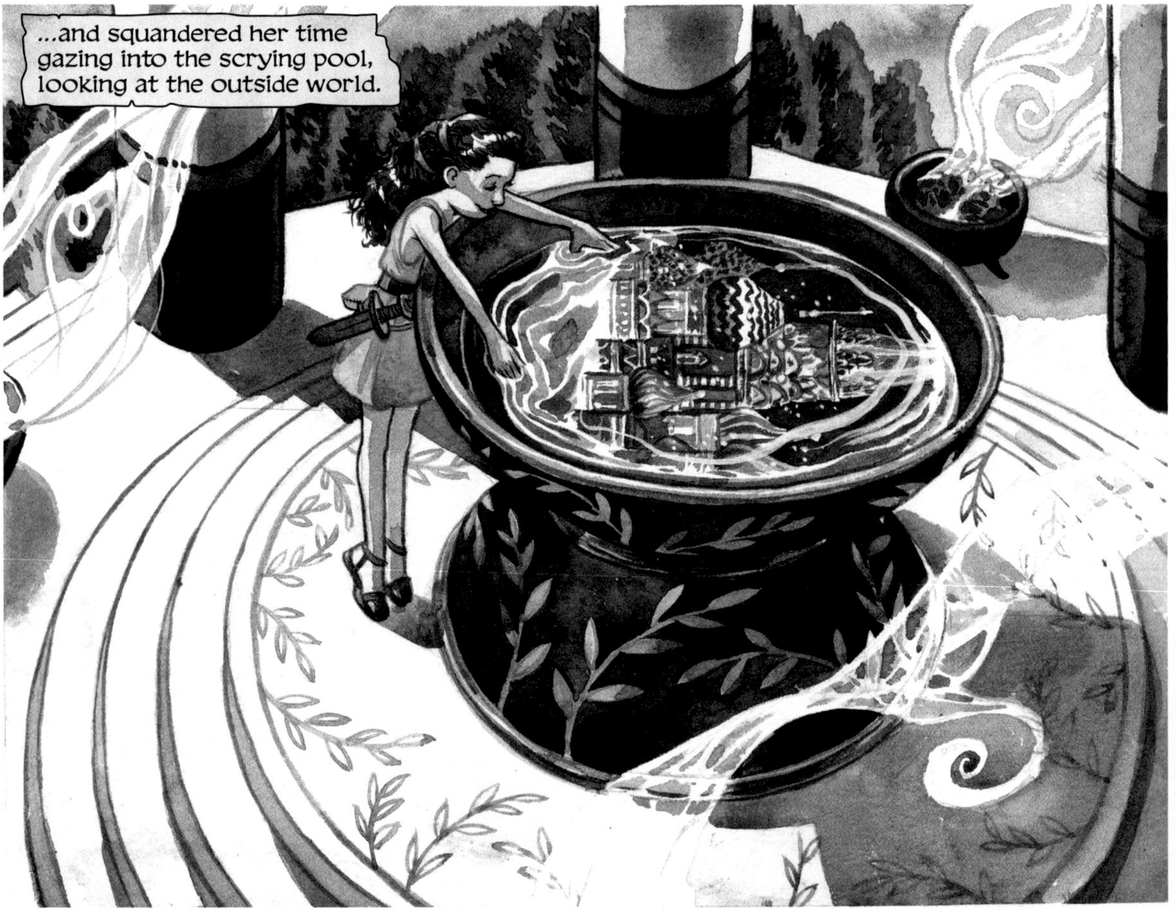
...and squandered her time gazing into the scrying pool, looking at the outside world.

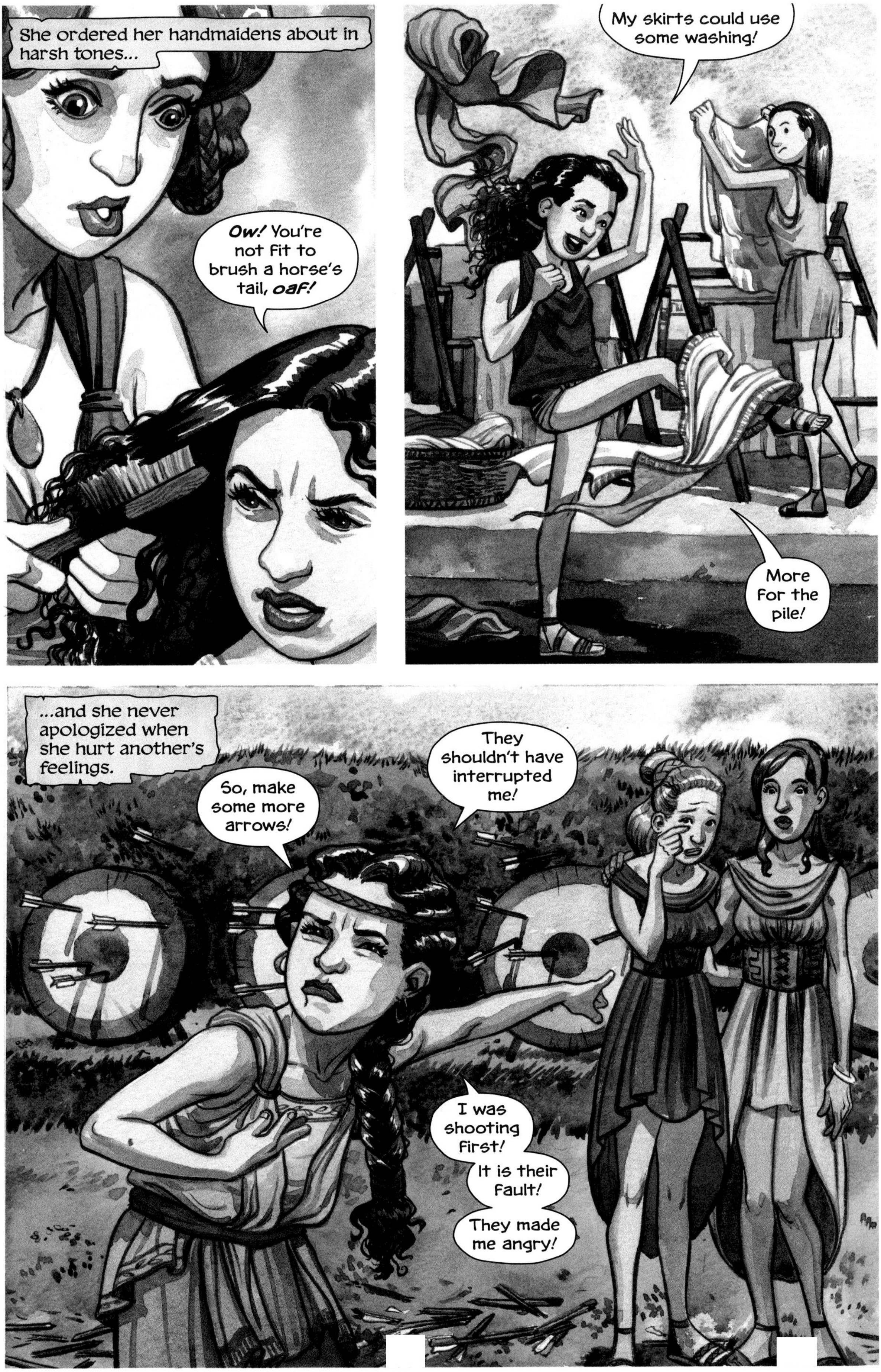
She ordered her handmaidens about in harsh tones...
Ow! You're not fit to brush a horse's tail, oaf!
My skirts could use some washing!
More for the pile!
...and she never apologized when she hurt another's feelings.
So, make some more arrows!
They shouldn't have interrupted me!
I was shooting first!
It is their fault!
They made me angry!

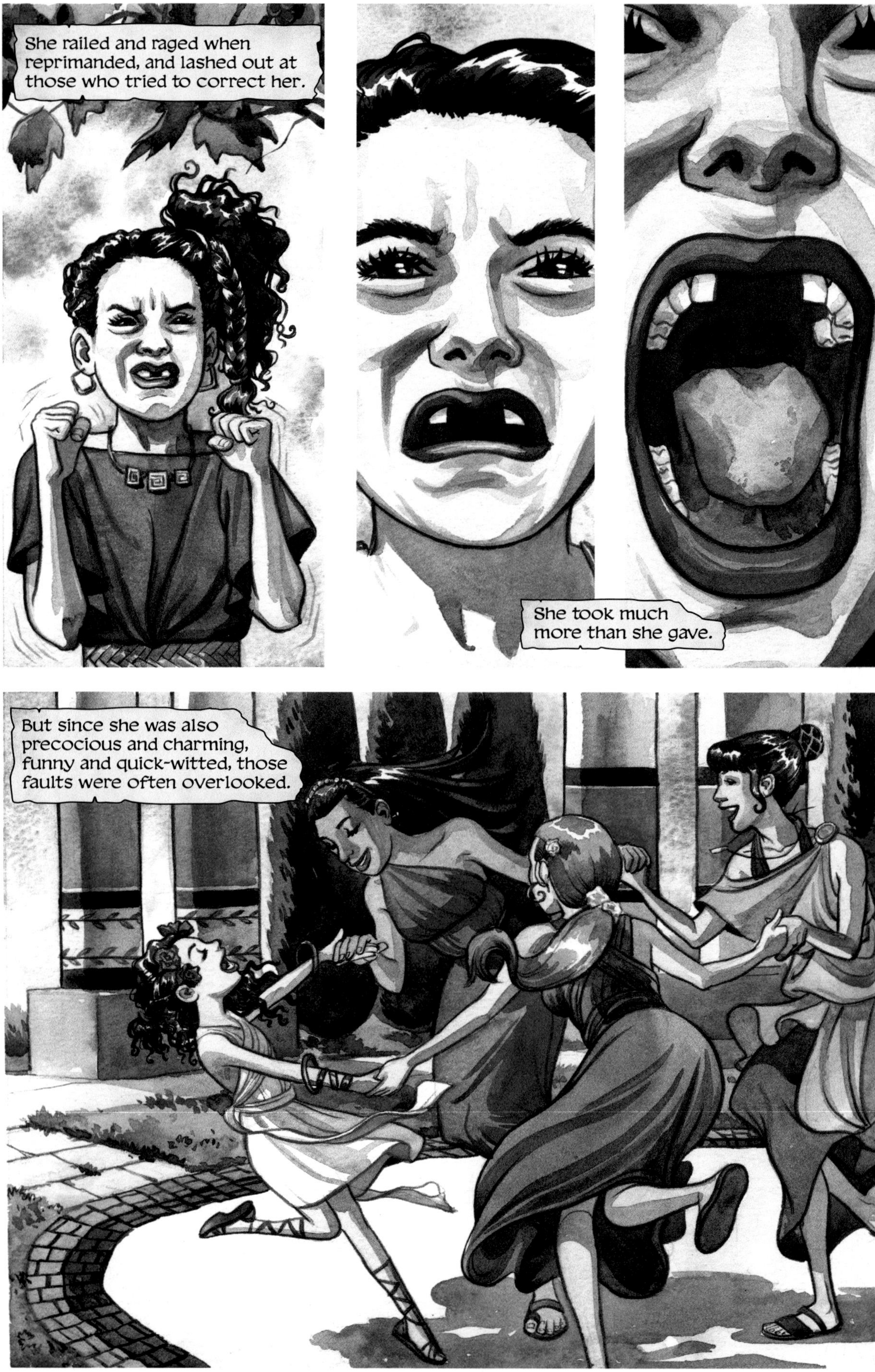
She railed and raged when reprimanded, and lashed out at those who tried to correct her.
She took much more than she gave.
But since she was also precocious and charming, funny and quick-witted, those faults were often overlooked.

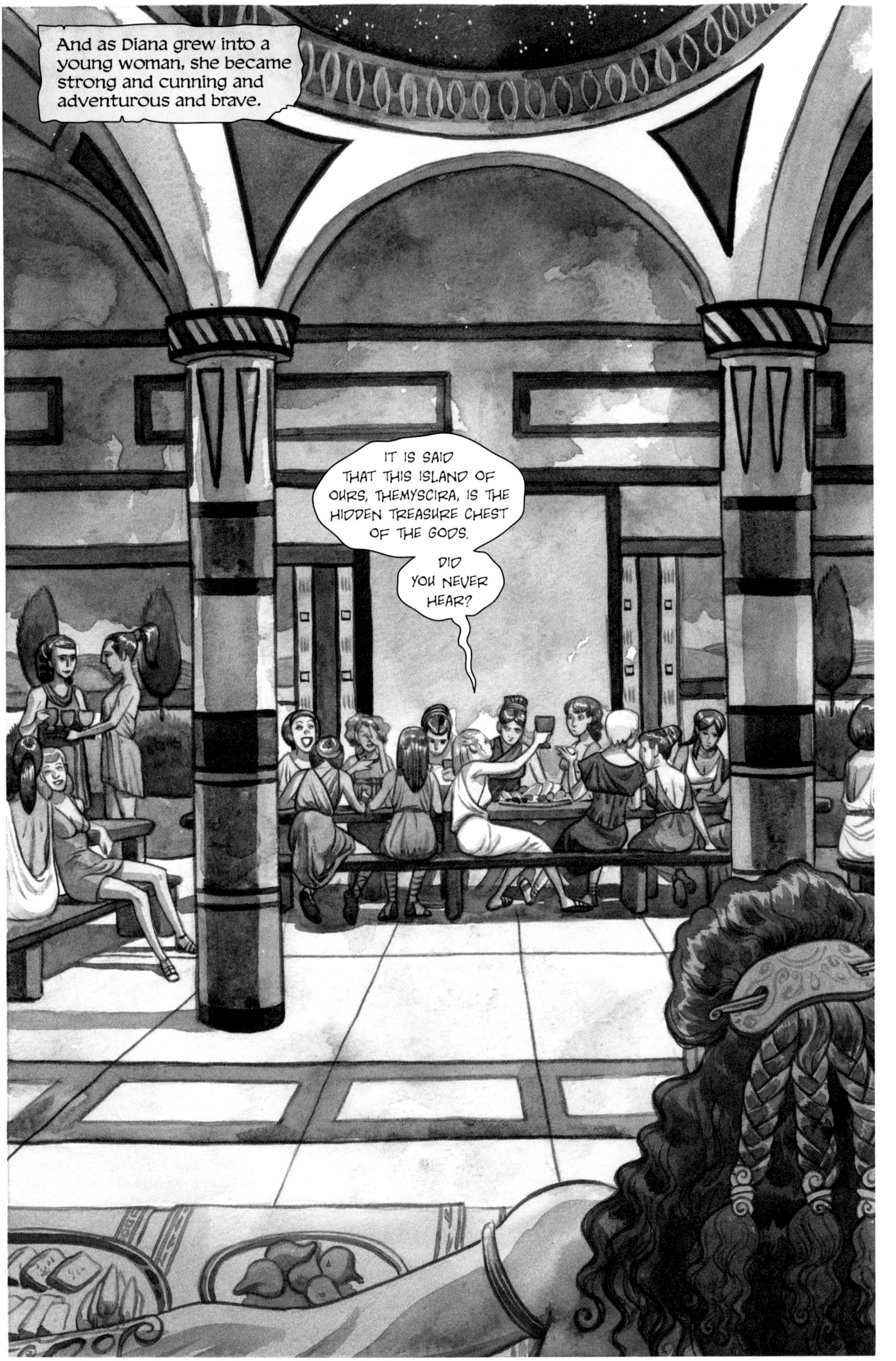
And as Diana grew into a young woman, she became strong and cunning and adventurous and brave.
IT IS SAID THAT THIS ISLAND OF OURS, THEMYSCIRA, IS THE HIDDEN TREASURE CHEST OF THE GODS.
DID YOU NEVER HEAR?

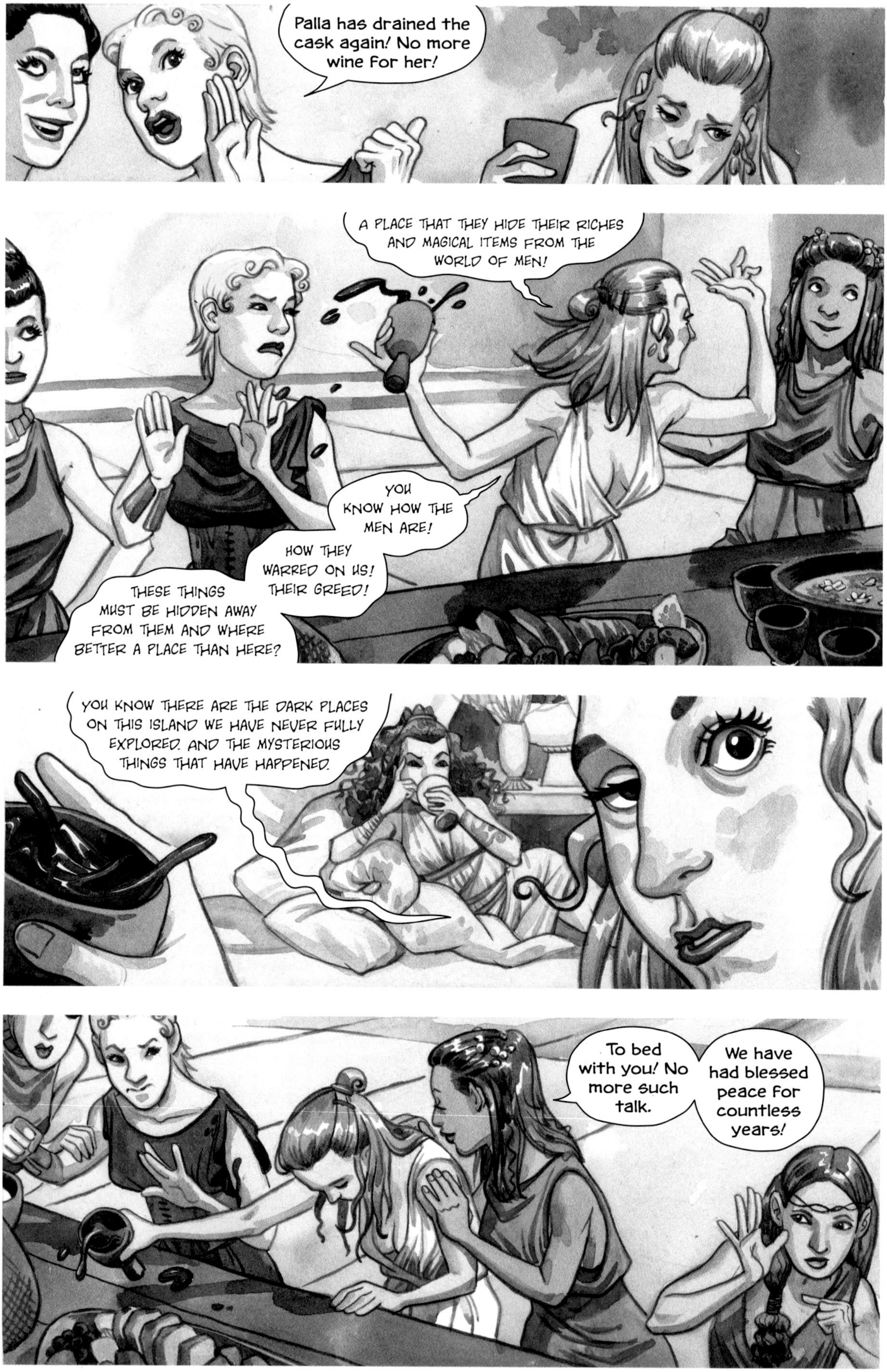
Palla has drained the cask again! No more wine for her!
A PLACE THAT THEY HIDE THEIR RICHES AND MAGICAL ITEMS FROM THE WORLD OF MEN!
YOU KNOW HOW THE MEN ARE!
HOW THEY WARRED ON US! THEIR GREED!
THESE THINGS MUST BE HIDDEN AWAY FROM THEM AND WHERE BETTER A PLACE THAN HERE?
YOU KNOW THERE ARE THE DARK PLACES ON THIS ISLAND WE HAVE NEVER FULLY EXPLORED. AND THE MYSTERIOUS THINGS THAT HAVE HAPPENED.
To bed with you! No more such talk.
We have had blessed peace for countless years!

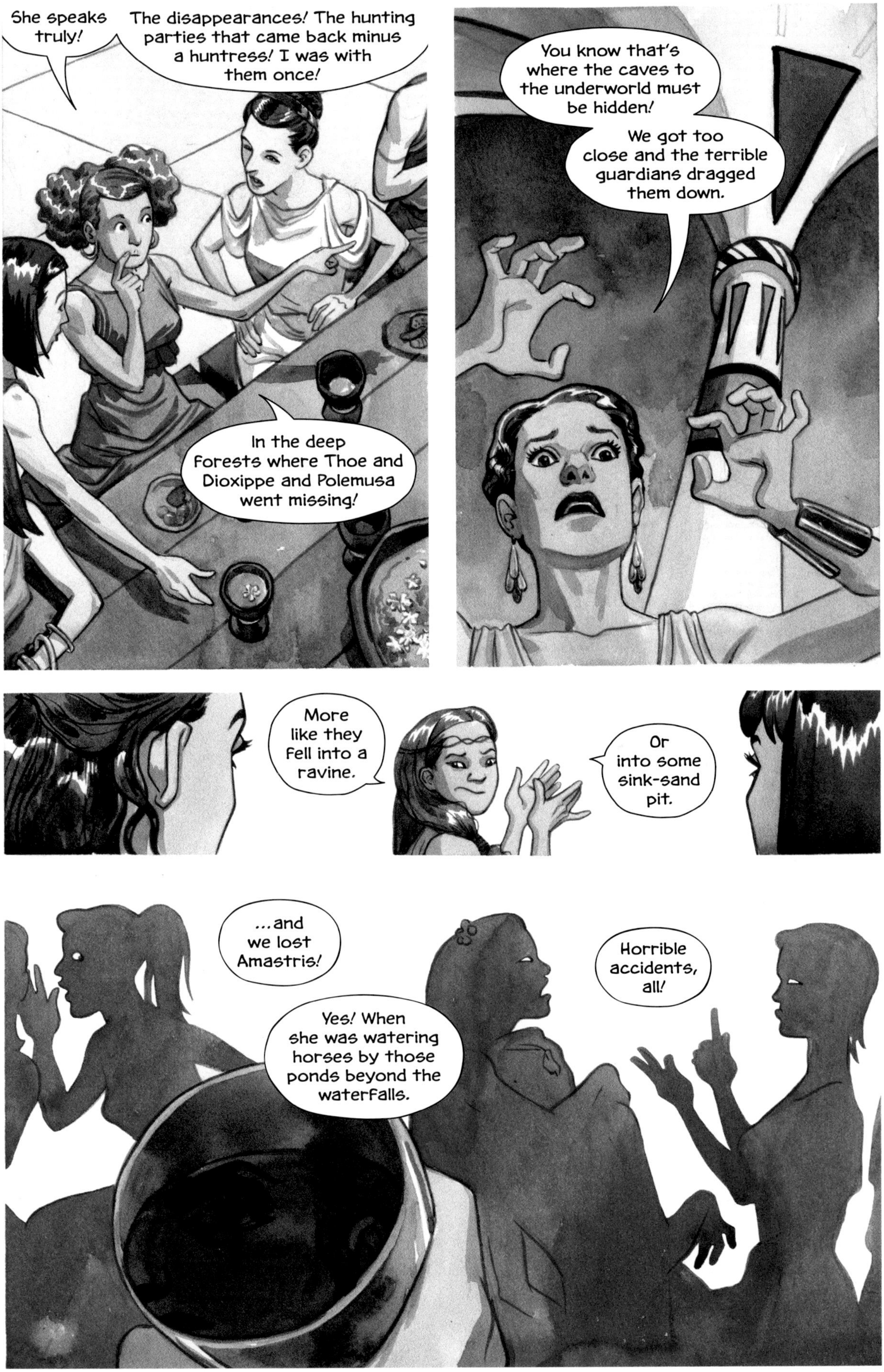
She speaks truly!
The disappearances! The hunting parties that came back minus a huntress! I was with them once!
In the deep forests where Thoe and Dioxippe and Polemusa went missing!
You know that's where the caves to the underworld must be hidden!
We got too close and the terrible guardians dragged them down.
More like they fell into a ravine.
Or into some sink-sand pit.
...and we lost Amastris!
Yes! When she was watering horses by those ponds beyond the waterfalls.
Horrible accidents, all!

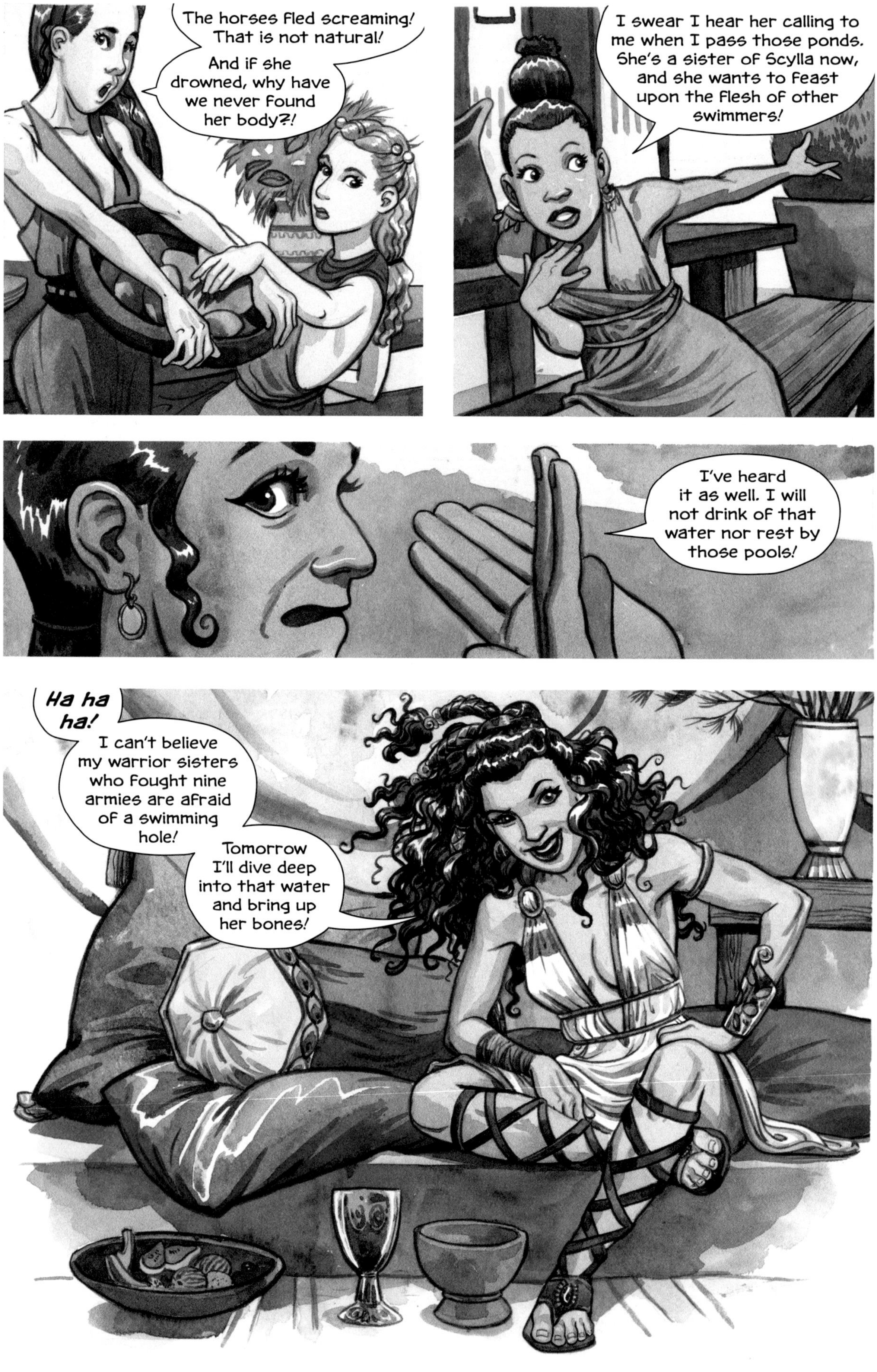
The horses fled screaming! That is not natural!
And if she drowned, why have we never found her body?!
I swear I hear her calling to me when I pass those ponds. She's a sister of Scylla now, and she wants to feast upon the flesh of other swimmers!
I've heard it as well. I will not drink of that water nor rest by those pools!
Ha ha ha!
I can't believe my warrior sisters who fought nine armies are afraid of a swimming hole!
Tomorrow I'll dive deep into that water and bring up her bones!

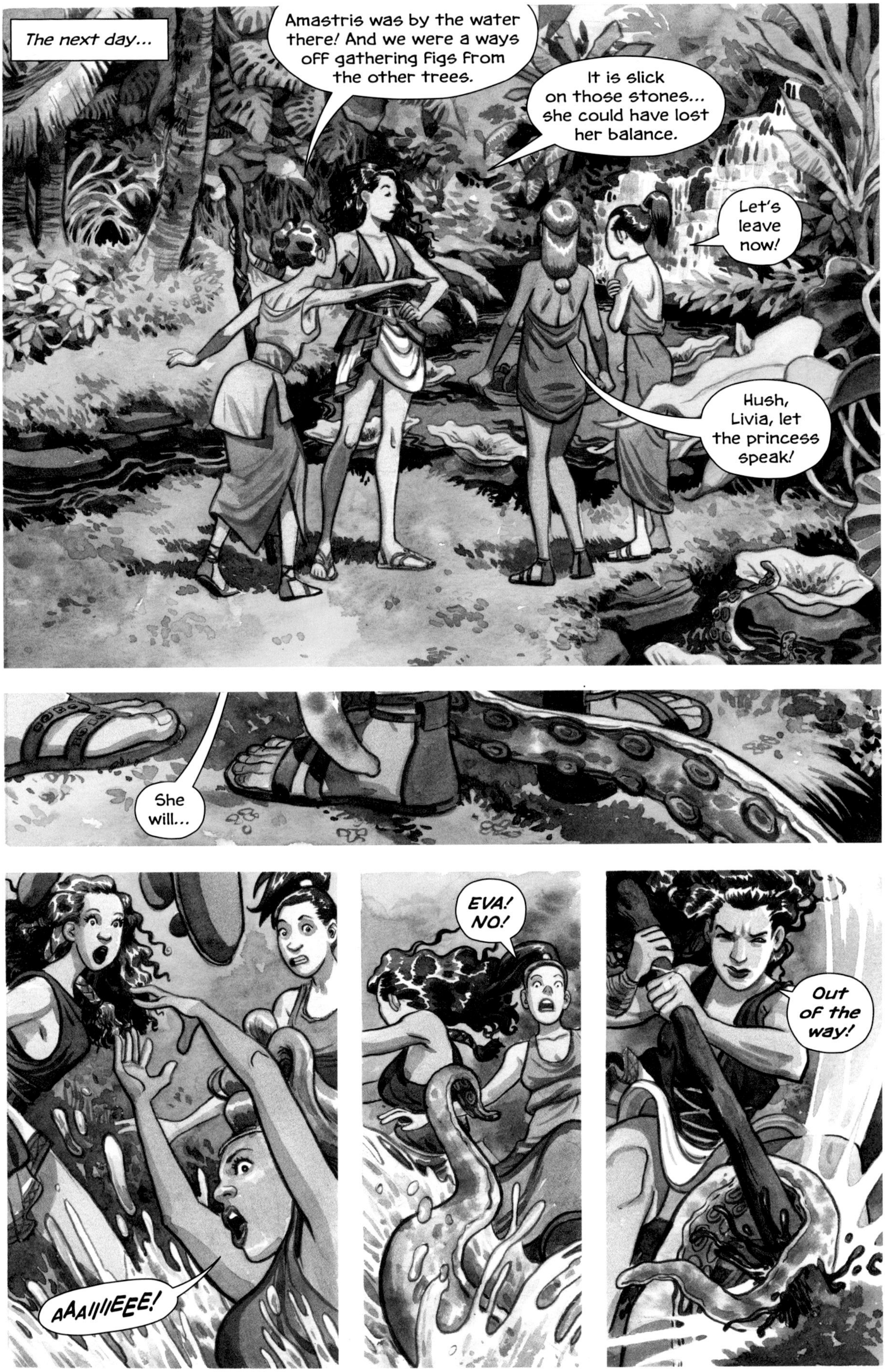
The next day...
Amastris was by the water there! And we were a ways off gathering figs from the other trees.
It is slick on those stones... she could have lost her balance.
Let's leave now!
Hush, Livia, let the princess speak!
She will...
AAAIIIIEEE!
EVA! NO!
Out of the way!

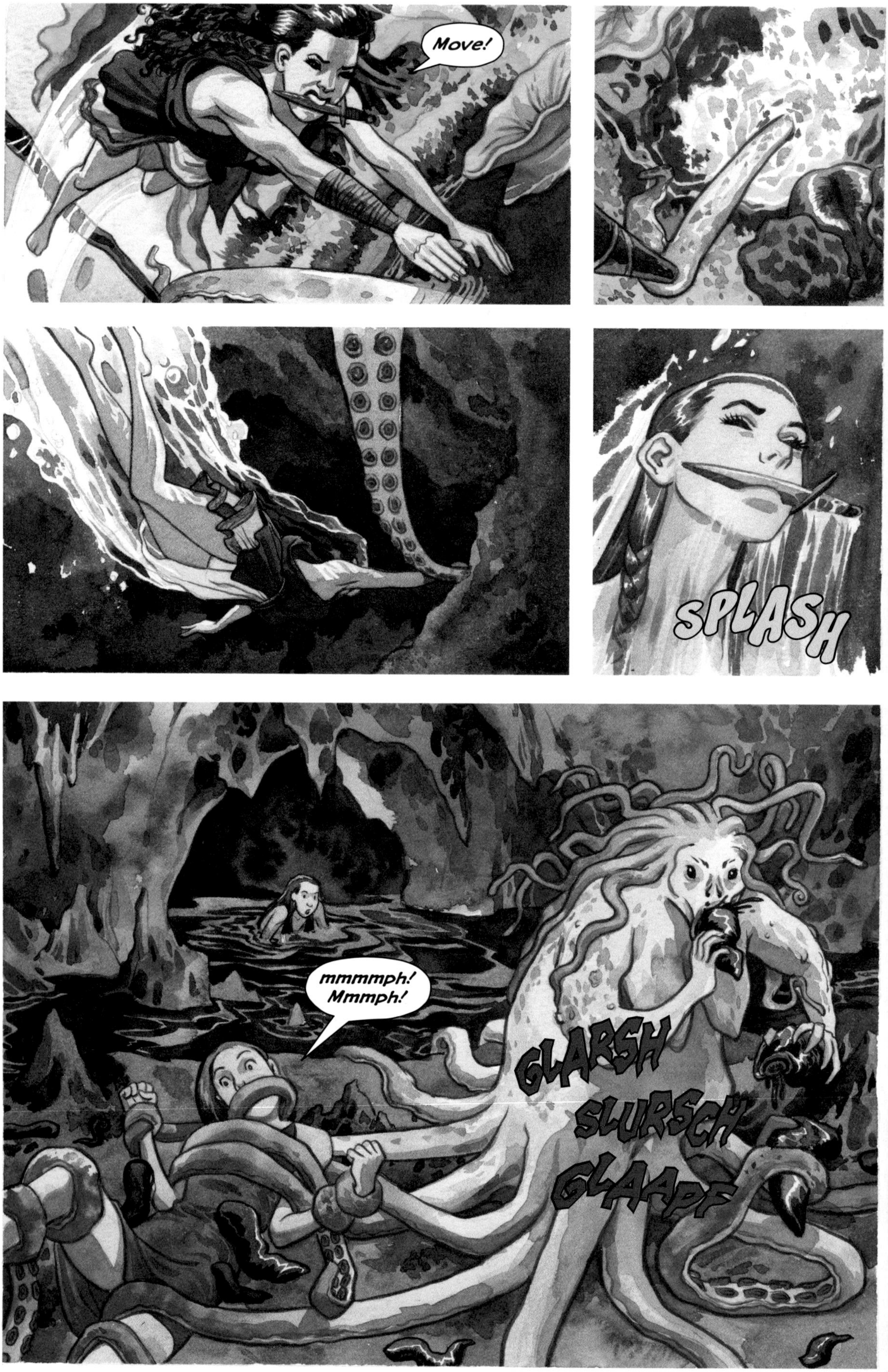
Move!
SPLASH
mmmmph! Mmmph!
GLARSH
SLURSCH
GLAAPF

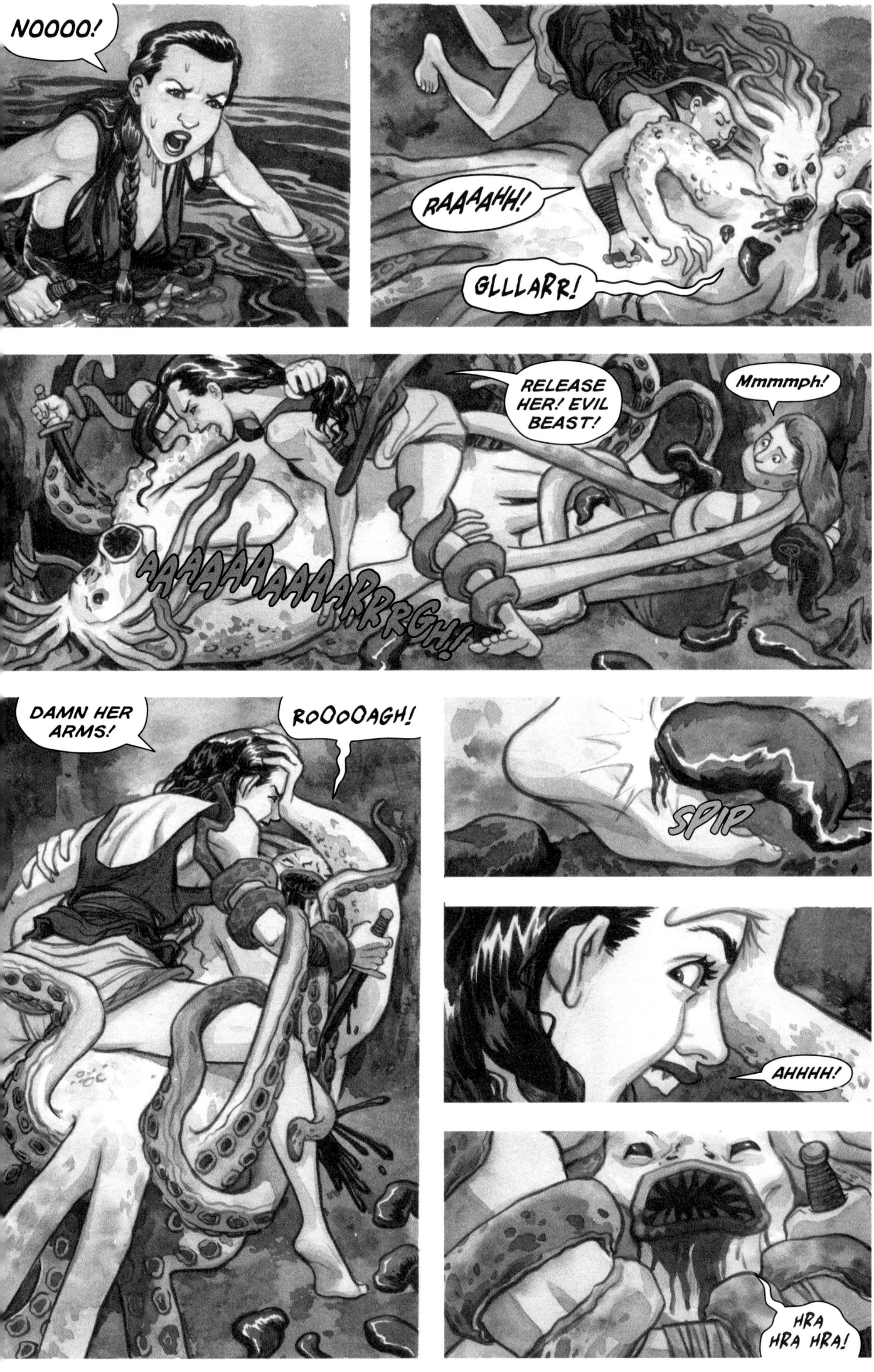
NOOOO!
RAAAAHH!
GLLLARR!
RELEASE HER! EVIL BEAST!
Mmmmph!
AAAAAAAAAAARRRGH!
DAMN HER ARMS!
ROOOOAGH!
SPIP
AHHHH!
HRA HRA HRA!

Evil bitch! You won't feast on my blood! Rrrr--

RAAAAHH!

Nor any Amazon blood!

EEEEEEEE!

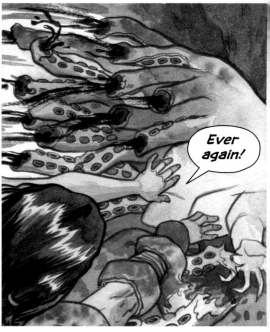

Ever again!

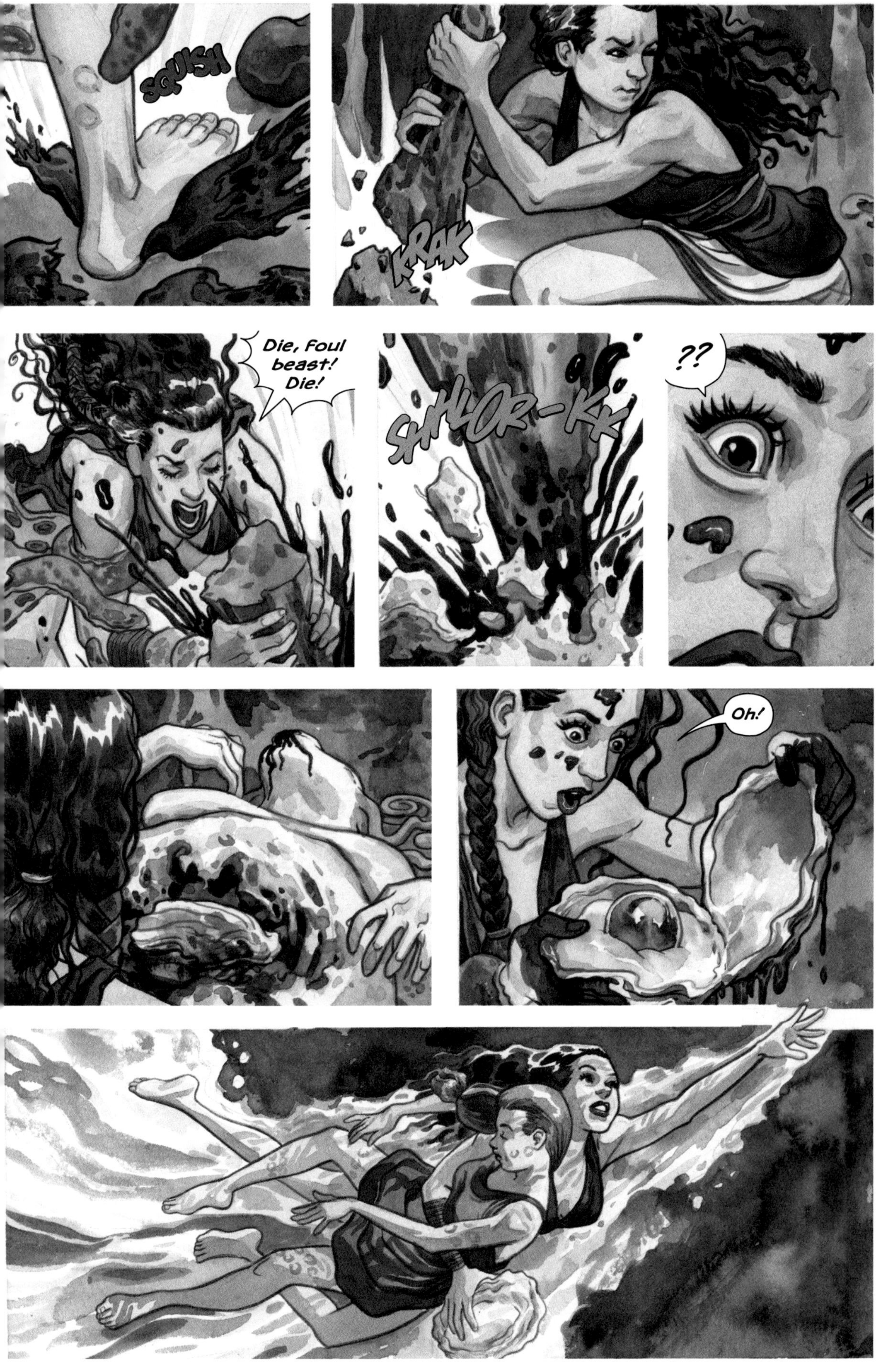
SQUISH
KRAK
Die, foul beast! Die!
SHHLOR-KK
??
Oh!

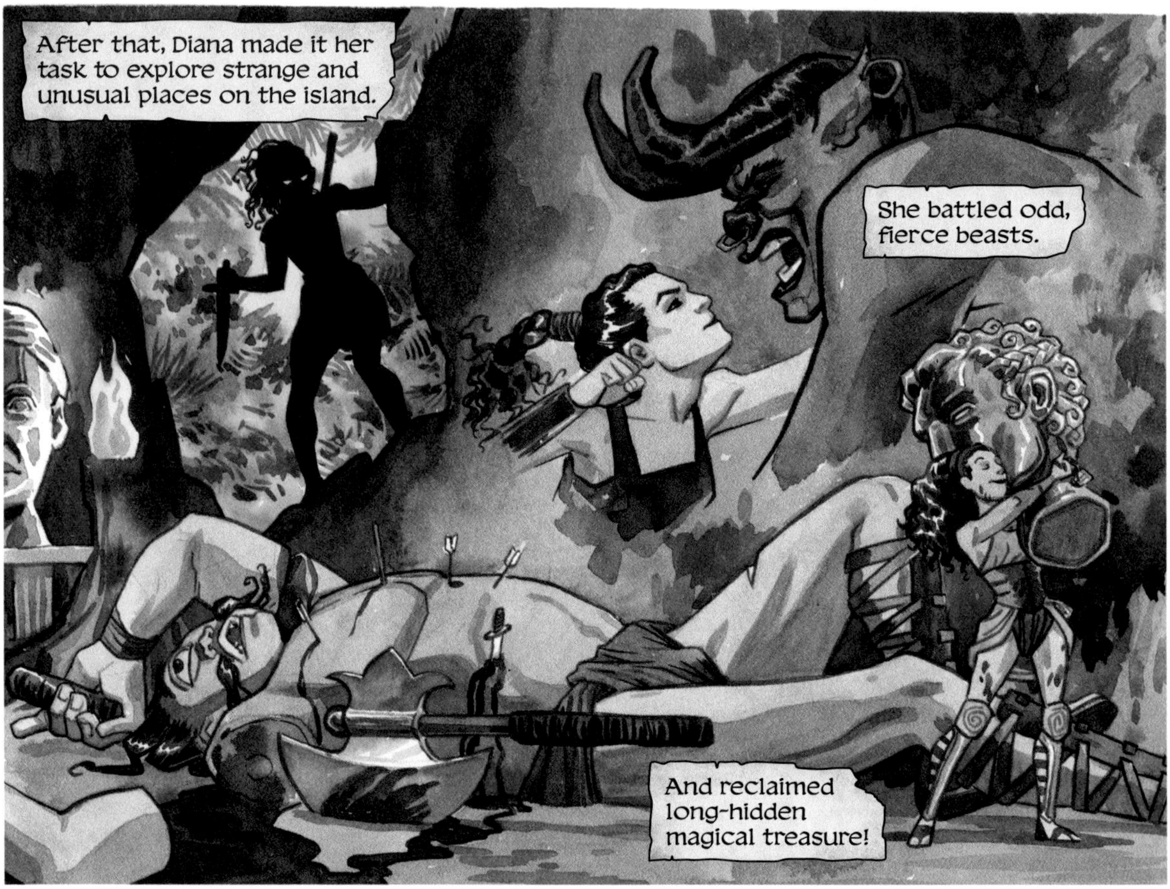
After that, Diana made it her task to explore strange and unusual places on the island.
She battled odd, fierce beasts.
And reclaimed long-hidden magical treasure!

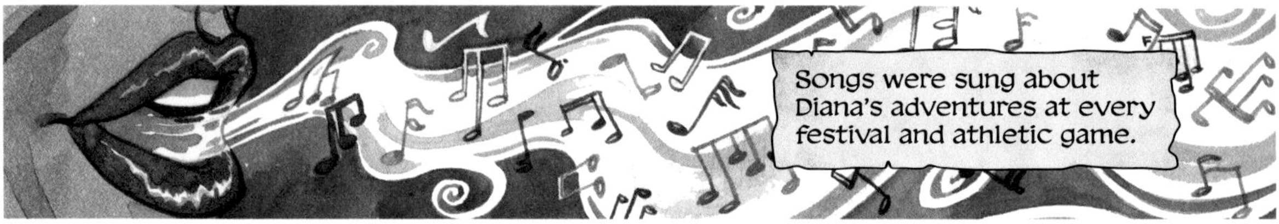
Songs were sung about Diana's adventures at every festival and athletic game.

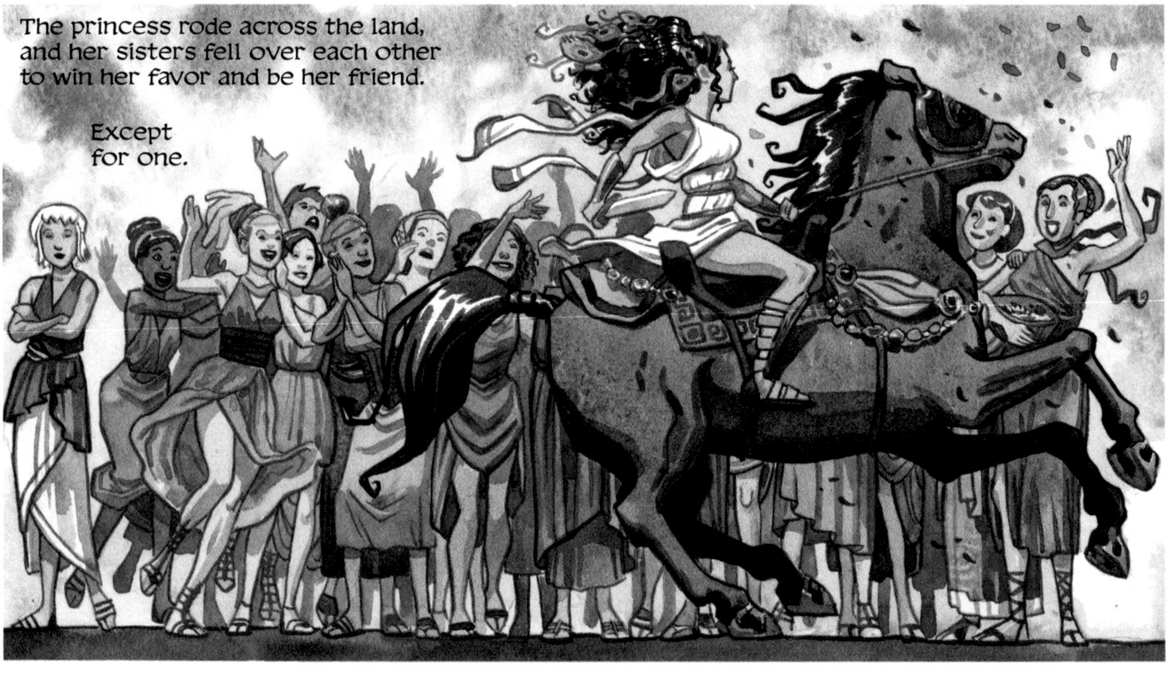
The princess rode across the land, and her sisters fell over each other to win her favor and be her friend.
Except for one.

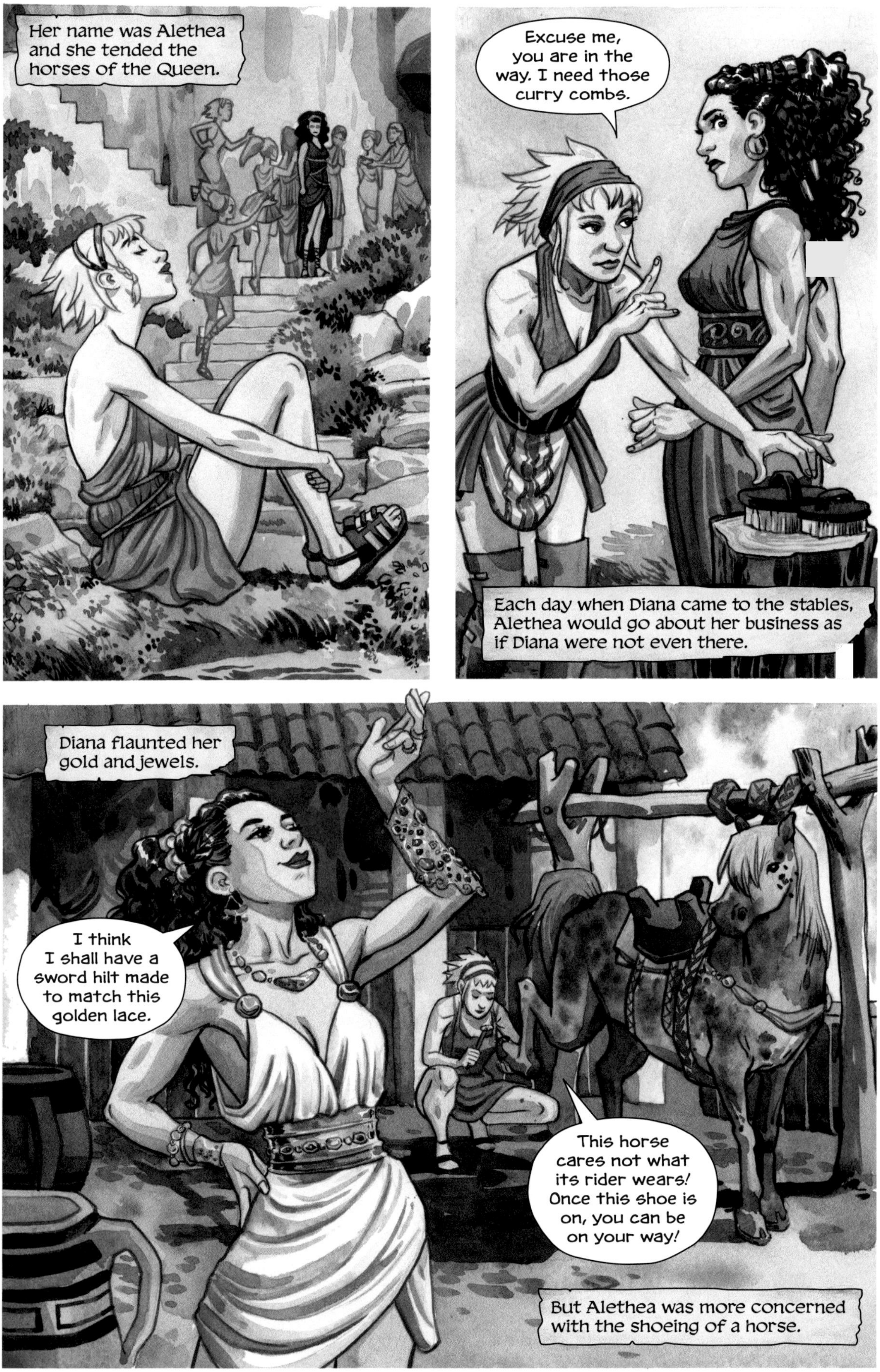

Her name was Alethea and she tended the horses of the Queen.
Excuse me, you are in the way. I need those curry combs.
Each day when Diana came to the stables, Alethea would go about her business as if Diana were not even there.
Diana flaunted her gold and jewels.
I think I shall have a sword hilt made to match this golden lace.
This horse cares not what its rider wears! Once this shoe is on, you can be on your way!
But Alethea was more concerned with the shoeing of a horse.

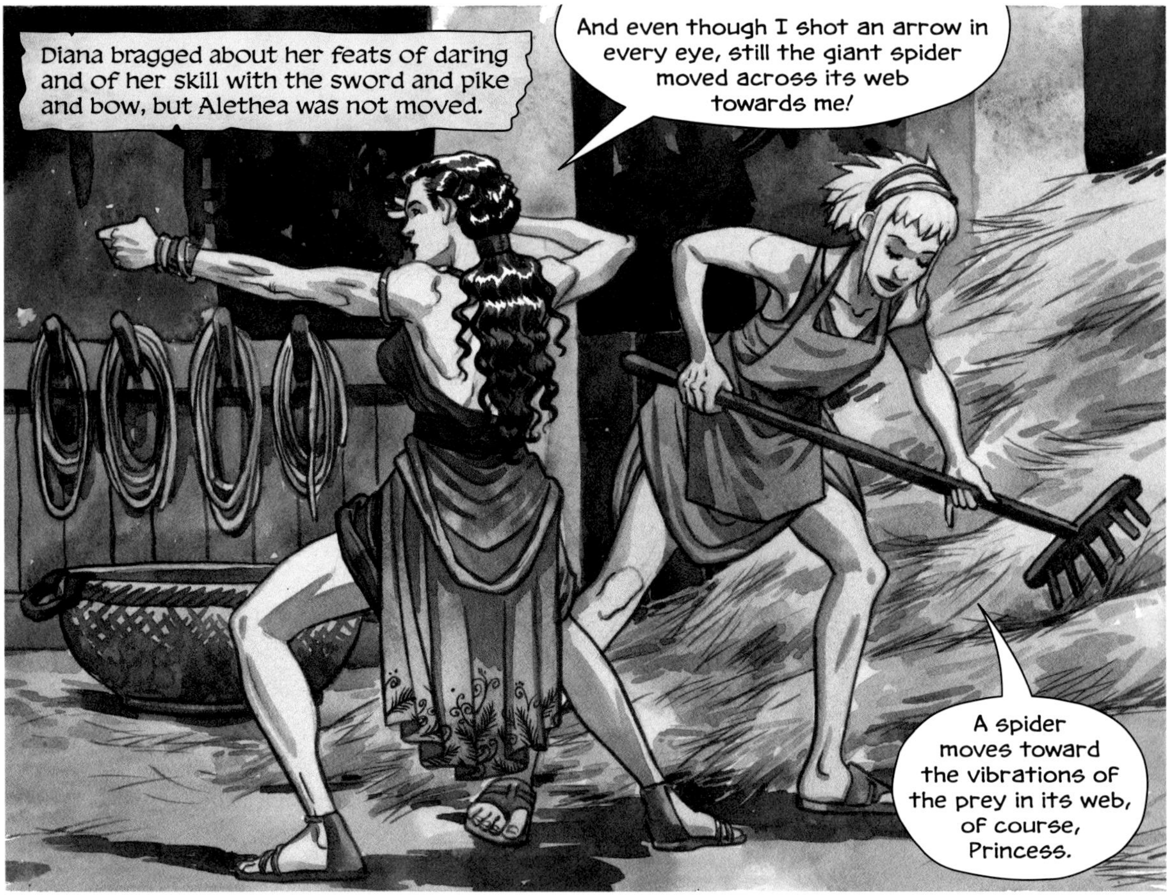
Diana bragged about her feats of daring and of her skill with the sword and pike and bow, but Alethea was not moved.
And even though I shot an arrow in every eye, still the giant spider moved across its web towards me!
A spider moves toward the vibrations of the prey in its web, of course, Princess.

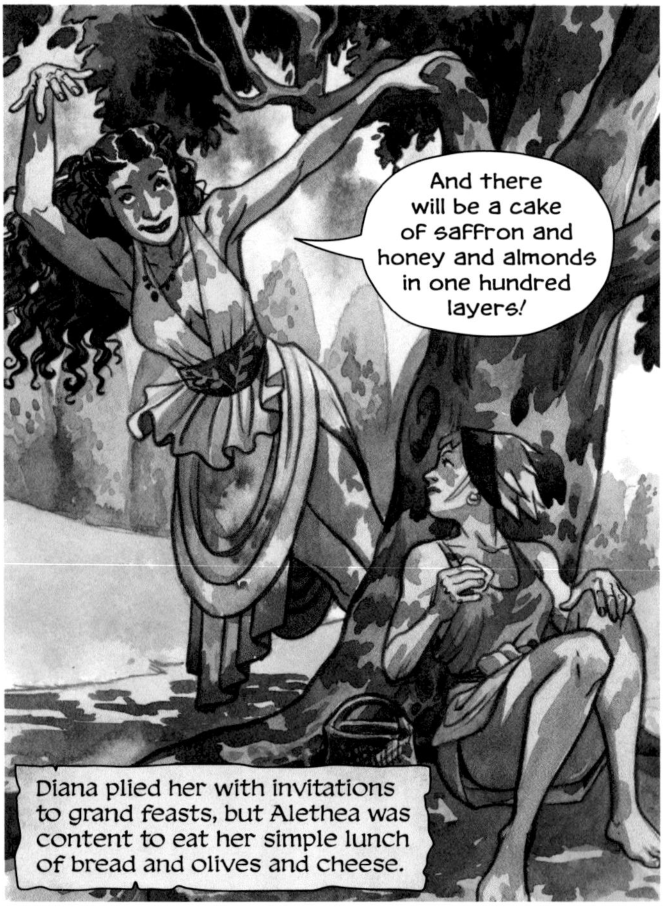
And there will be a cake of saffron and honey and almonds in one hundred layers!
Diana plied her with invitations to grand feasts, but Alethea was content to eat her simple lunch of bread and olives and cheese.

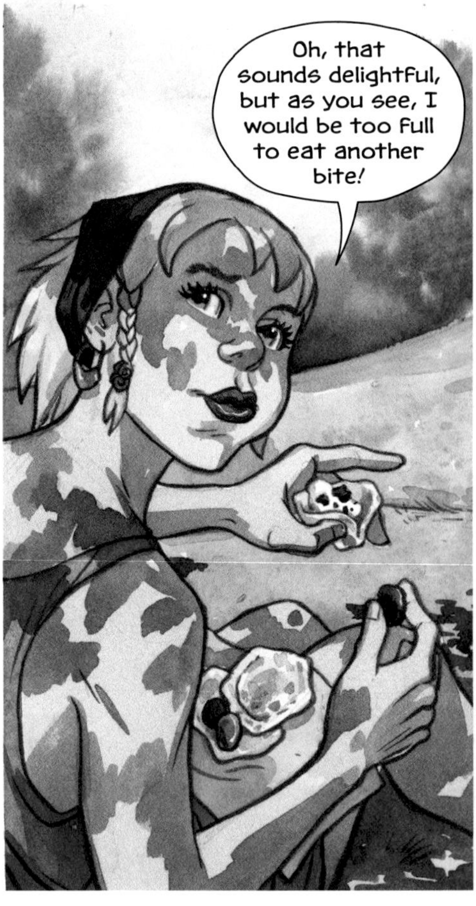
Oh, that sounds delightful, but as you see, I would be too full to eat another bite!

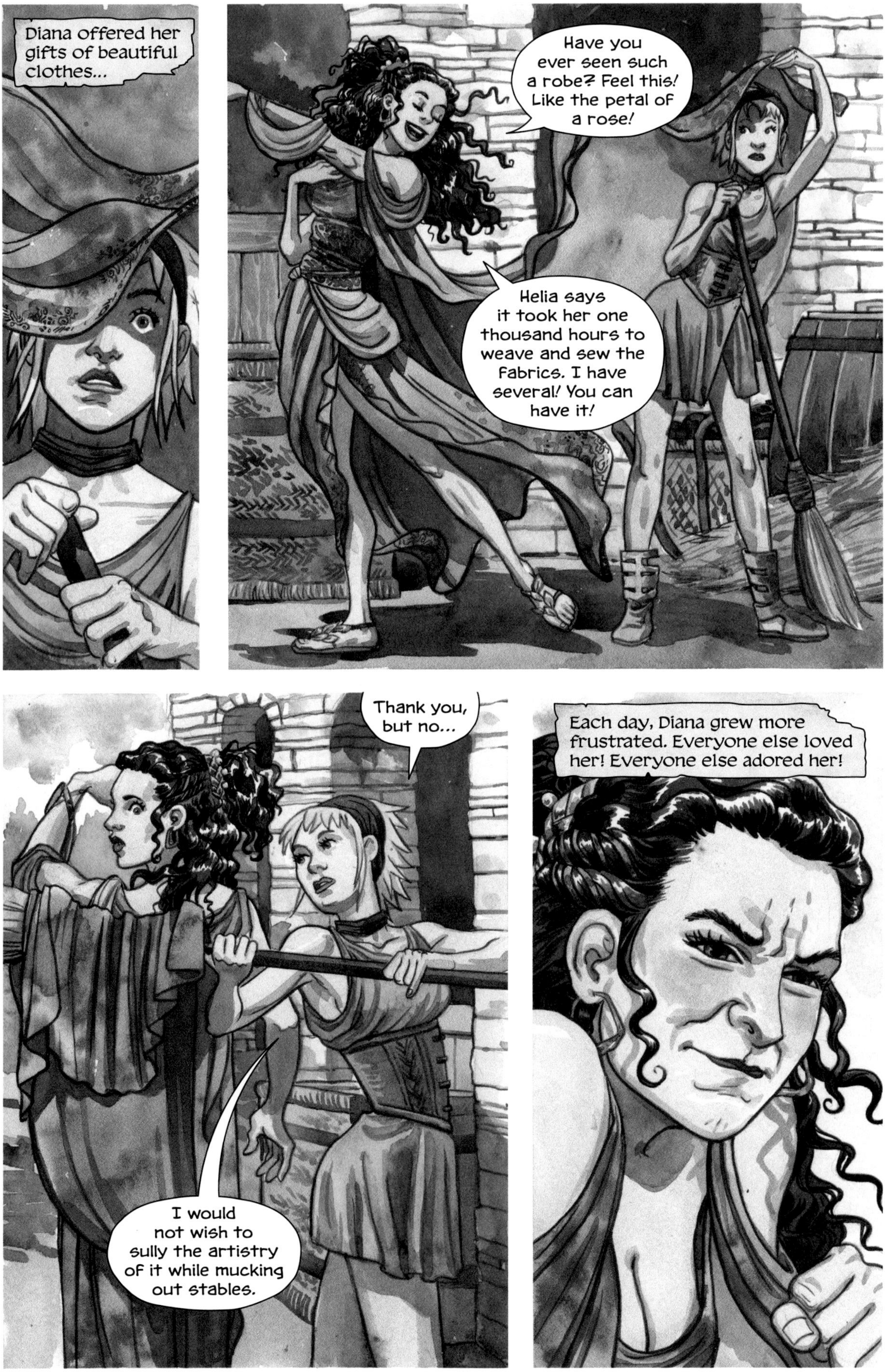
Diana offered her gifts of beautiful clothes...
Have you ever seen such a robe? Feel this! Like the petal of a rose!
Helia says it took her one thousand hours to weave and sew the fabrics. I have several! You can have it!
Thank you, but no...
I would not wish to sully the artistry of it while mucking out stables.
Each day, Diana grew more frustrated. Everyone else loved her! Everyone else adored her!

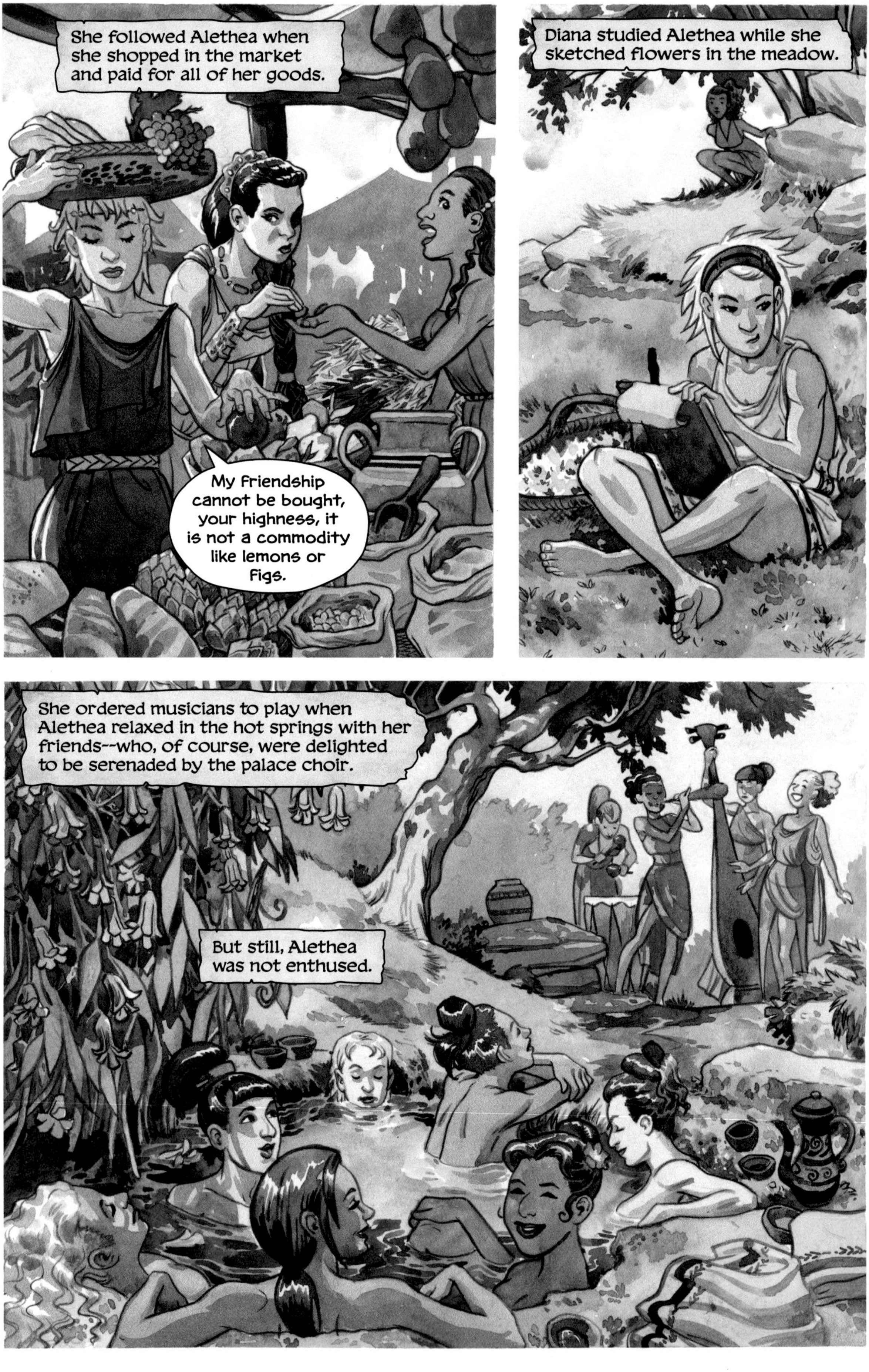
She followed Alethea when she shopped in the market and paid for all of her goods.
My friendship cannot be bought, your highness, it is not a commodity like lemons or figs.
Diana studied Alethea while she sketched flowers in the meadow.
She ordered musicians to play when Alethea relaxed in the hot springs with her friends--who, of course, were delighted to be serenaded by the palace choir.
But still, Alethea was not enthused.

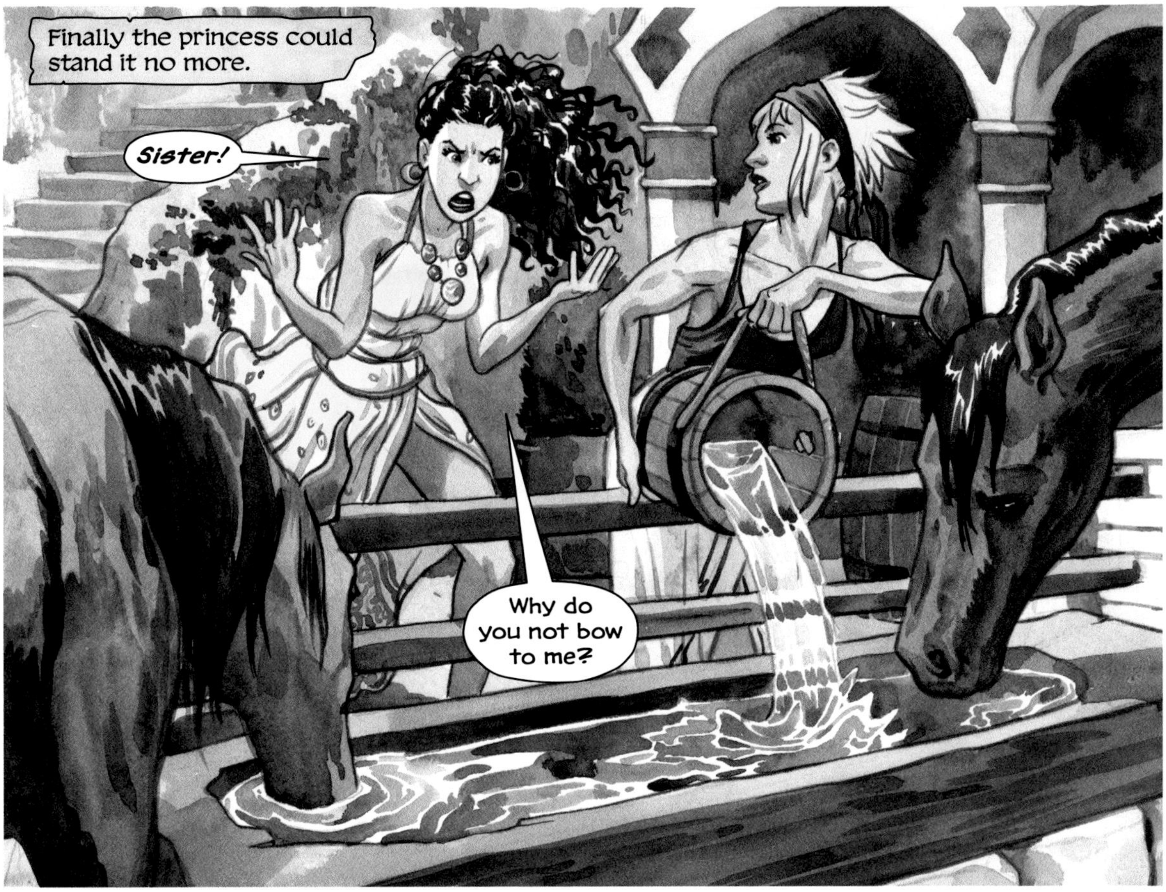
Finally the princess could stand it no more.
Sister!
Why do you not bow to me?

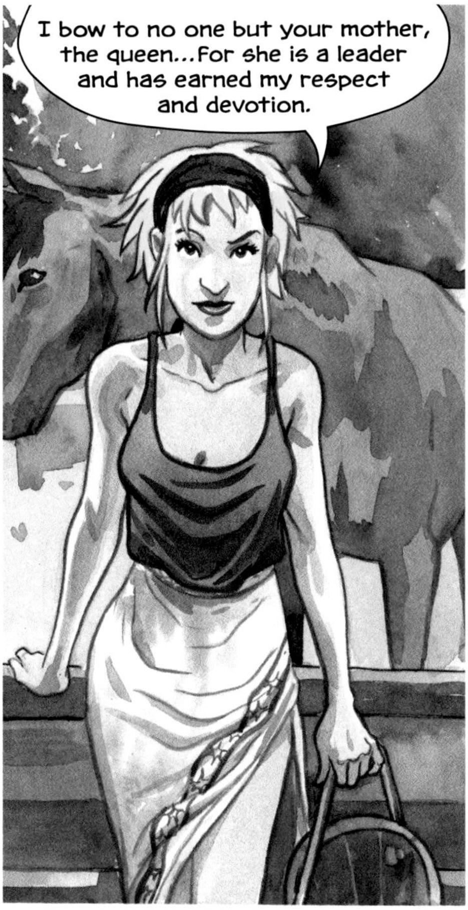
I bow to no one but your mother, the queen...For she is a leader and has earned my respect and devotion.

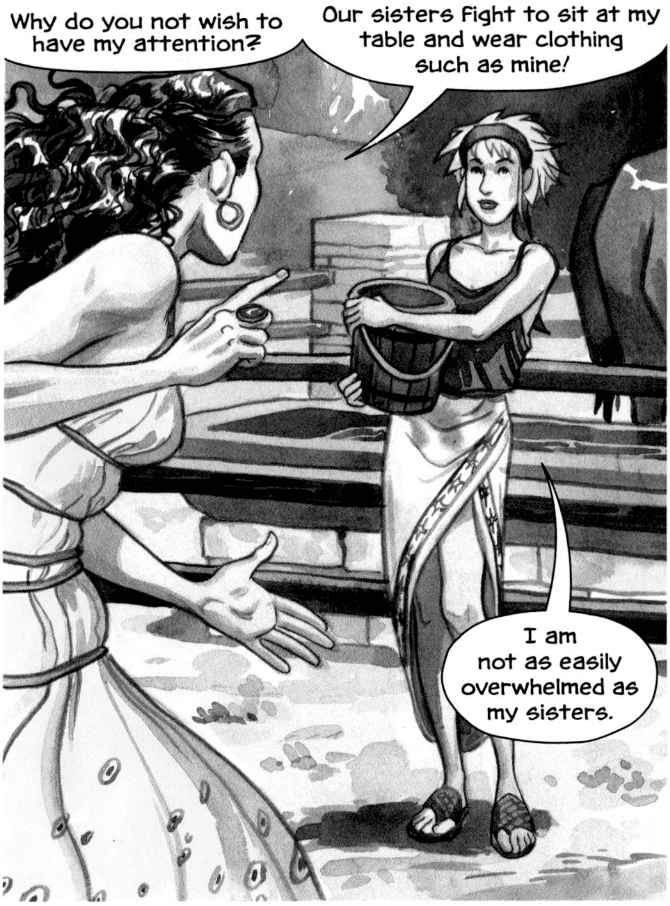
Why do you not wish to have my attention?
Our sisters fight to sit at my table and wear clothing such as mine!
I am not as easily overwhelmed as my sisters.

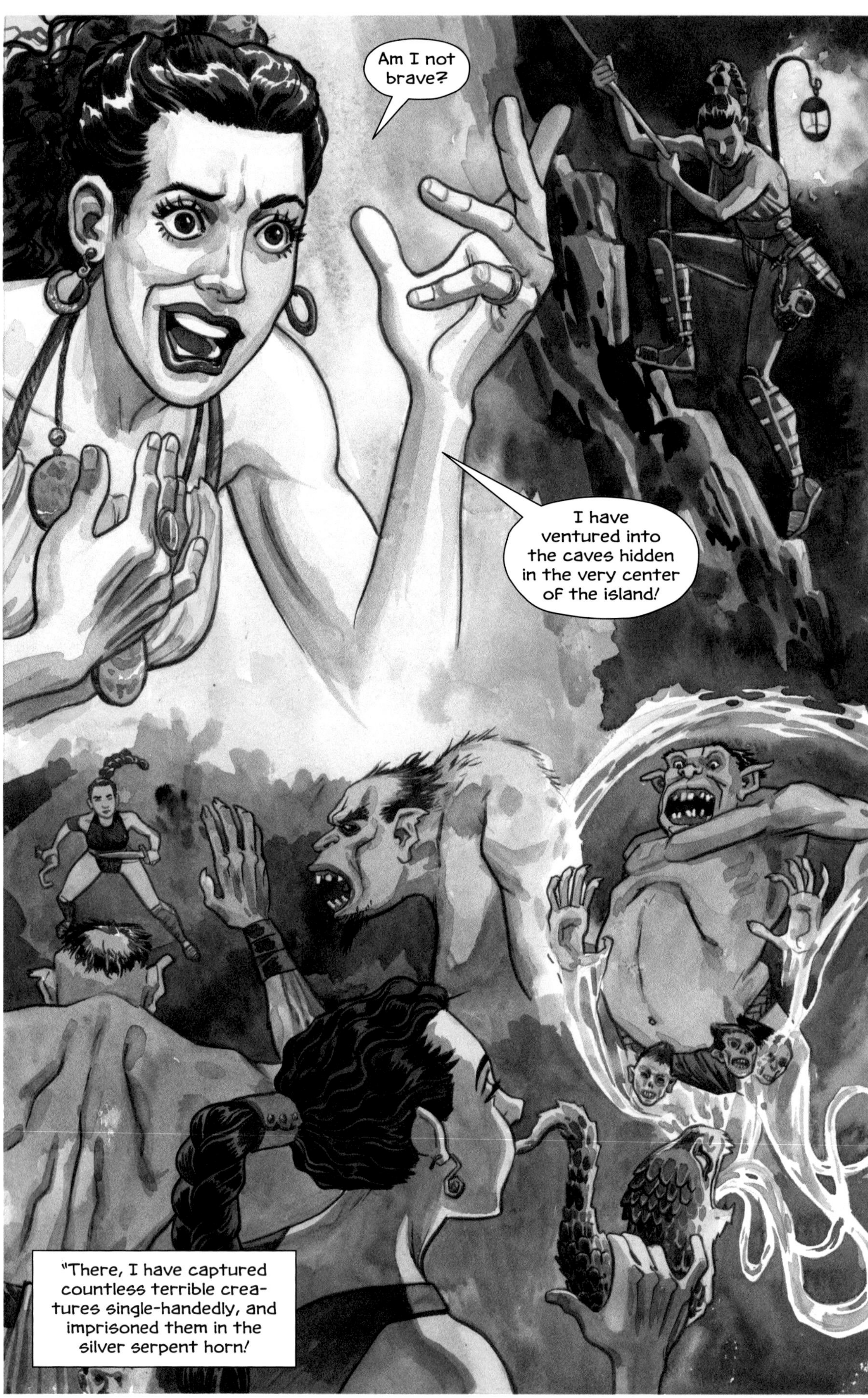
Am I not brave?
I have ventured into the caves hidden in the very center of the island!
"There, I have captured countless terrible creatures single-handedly, and imprisoned them in the silver serpent horn!

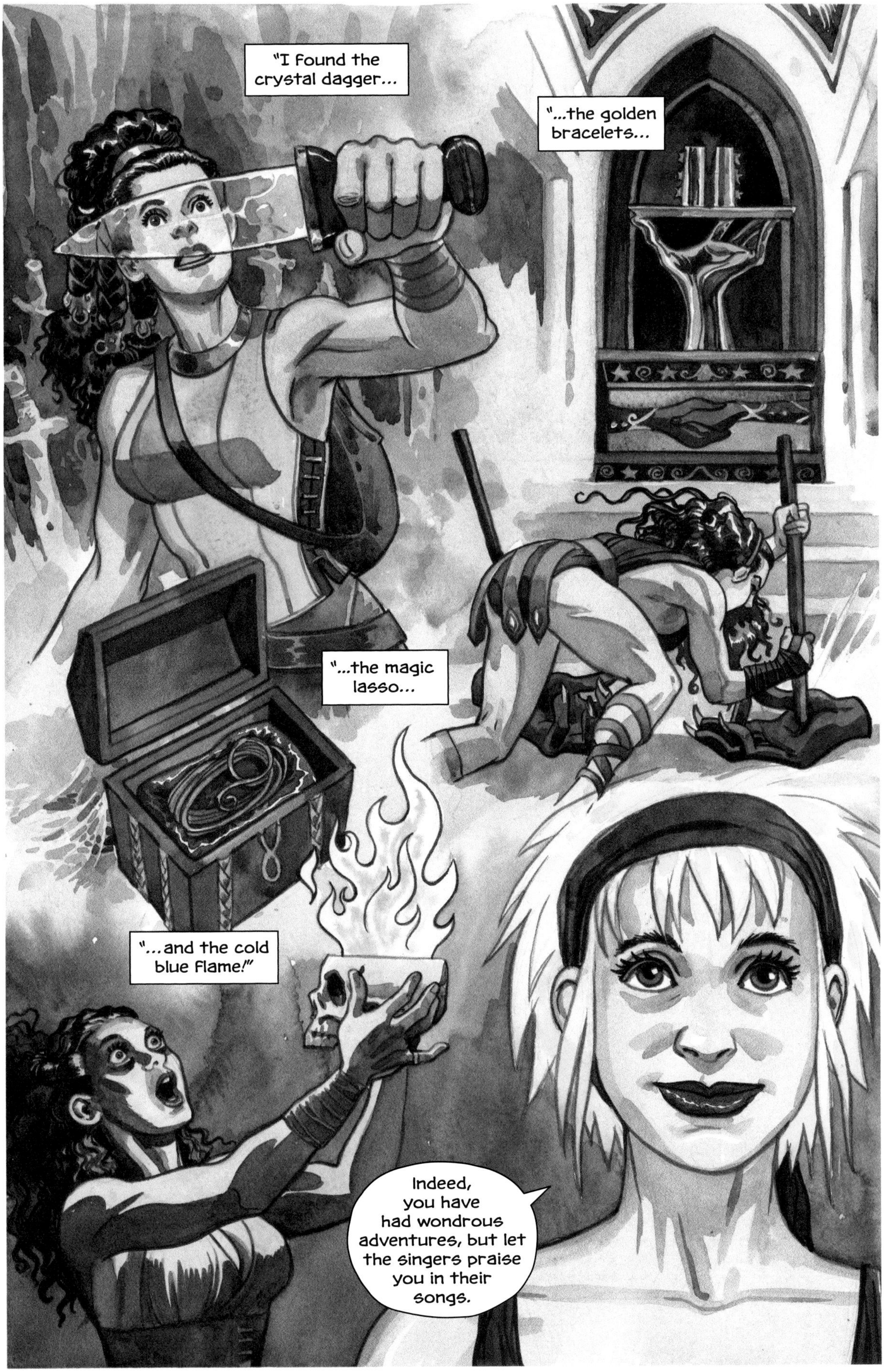
"I found the crystal dagger...
"...the golden bracelets...
"...the magic lasso...
"...and the cold blue flame!"
Indeed, you have had wondrous adventures, but let the singers praise you in their songs.

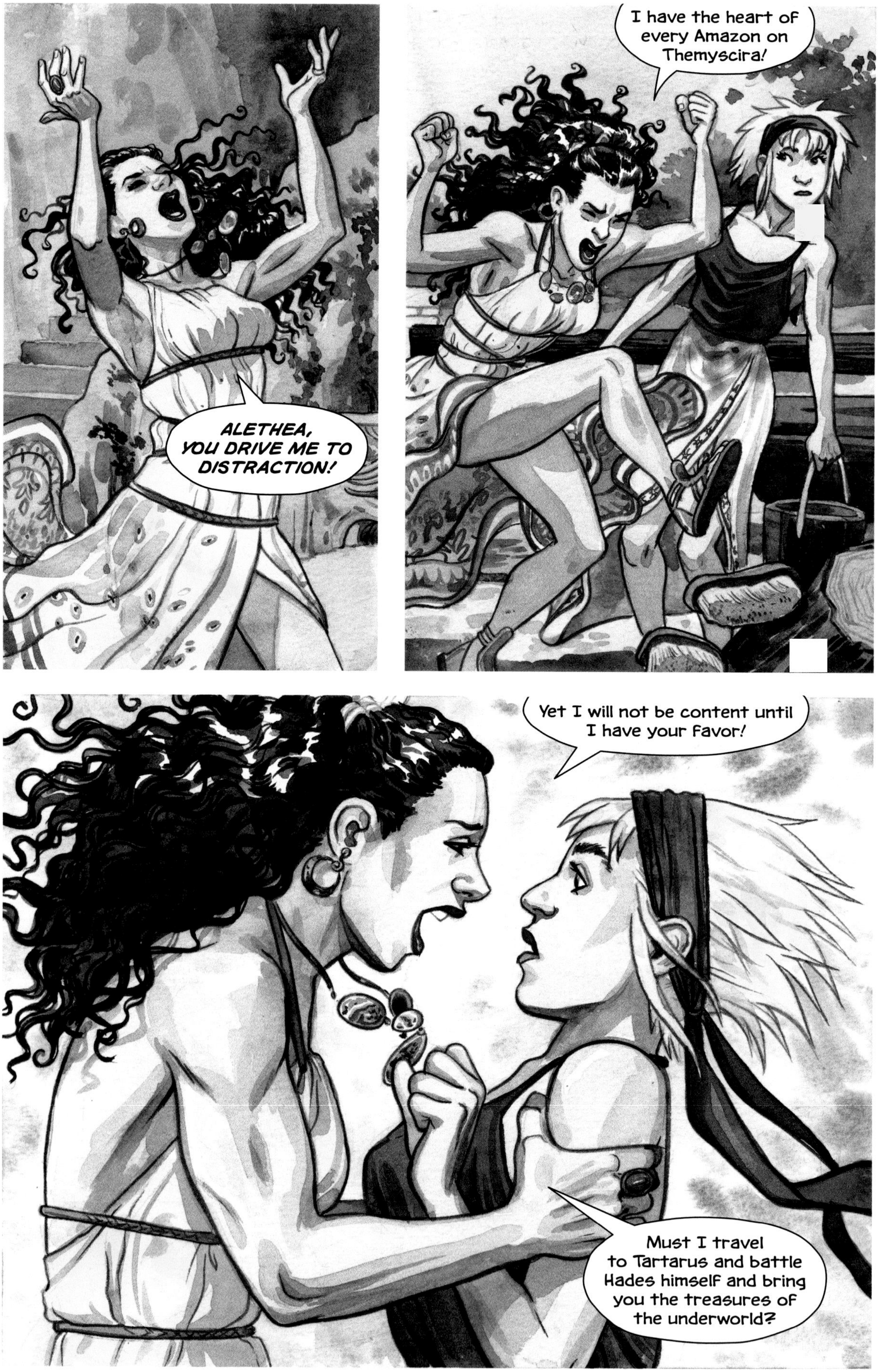
ALETHEA, YOU DRIVE ME TO DISTRACTION!
I have the heart of every Amazon on Themyscira!
Yet I will not be content until I have your favor!
Must I travel to Tartarus and battle Hades himself and bring you the treasures of the underworld?

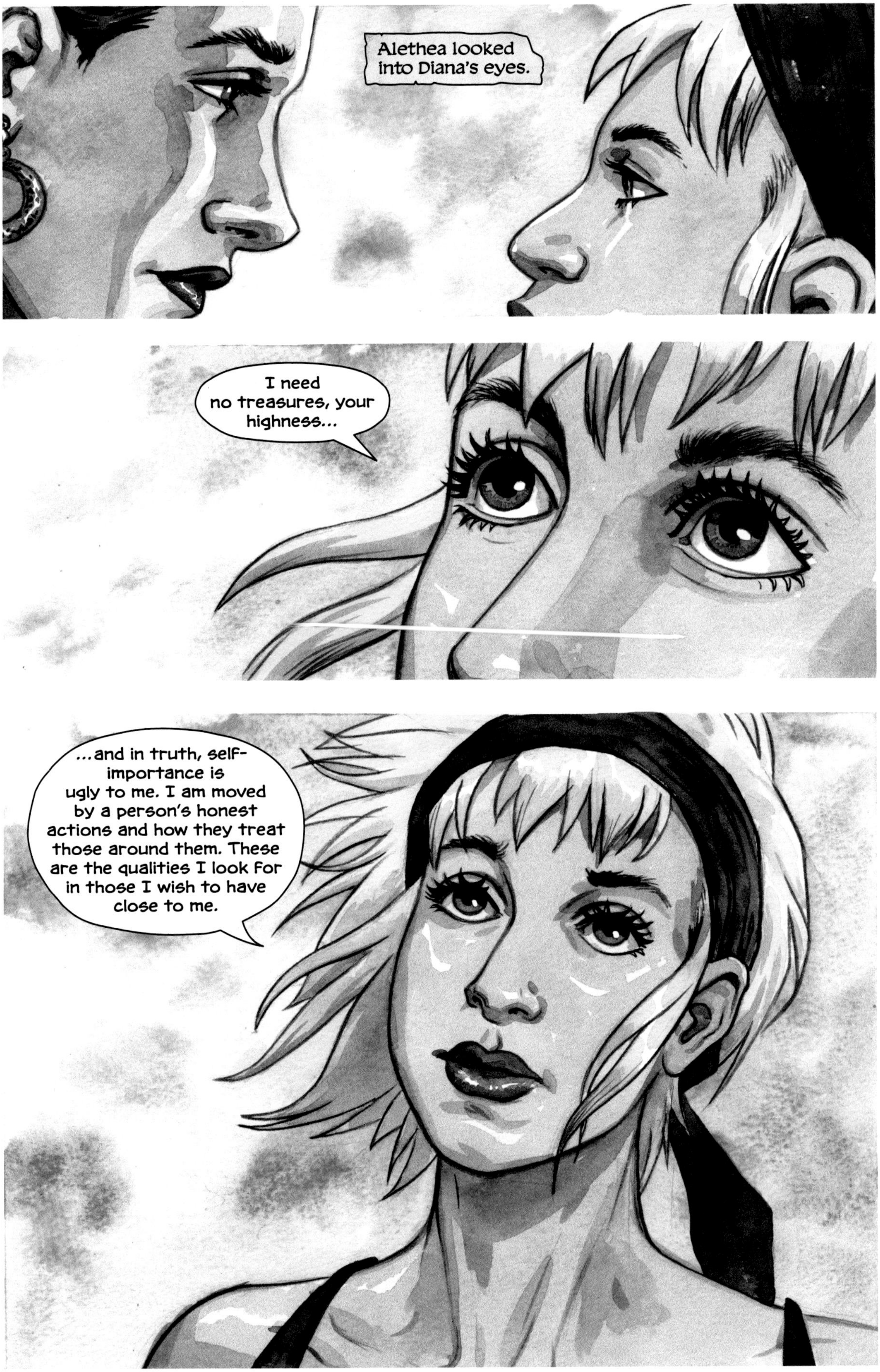
Alethea looked into Diana's eyes.
I need no treasures, your highness...
...and in truth, self-importance is ugly to me. I am moved by a person's honest actions and how they treat those around them. These are the qualities I look for in those I wish to have close to me.

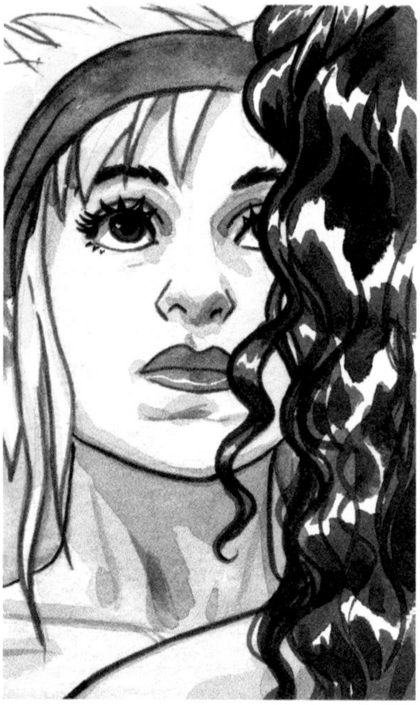

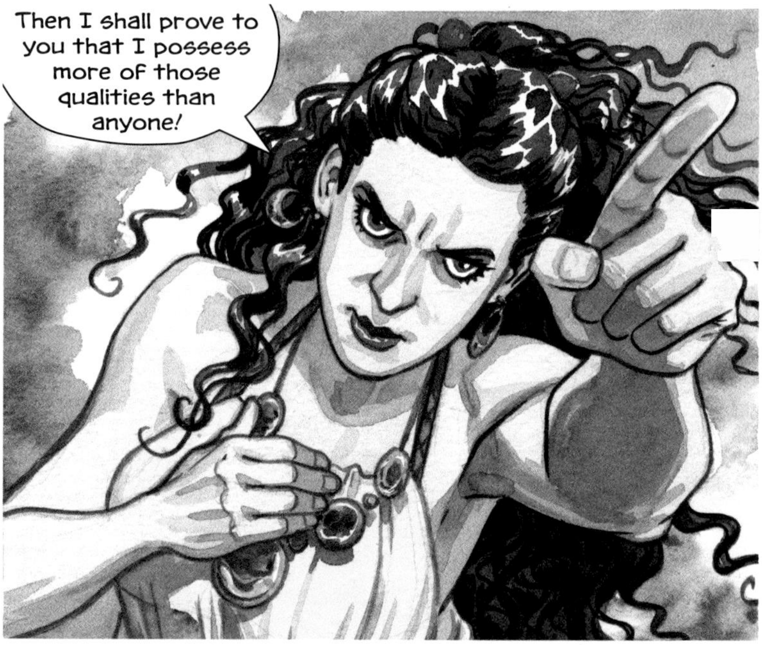

Then I shall prove to you that I possess more of those qualities than anyone!

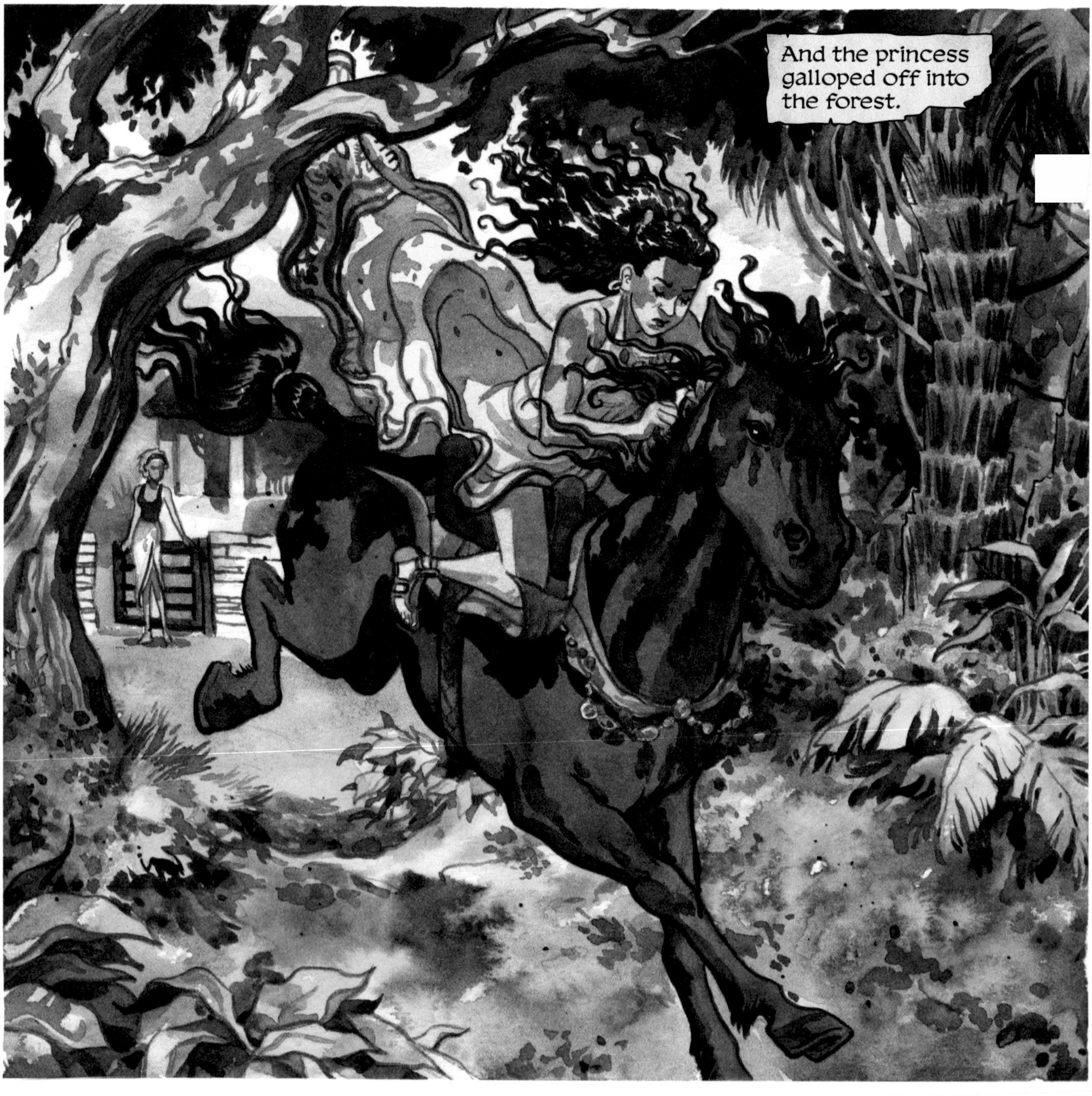

And the princess galloped off into the forest.

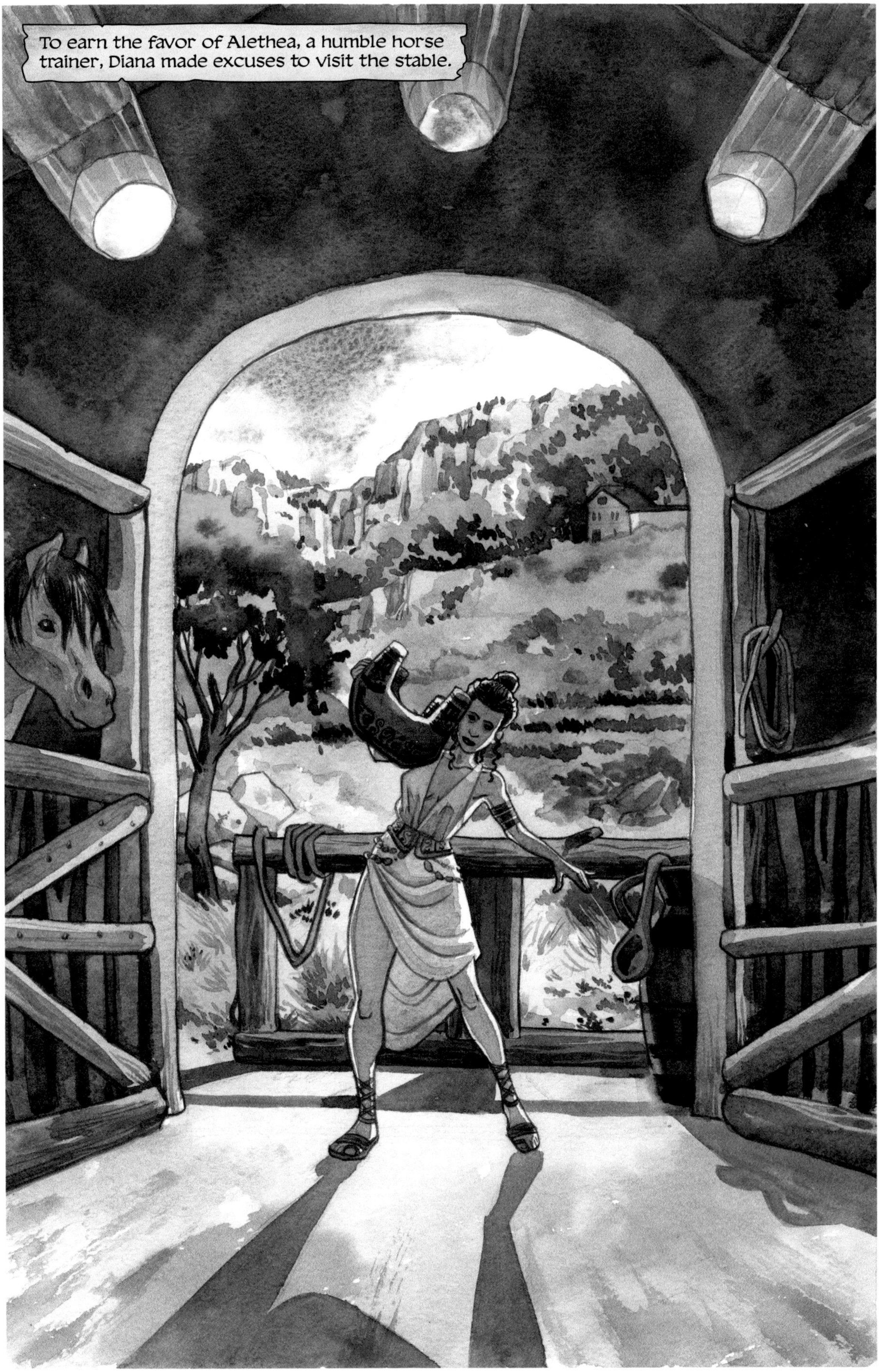
To earn the favor of Alethea, a humble horse trainer, Diana made excuses to visit the stable.

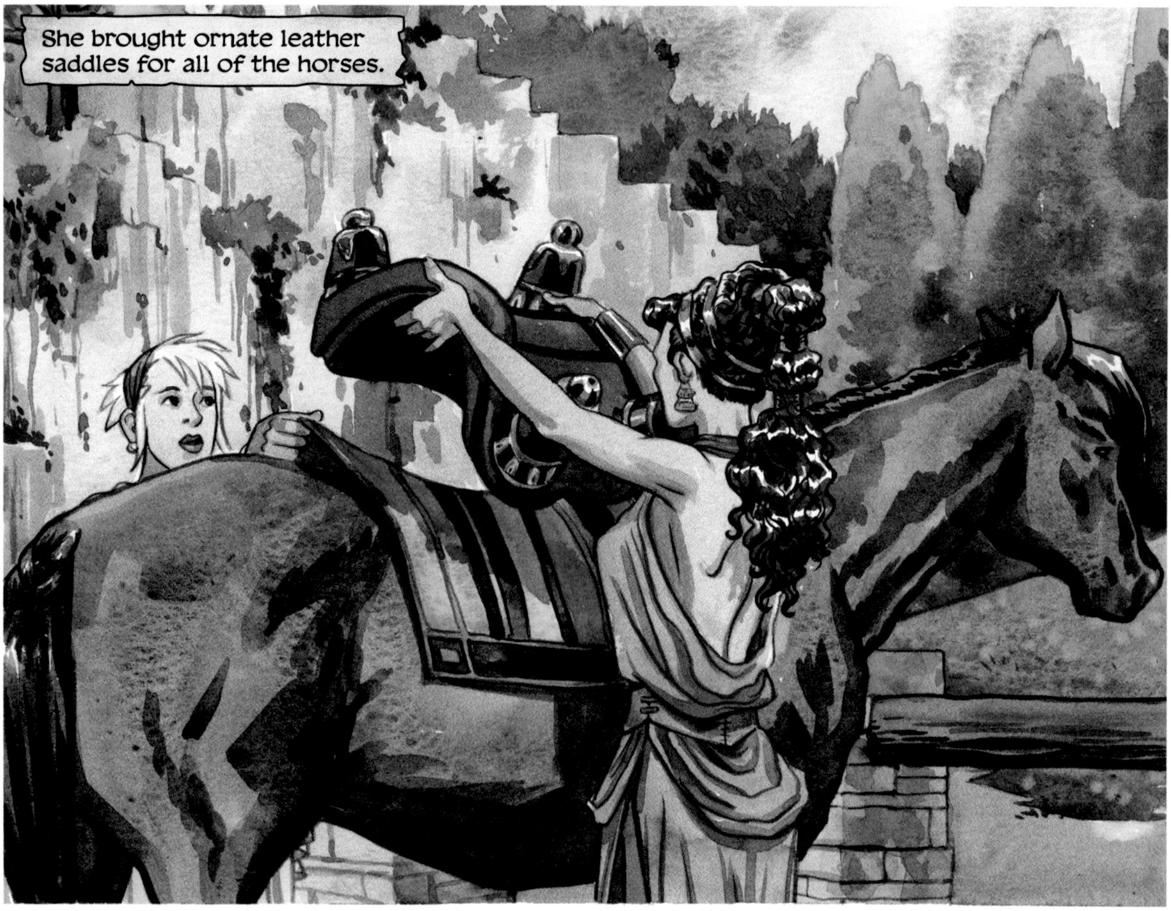
She brought ornate leather saddles for all of the horses.

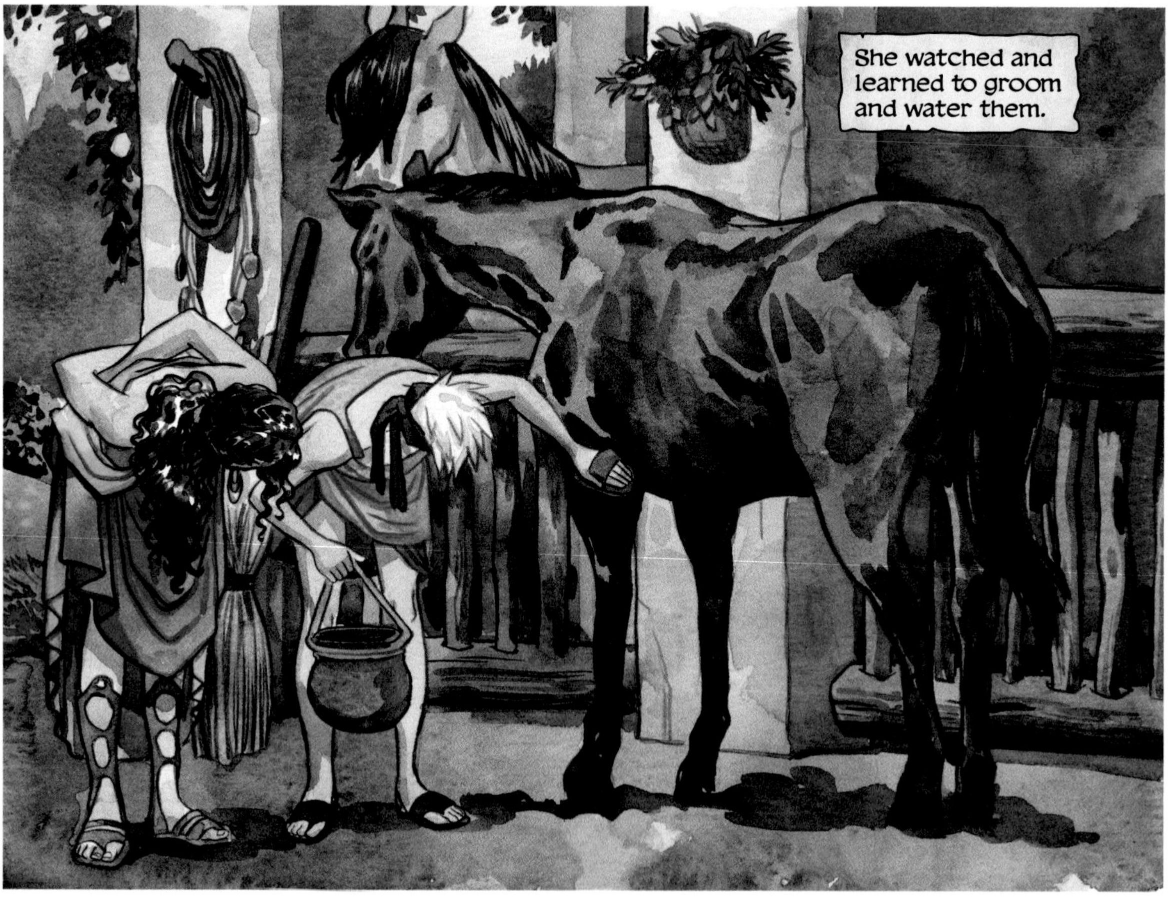
She watched and learned to groom and water them.

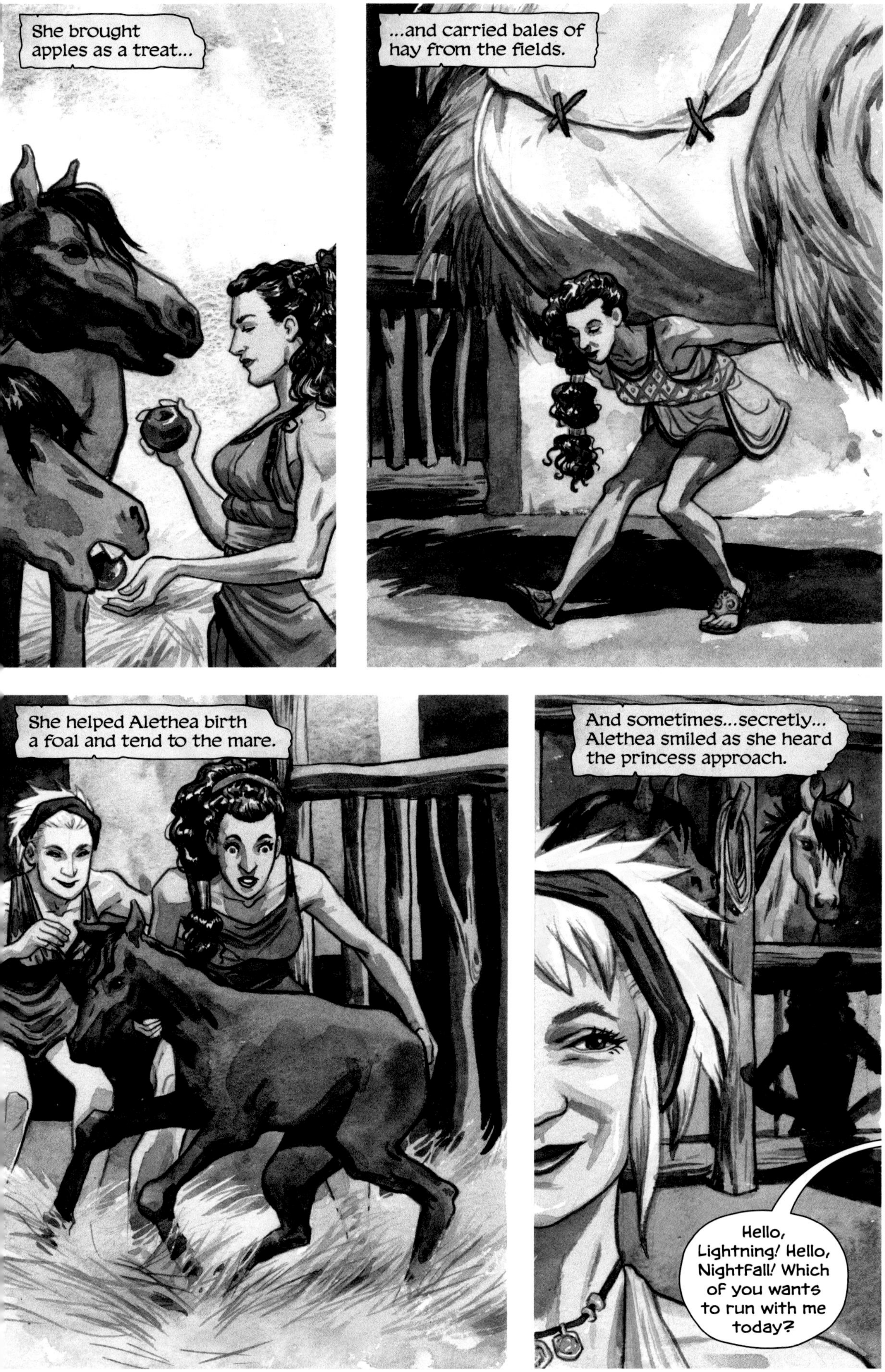
She brought apples as a treat...
...and carried bales of hay from the fields.
She helped Alethea birth a foal and tend to the mare.
And sometimes...secretly... Alethea smiled as she heard the princess approach.
Hello, Lightning! Hello, Nightfall! Which of you wants to run with me today?

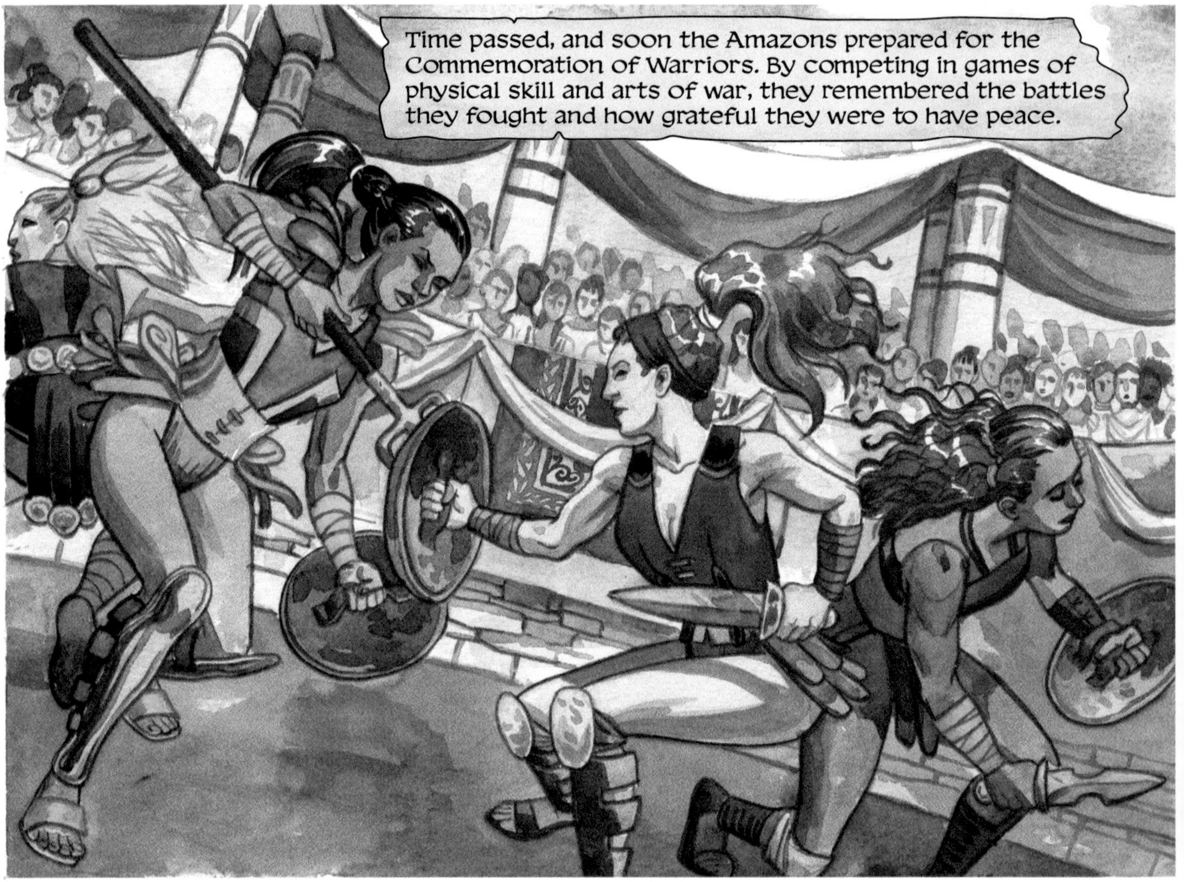
Time passed, and soon the Amazons prepared for the Commemoration of Warriors. By competing in games of physical skill and arts of war, they remembered the battles they fought and how grateful they were to have peace.

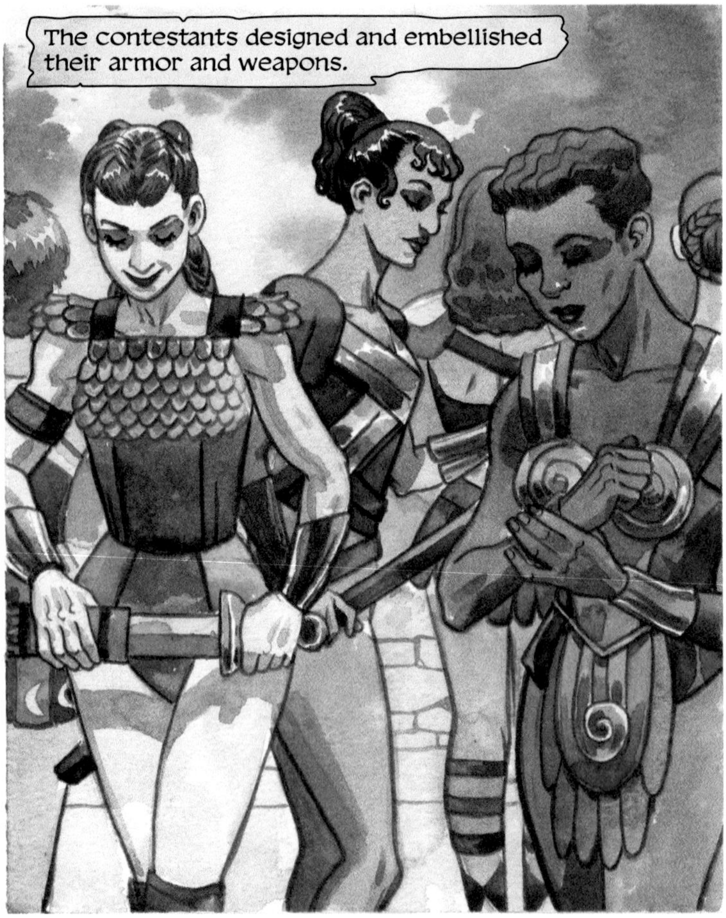
The contestants designed and embellished their armor and weapons.

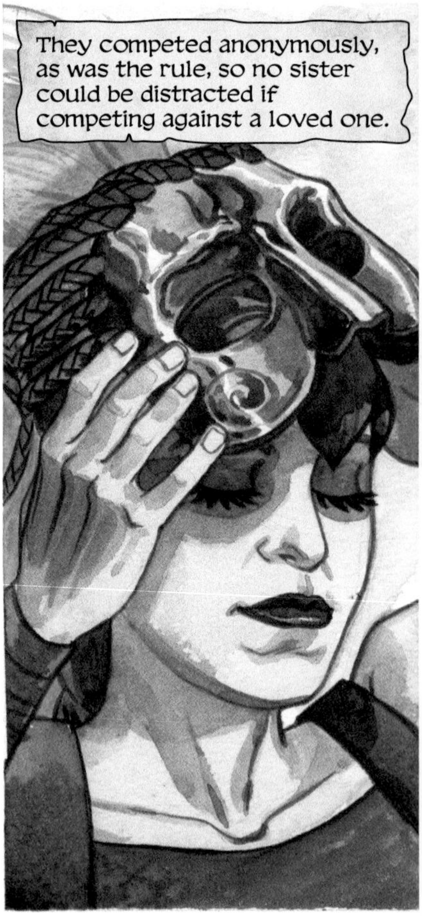
They competed anonymously, as was the rule, so no sister could be distracted if competing against a loved one.

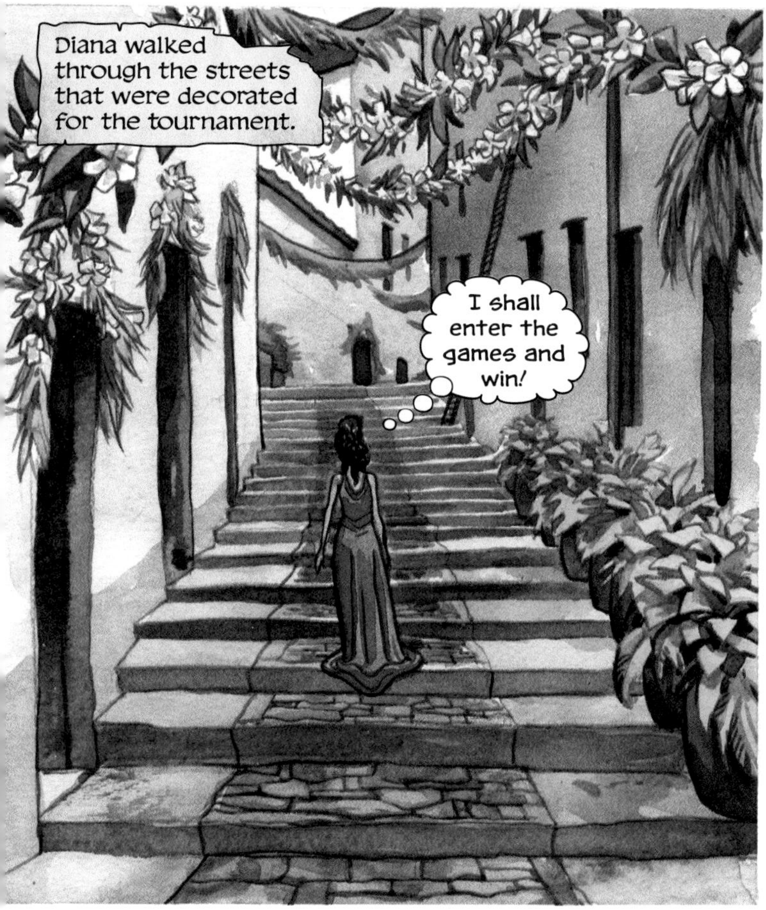
Diana walked through the streets that were decorated for the tournament.
I shall enter the games and win!
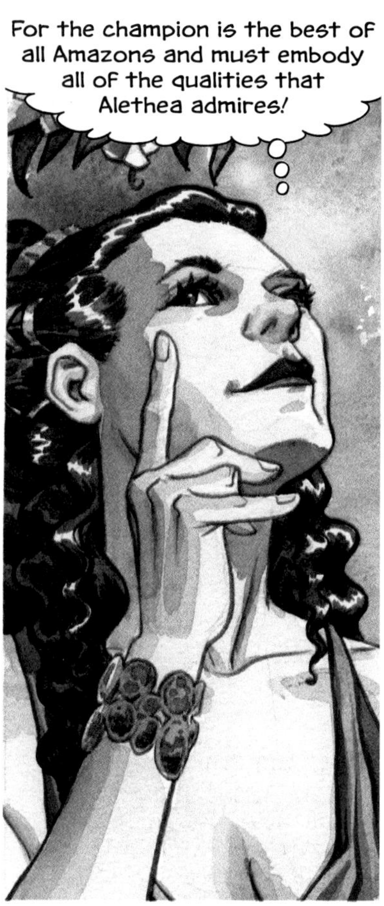
For the champion is the best of all Amazons and must embody all of the qualities that Alethea admires!
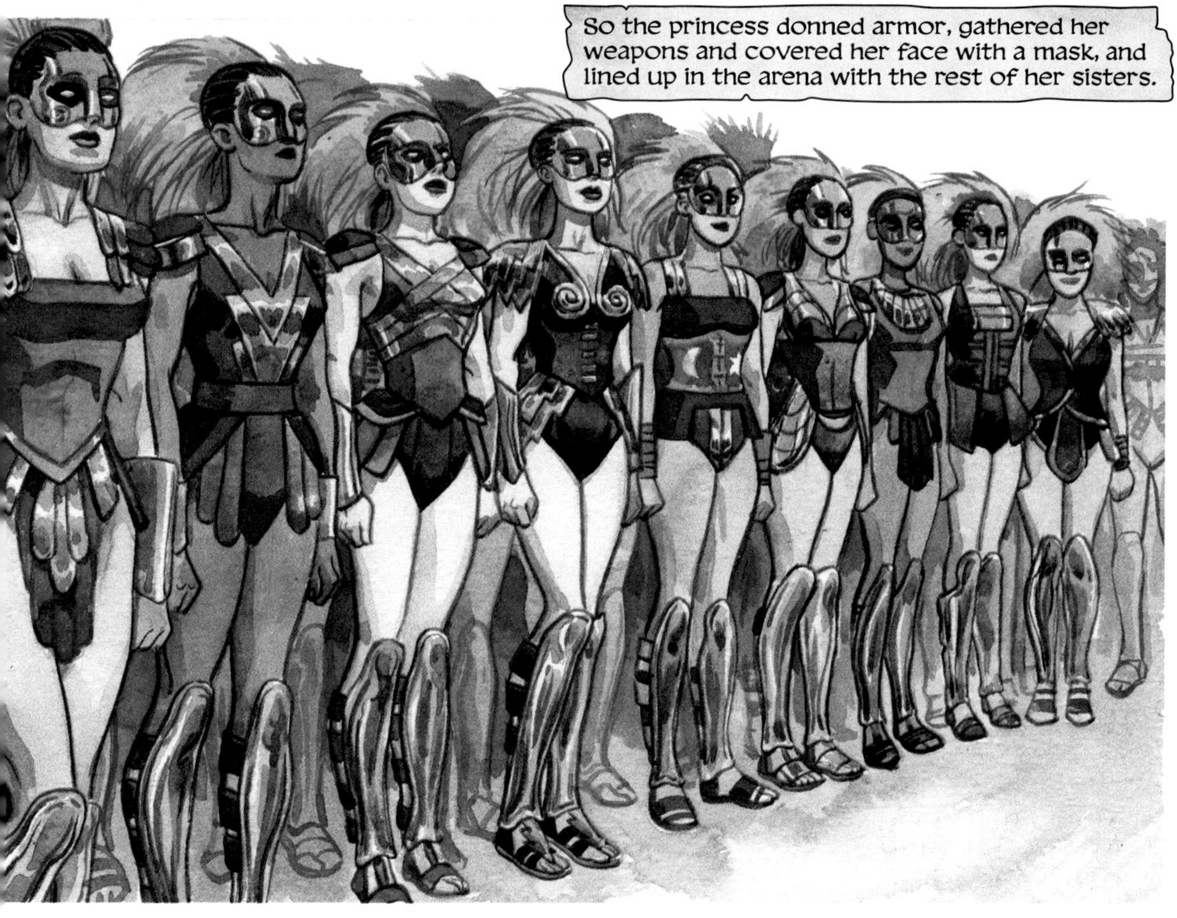
So the princess donned armor, gathered her weapons and covered her face with a mask, and lined up in the arena with the rest of her sisters.

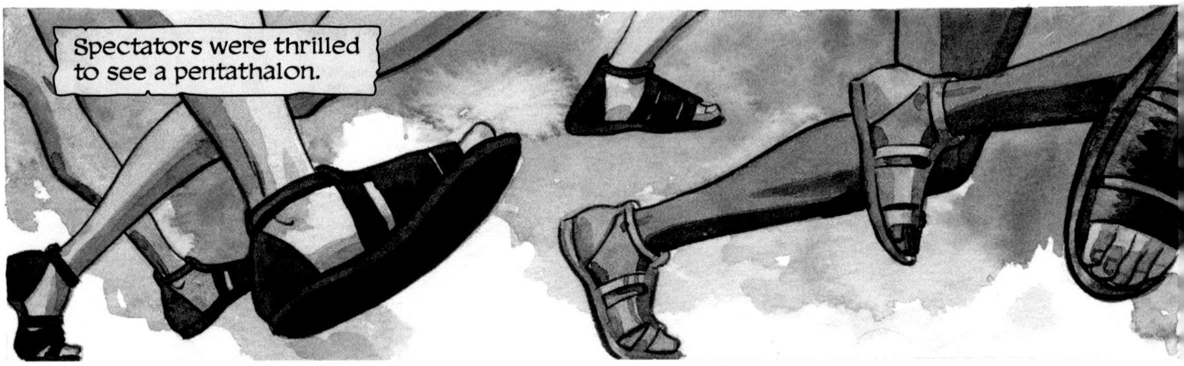
Spectators were thrilled to see a pentathalon.

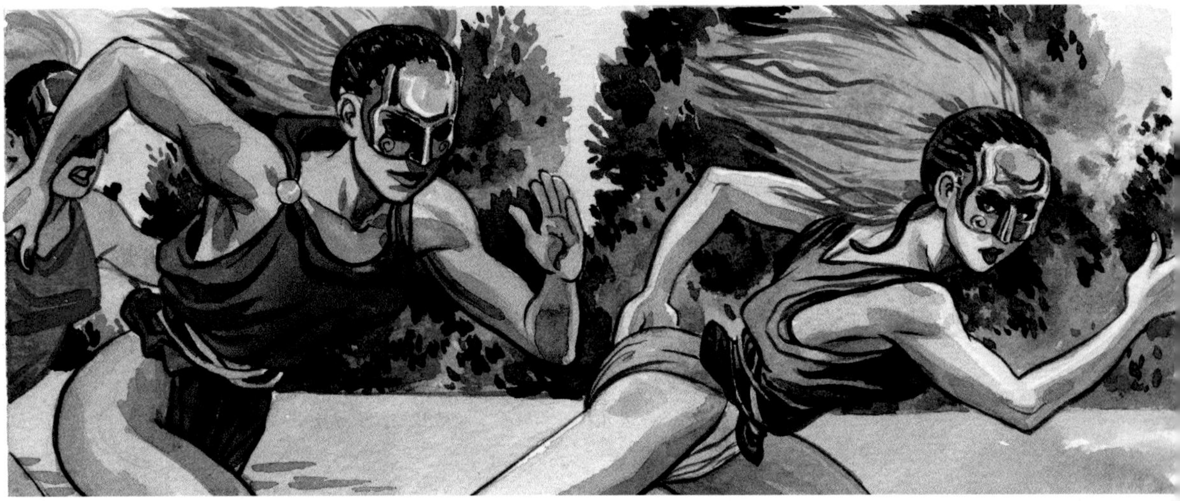

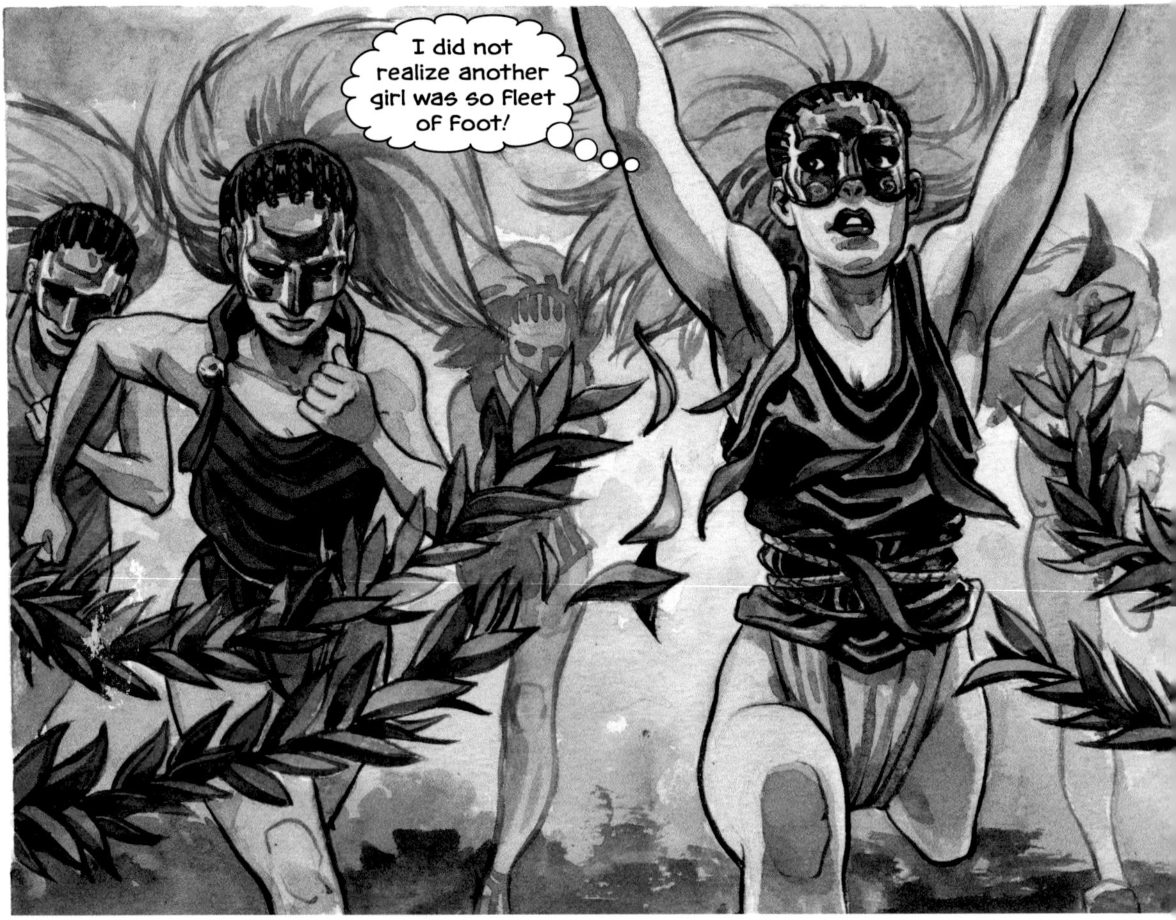
I did not realize another girl was so fleet of foot!

There were games of archery.

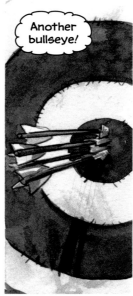

Another bullseye!

The only way I can win...is...

Yes!! I have split her arrow! Ha!!

Uuuuff! *Finally!* I disarmed her!

Her swordsmanship is impressive!

And swordplay.

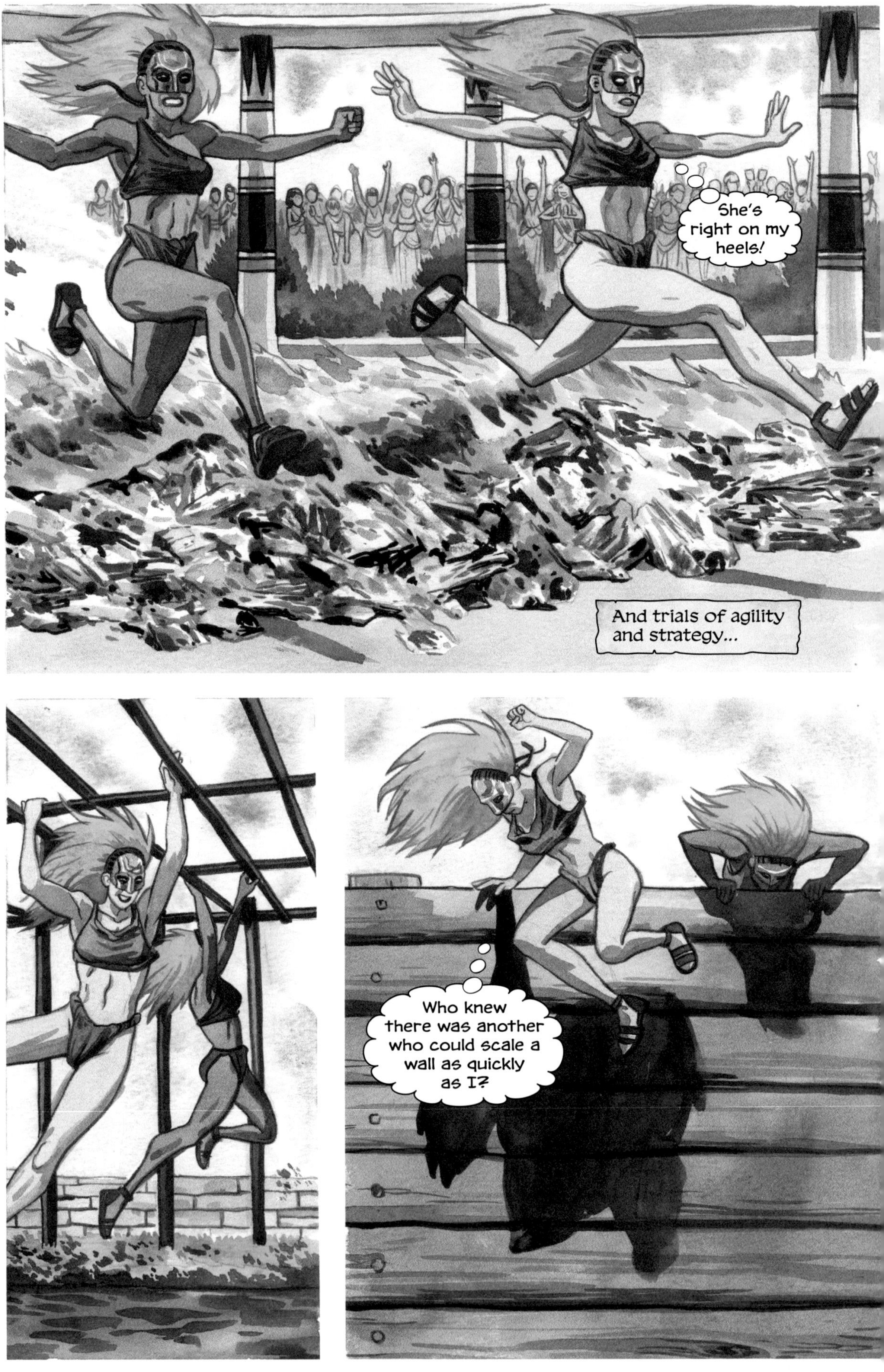
She's right on my heels!
And trials of agility and strategy...
Who knew there was another who could scale a wall as quickly as I?

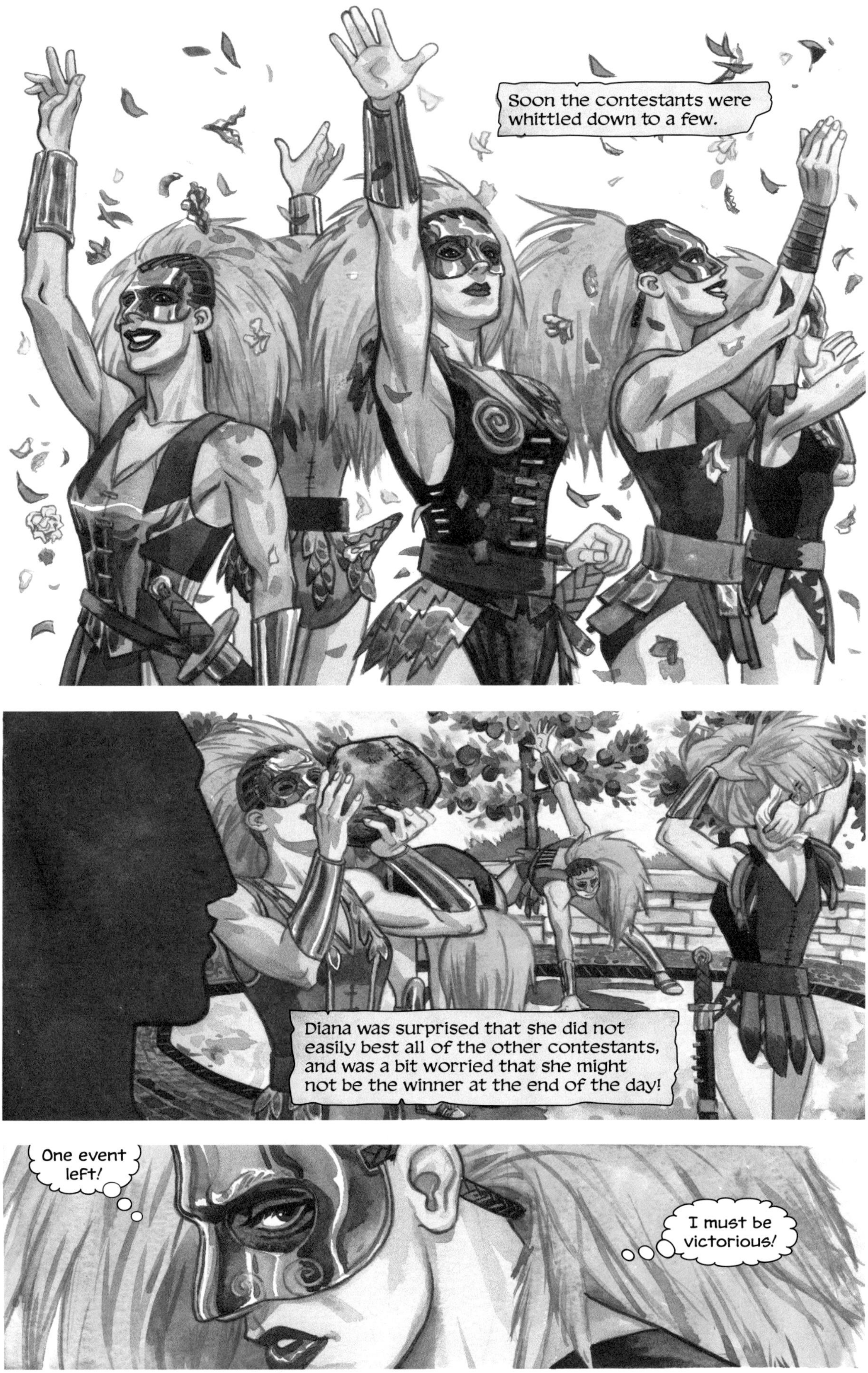
Soon the contestants were whittled down to a few.
Diana was surprised that she did not easily best all of the other contestants, and was a bit worried that she might not be the winner at the end of the day!
One event left!
I must be victorious!

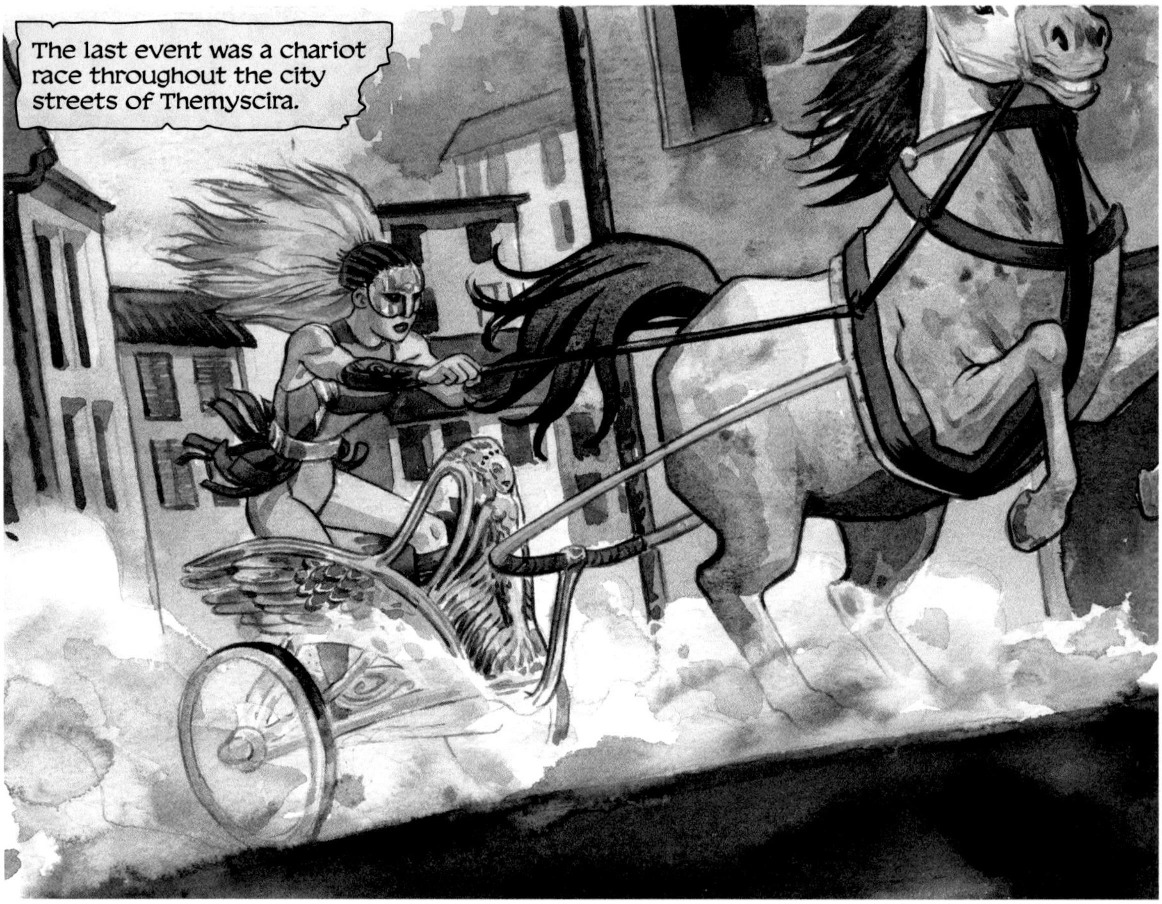
The last event was a chariot race throughout the city streets of Themyscira.

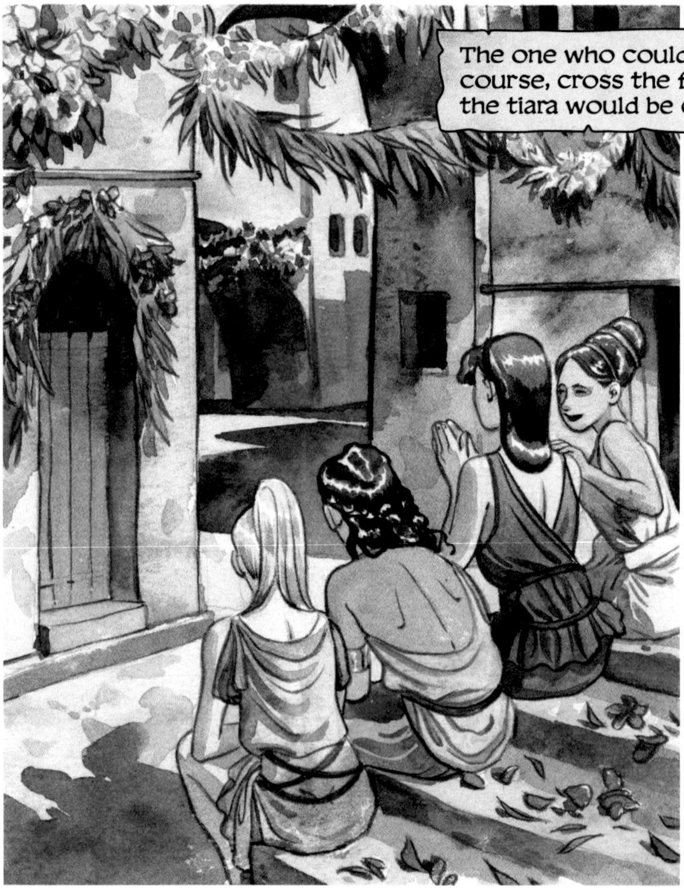
The one who could navigate the winding course, cross the finish line and grab the tiara would be crowned champion.

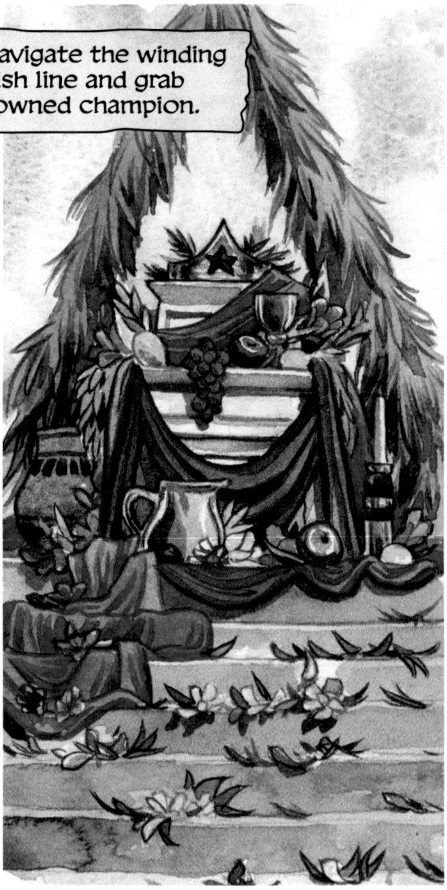

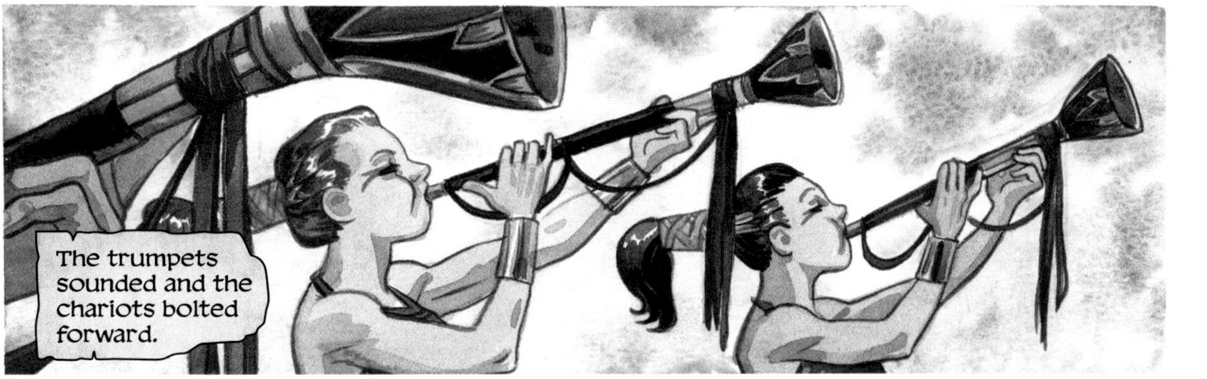
The trumpets sounded and the chariots bolted forward.

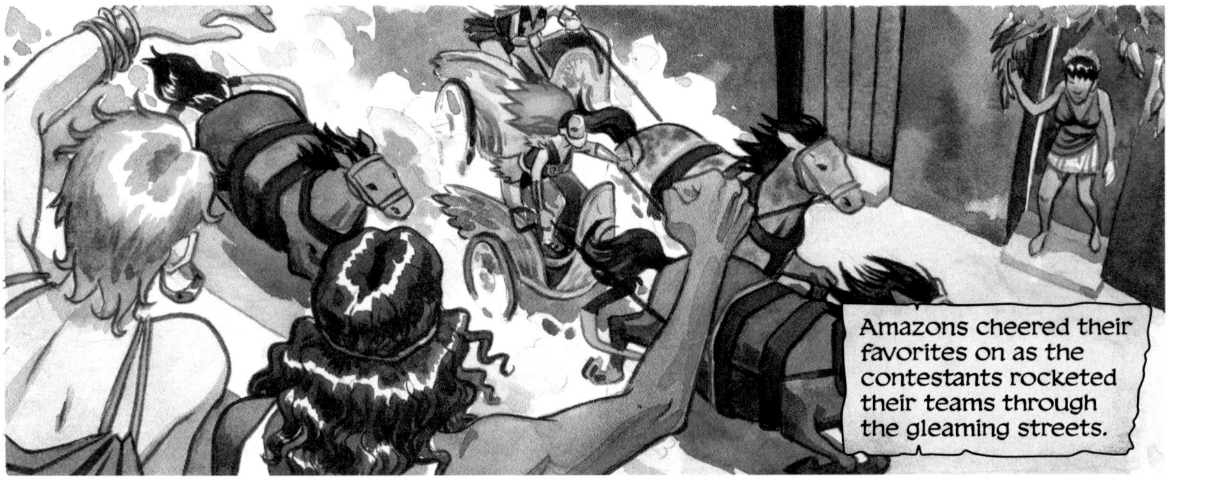
Amazons cheered their favorites on as the contestants rocketed their teams through the gleaming streets.

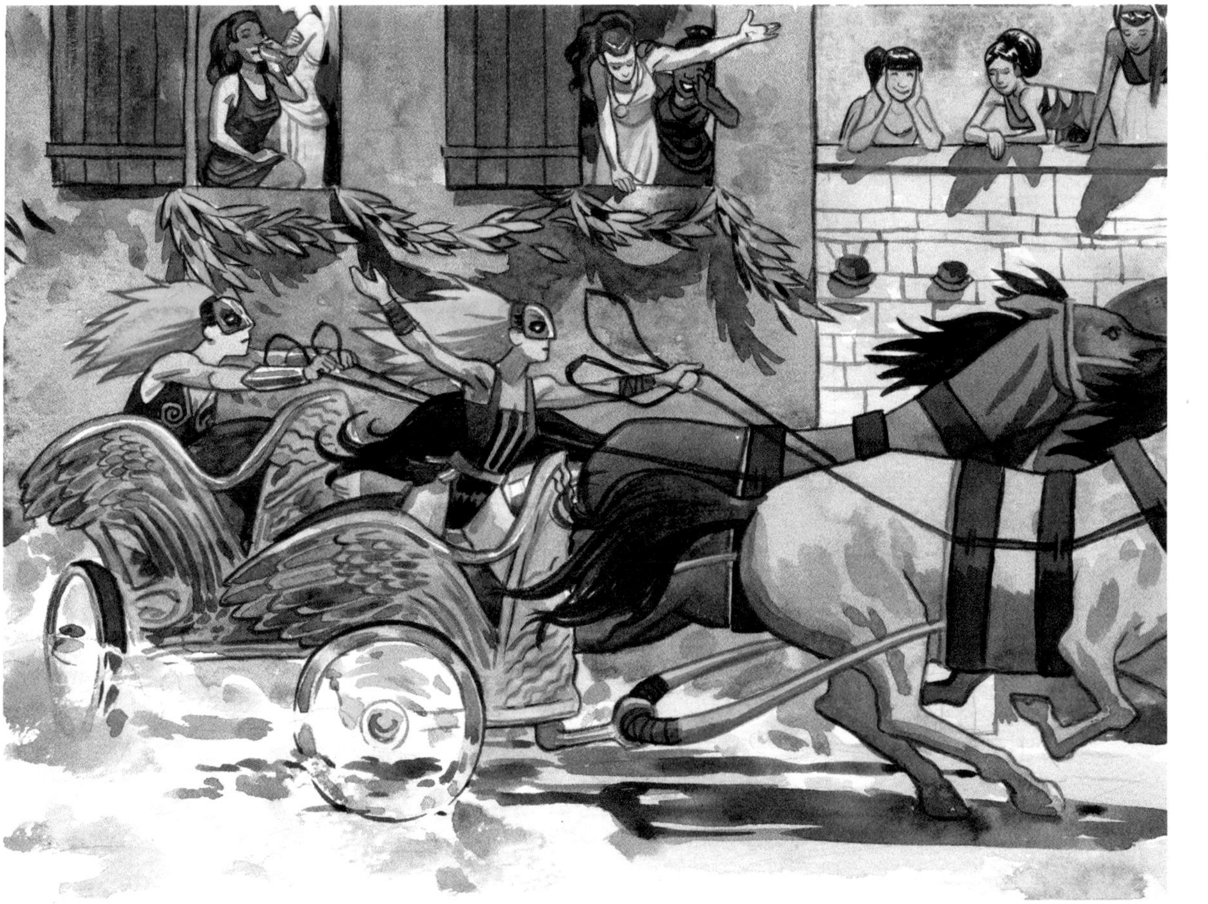

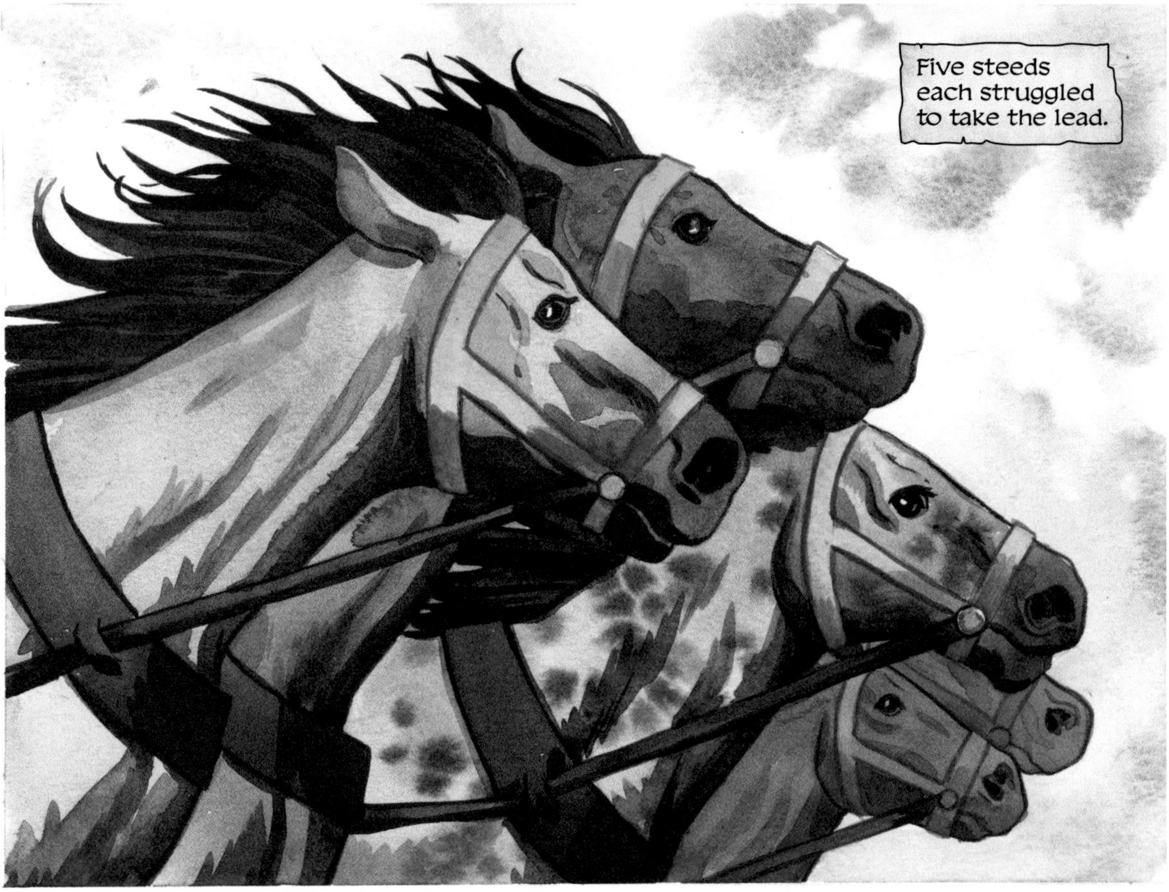
Five steeds
each struggled
to take the lead.

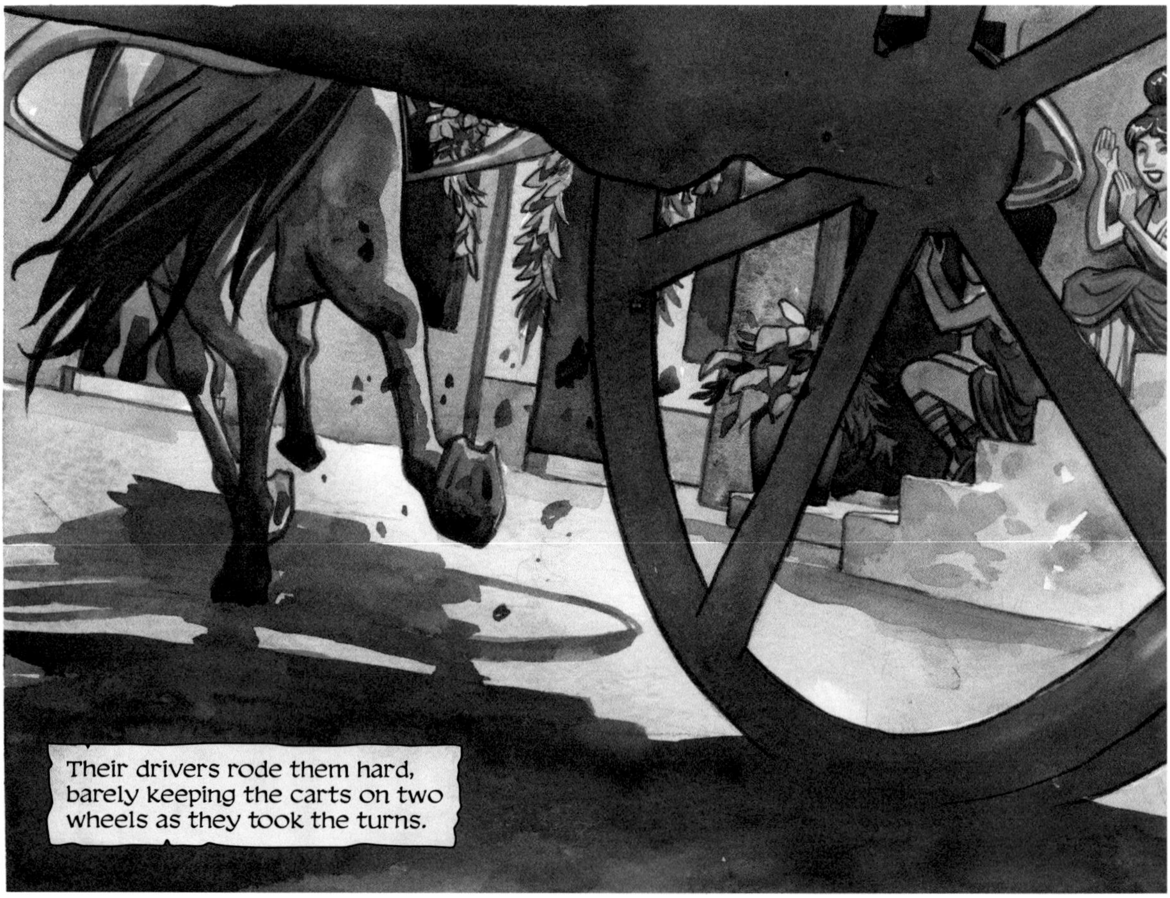
Their drivers rode them hard,
barely keeping the carts on two
wheels as they took the turns.

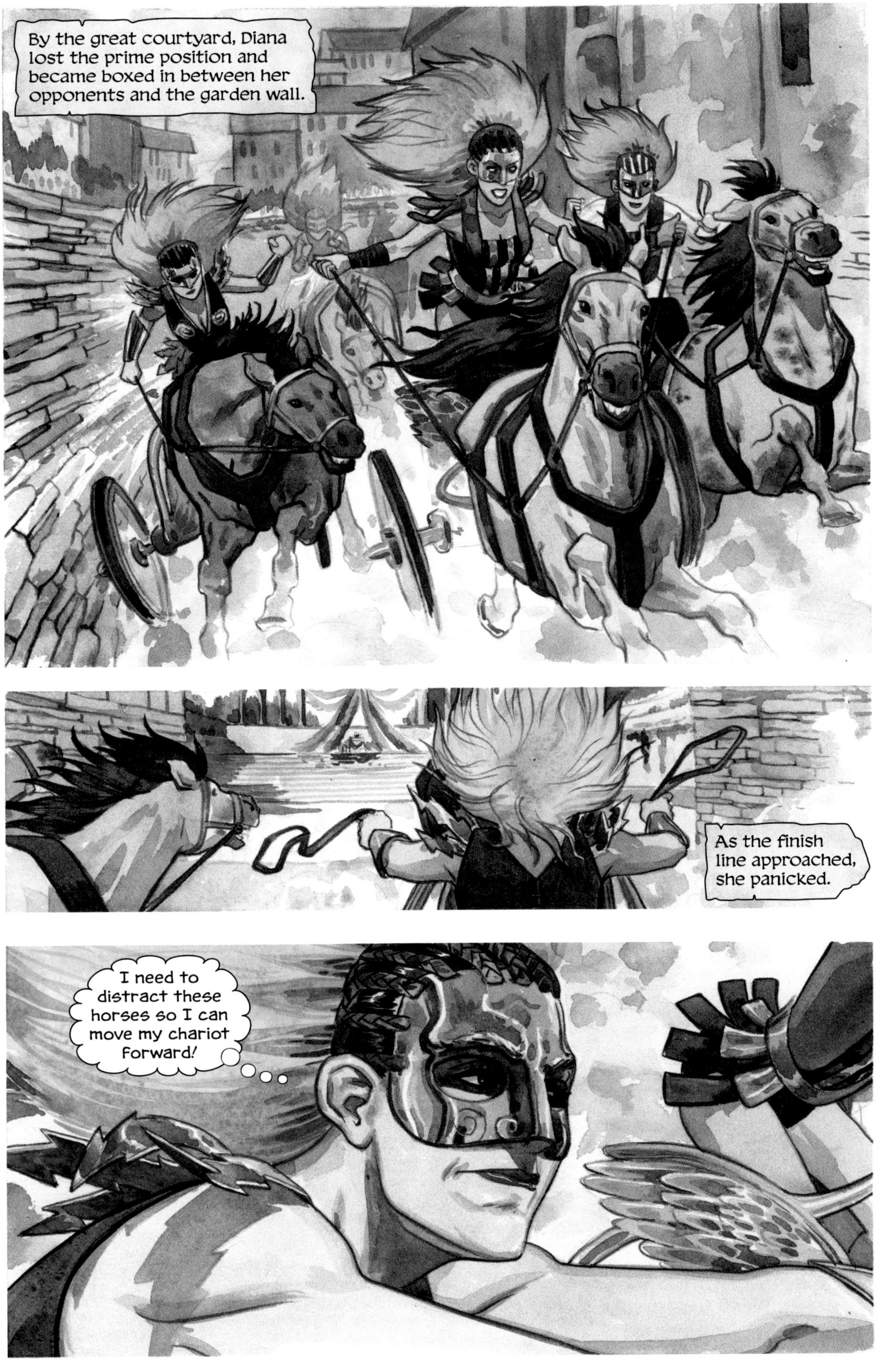
By the great courtyard, Diana lost the prime position and became boxed in between her opponents and the garden wall.
As the finish line approached, she panicked.
I need to distract these horses so I can move my chariot forward!

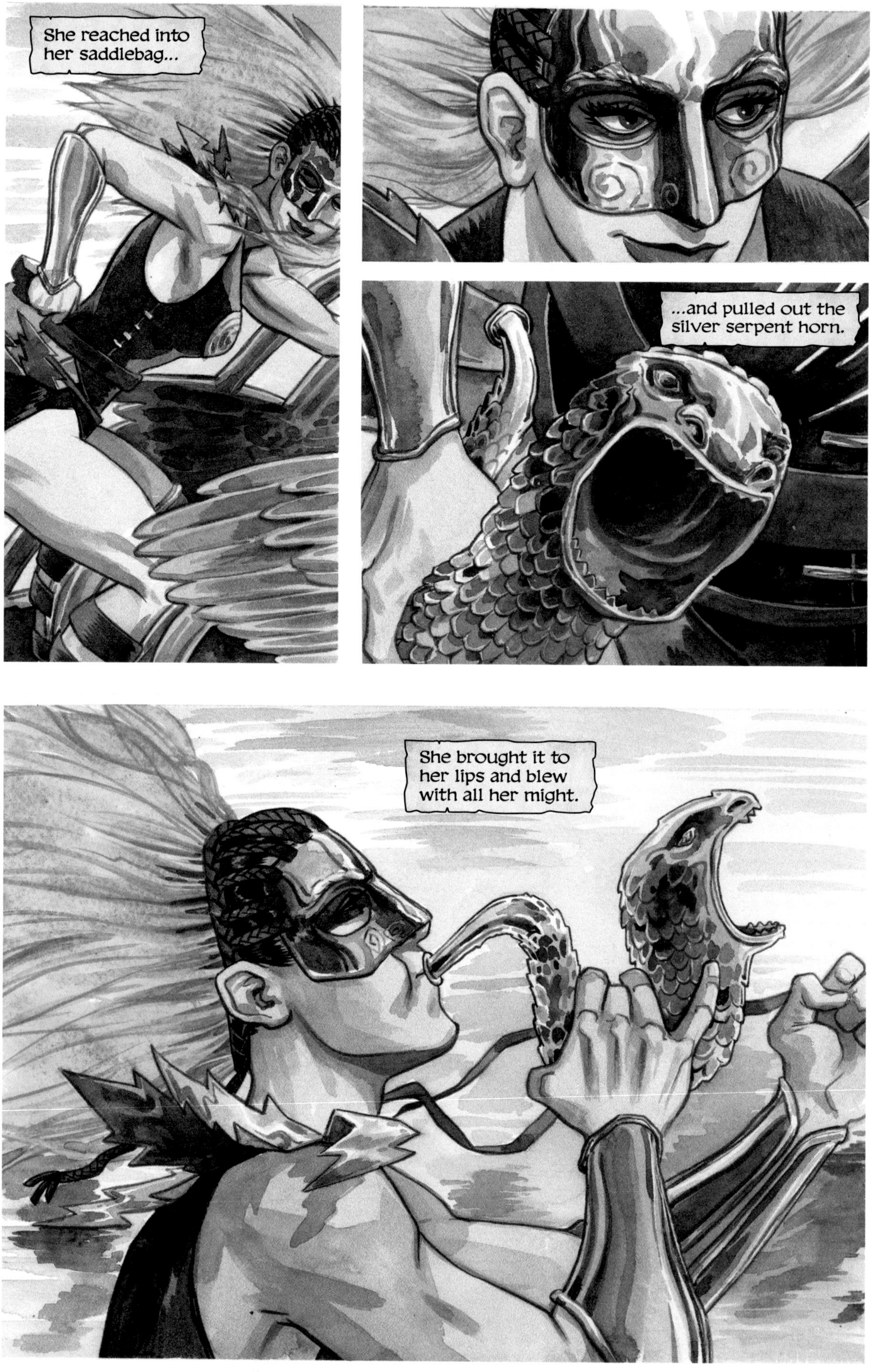
She reached into her saddlebag...
...and pulled out the silver serpent horn.
She brought it to her lips and blew with all her might.

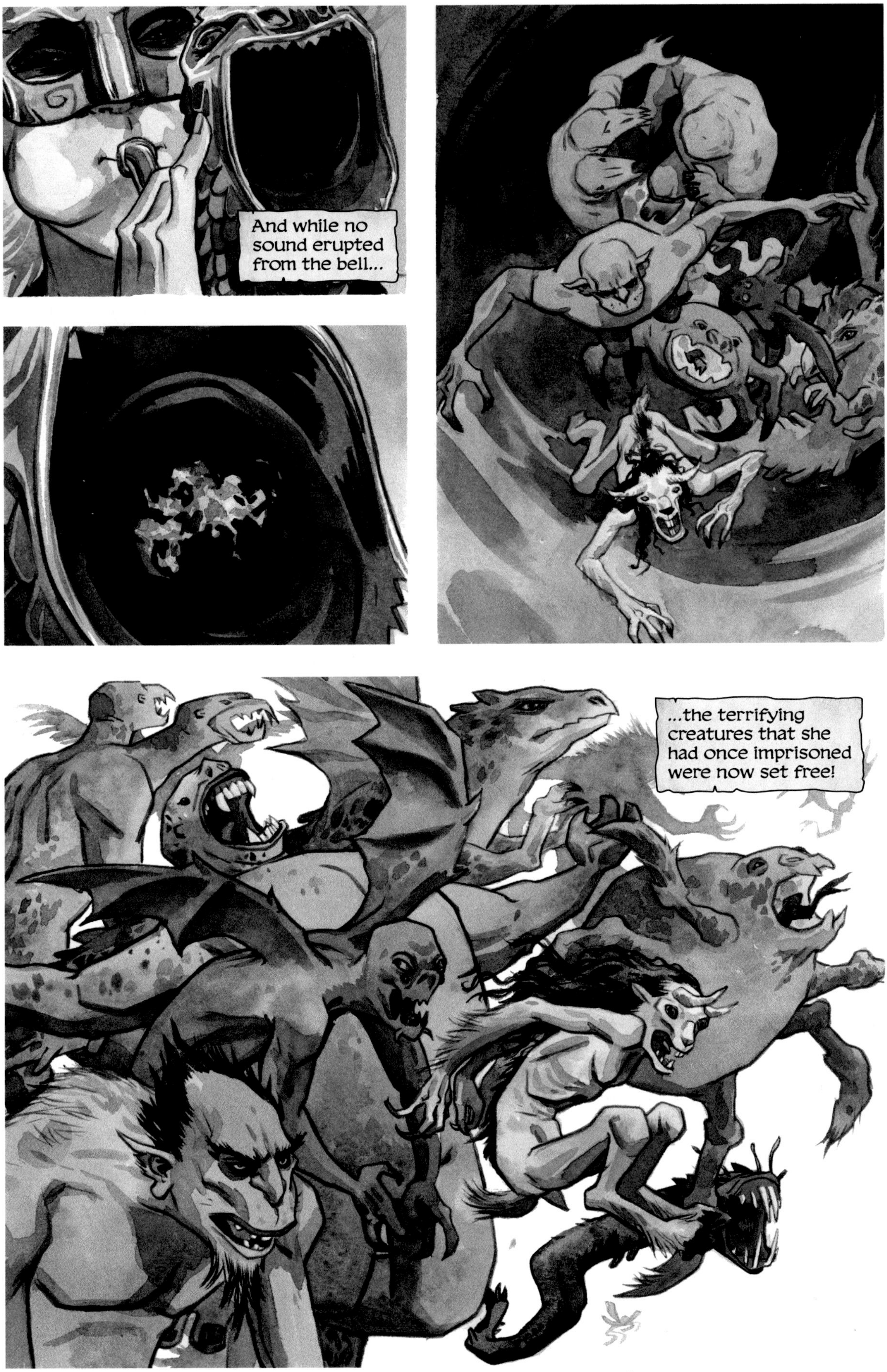
And while no sound erupted from the bell...
...the terrifying creatures that she had once imprisoned were now set free!

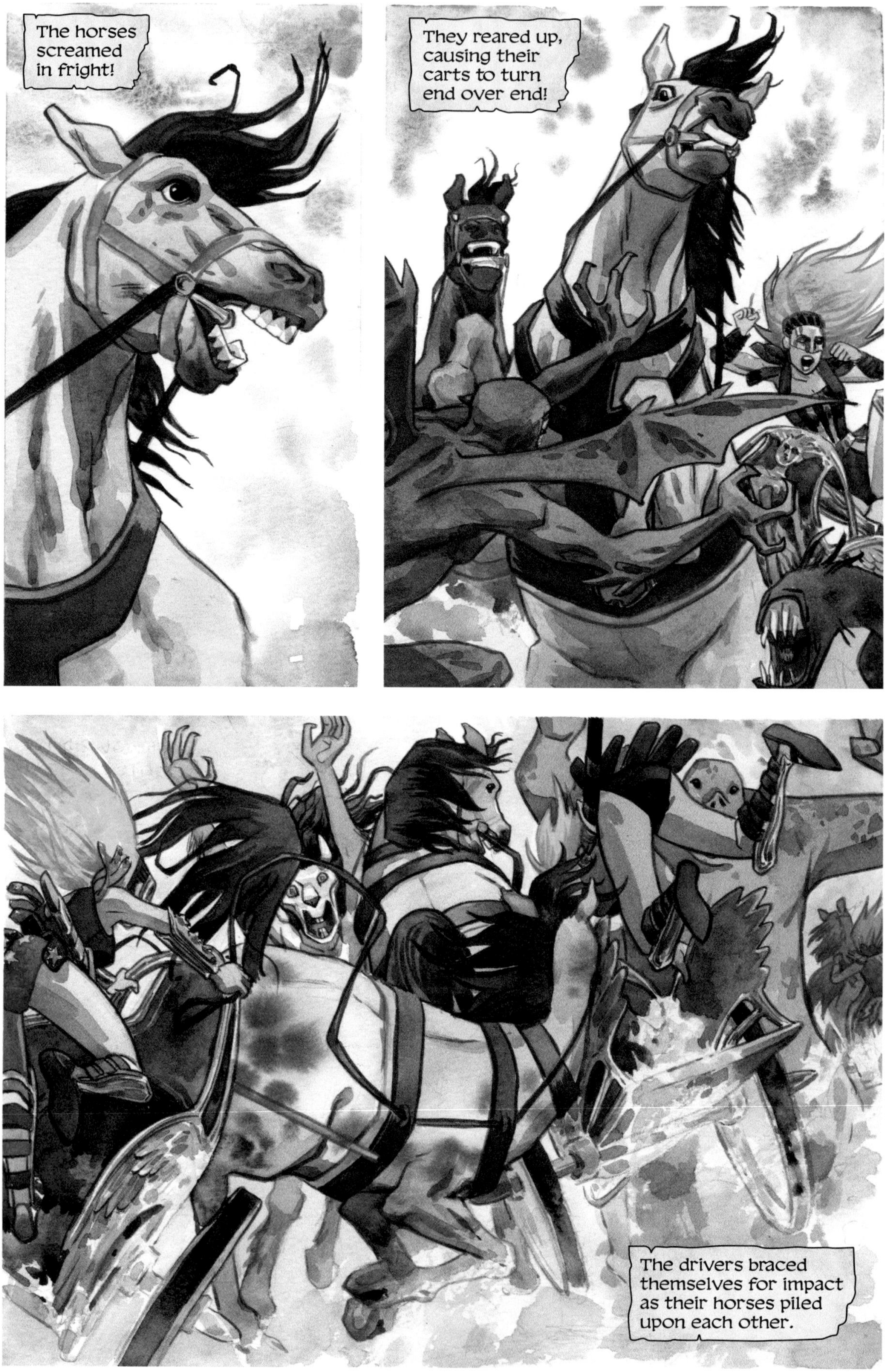
The horses screamed in fright!
They reared up, causing their carts to turn end over end!
The drivers braced themselves for impact as their horses piled upon each other.

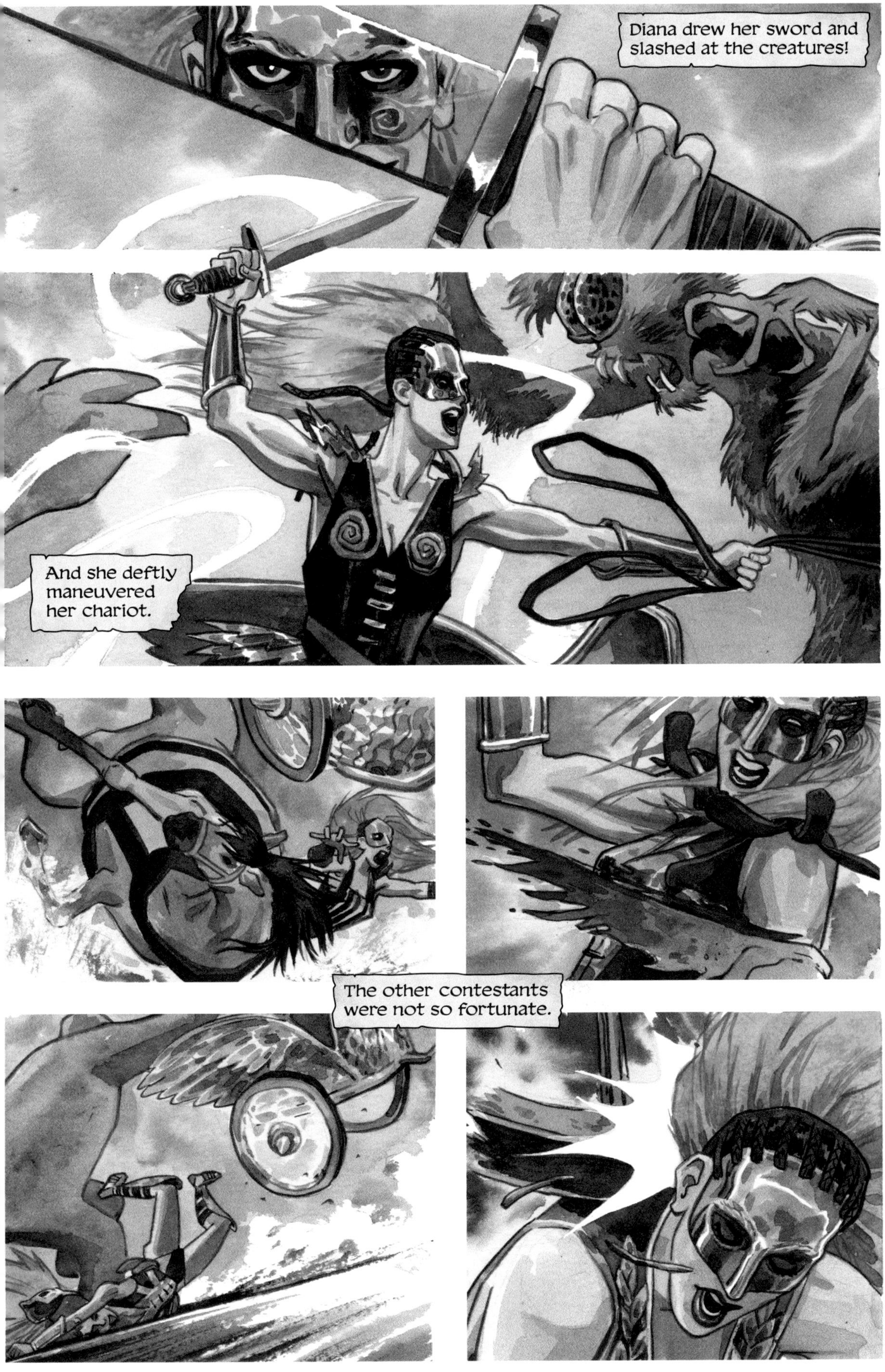

Diana drew her sword and slashed at the creatures!
And she deftly maneuvered her chariot.
The other contestants were not so fortunate.

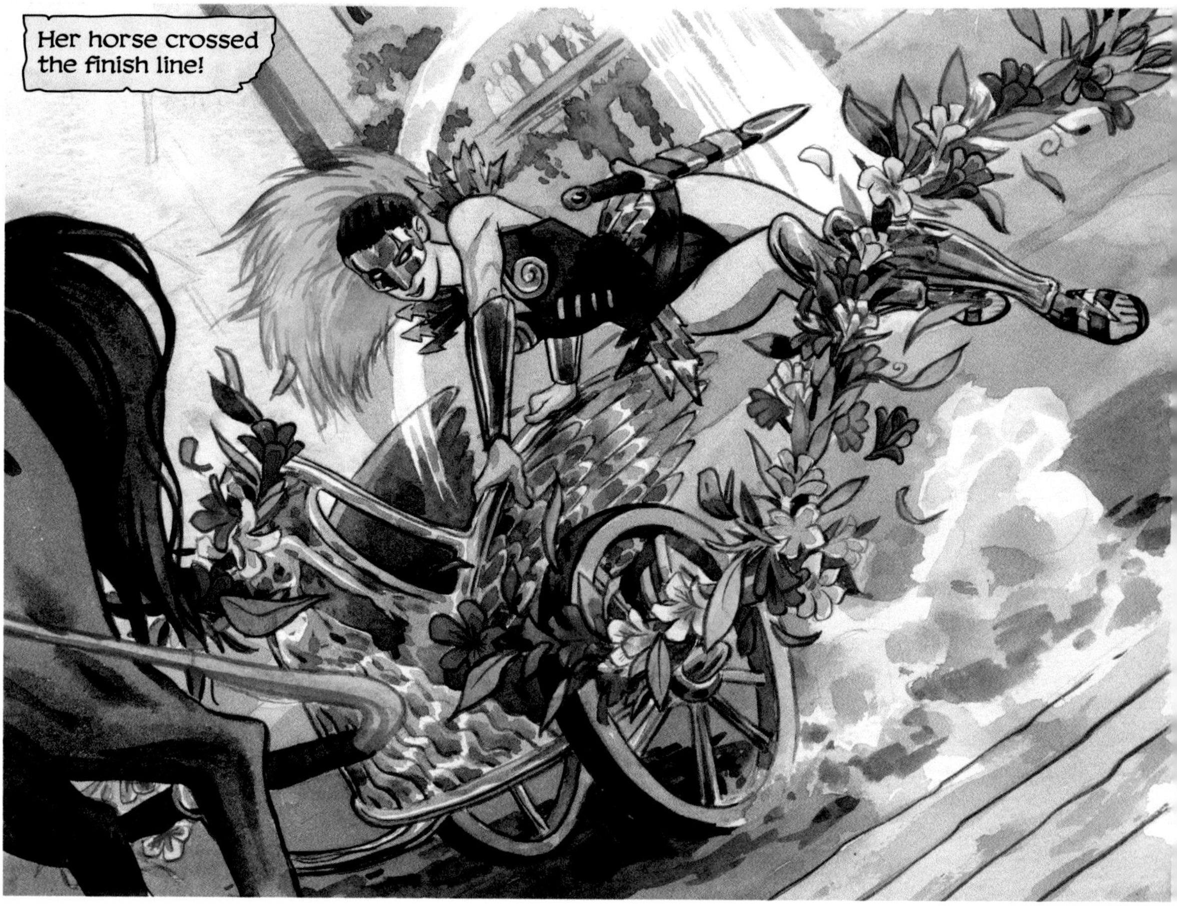
Her horse crossed the finish line!

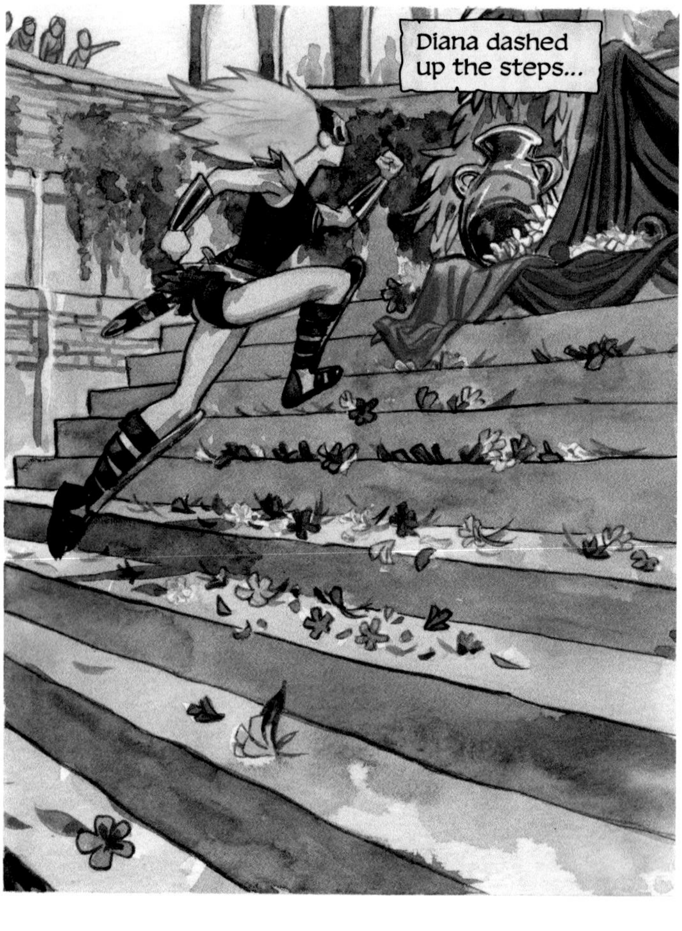
Diana dashed up the steps...

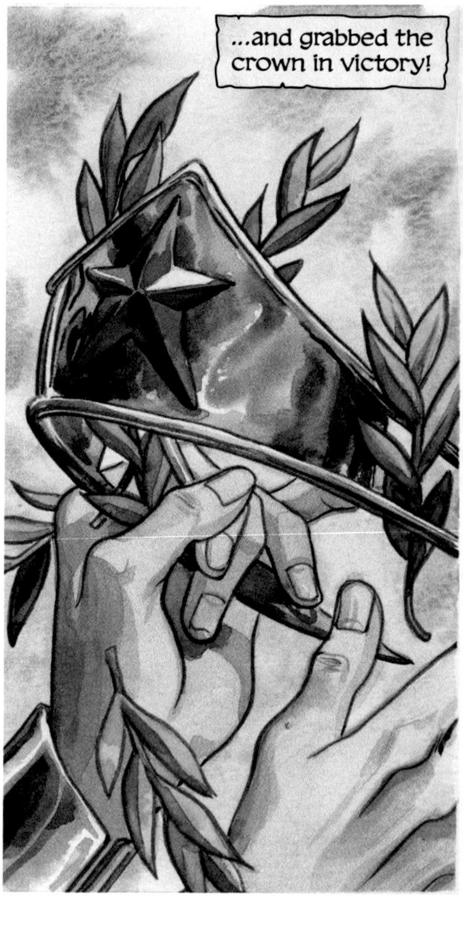
...and grabbed the crown in victory!

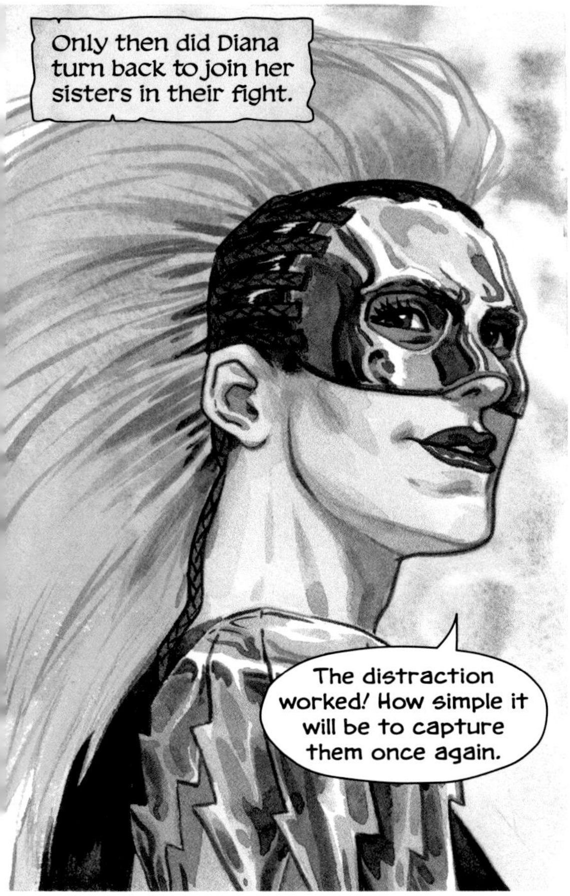
Only then did Diana turn back to join her sisters in their fight.
The distraction worked! How simple it will be to capture them once again.

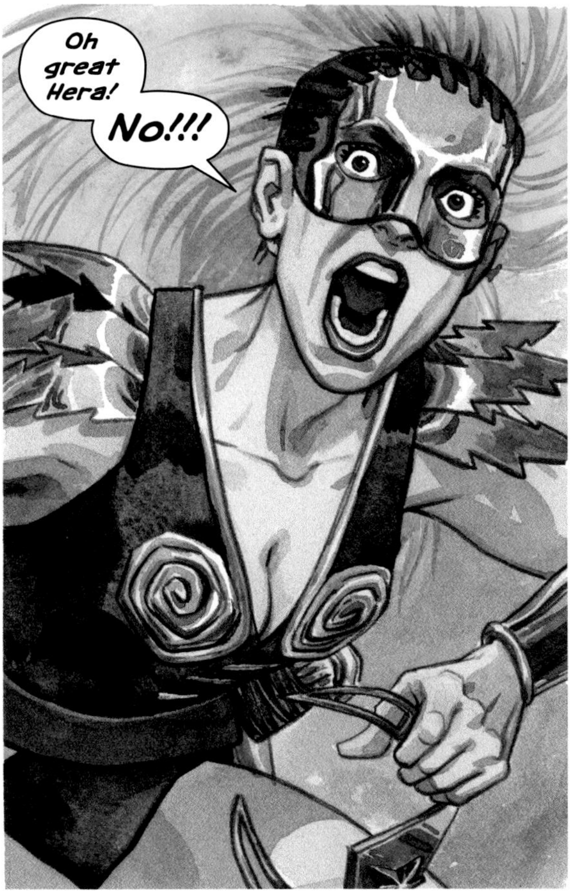
Oh great Hera!
No!!!

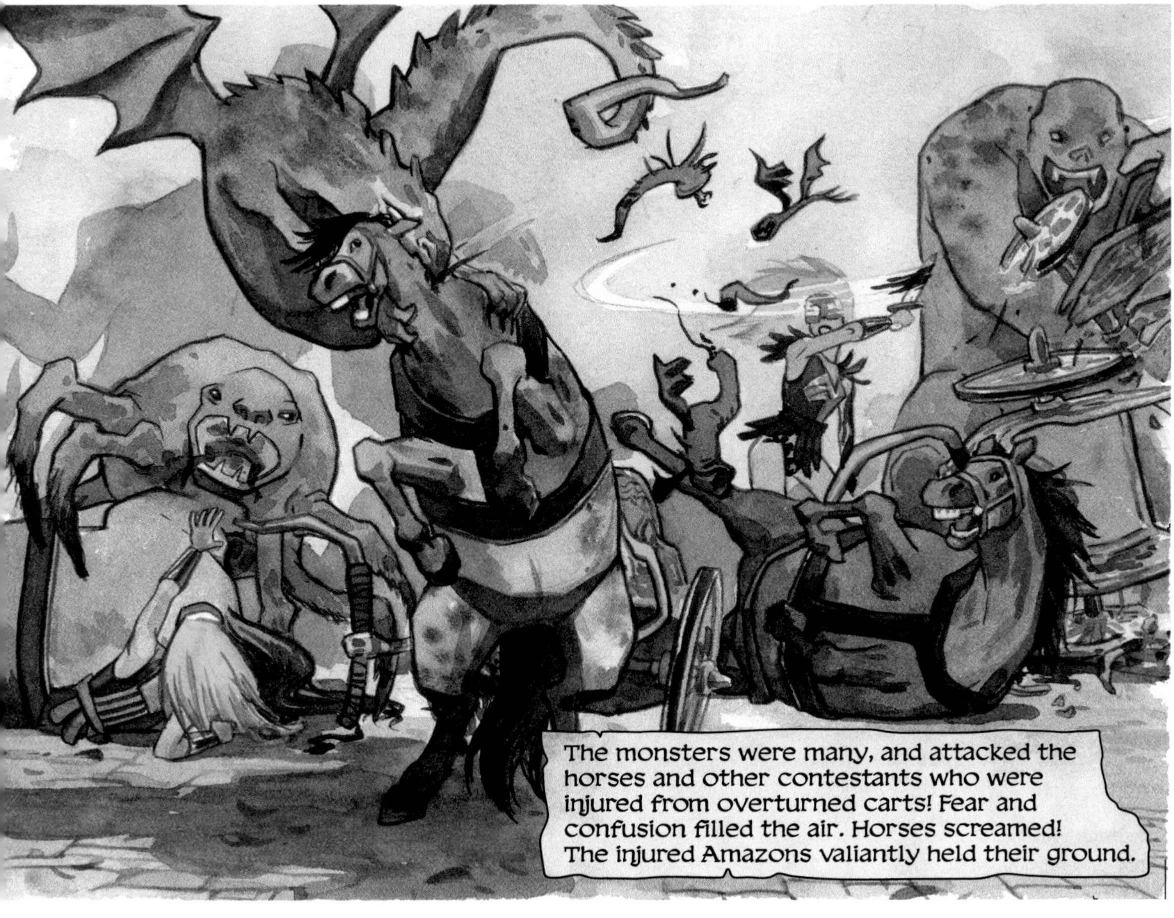
The monsters were many, and attacked the horses and other contestants who were injured from overturned carts! Fear and confusion filled the air. Horses screamed! The injured Amazons valiantly held their ground.

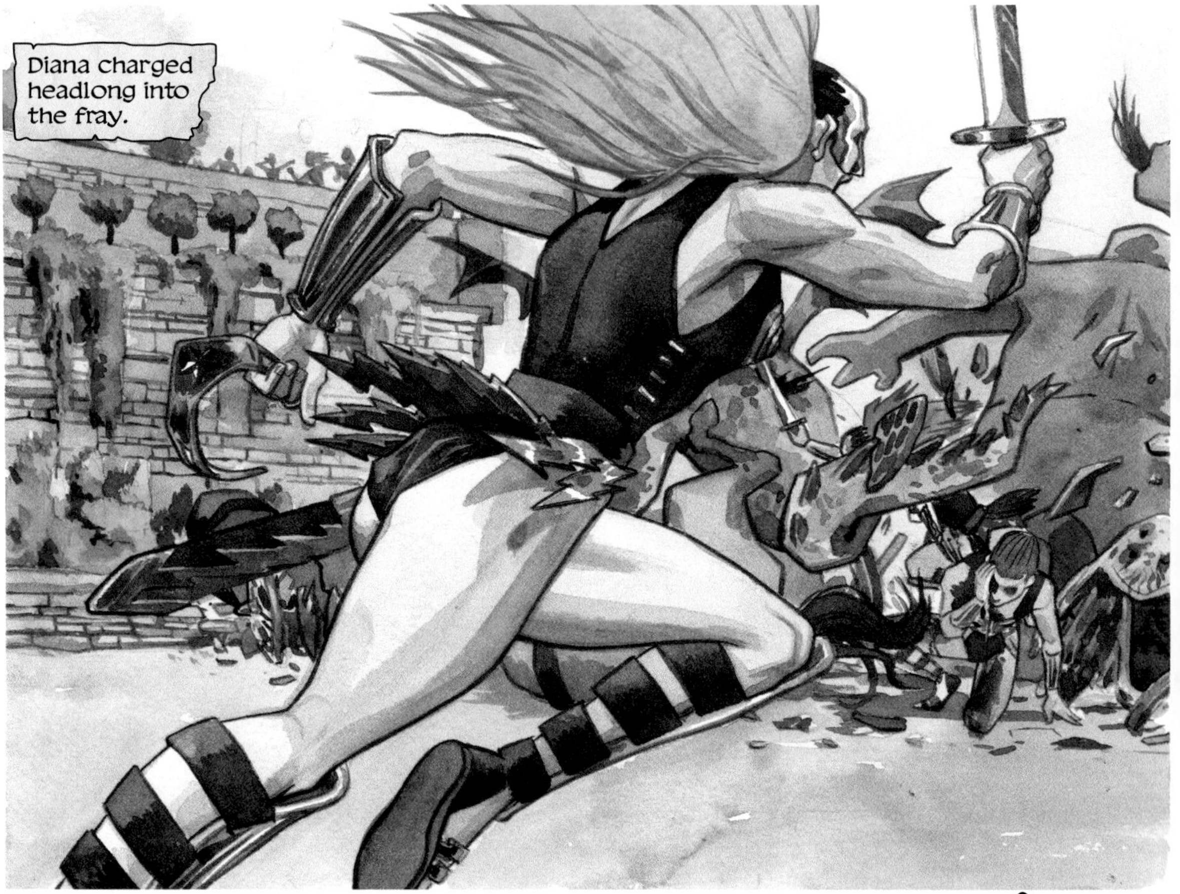
Diana charged headlong into the fray.

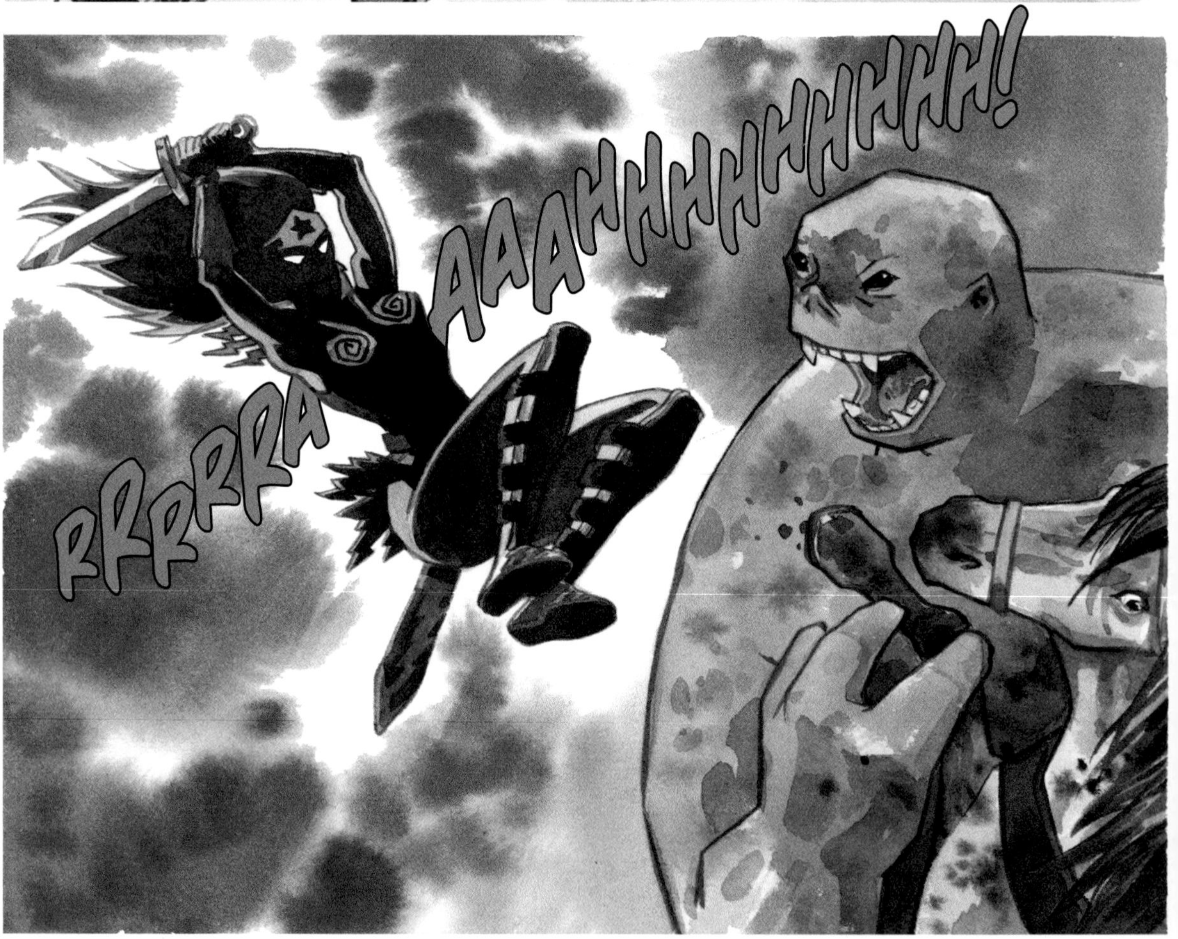
RRRRRAAAAHHHHHHHHHHH!

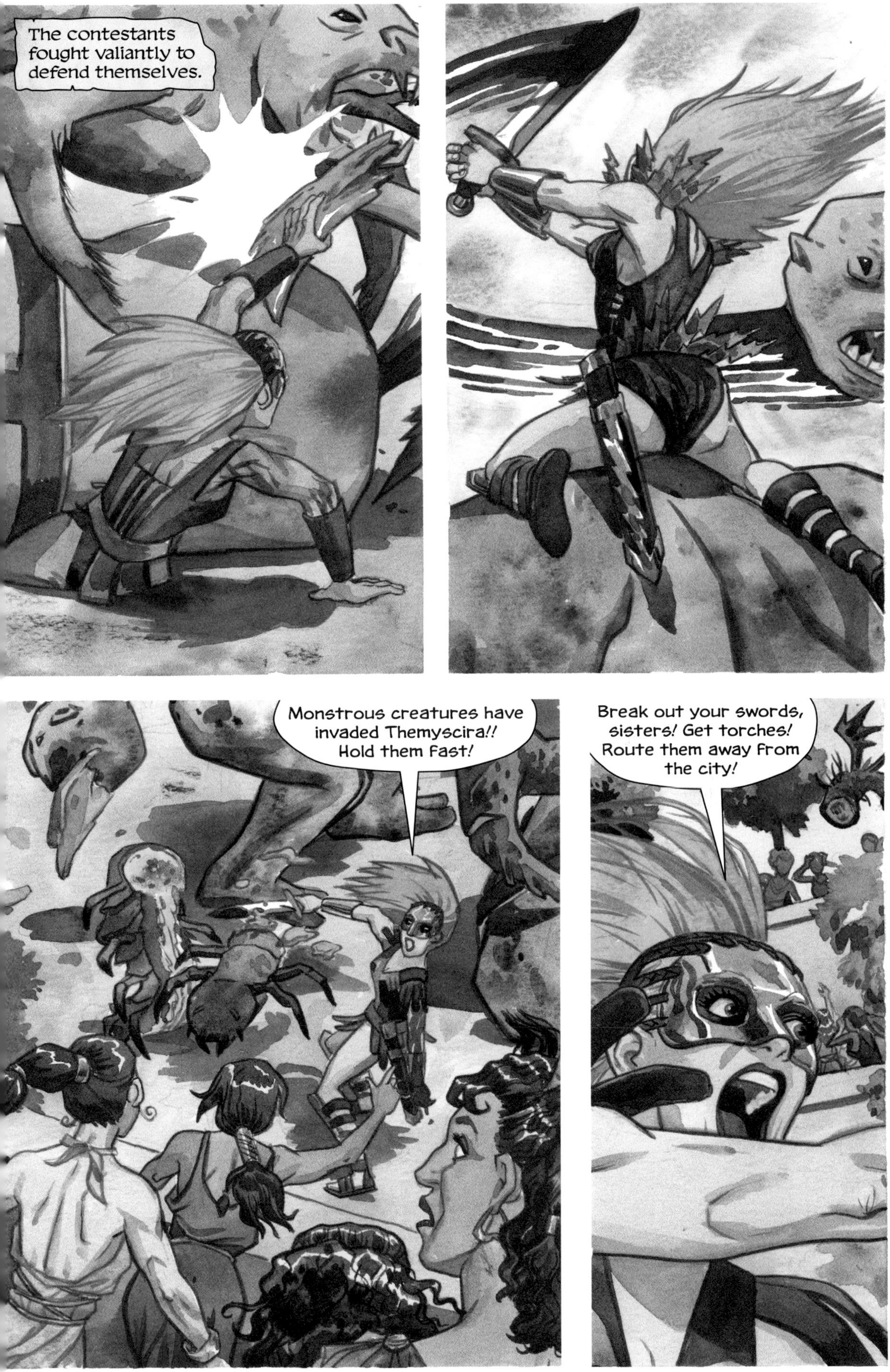
The contestants fought valiantly to defend themselves.
Monstrous creatures have invaded Themyscira!! Hold them fast!
Break out your swords, sisters! Get torches! Route them away from the city!

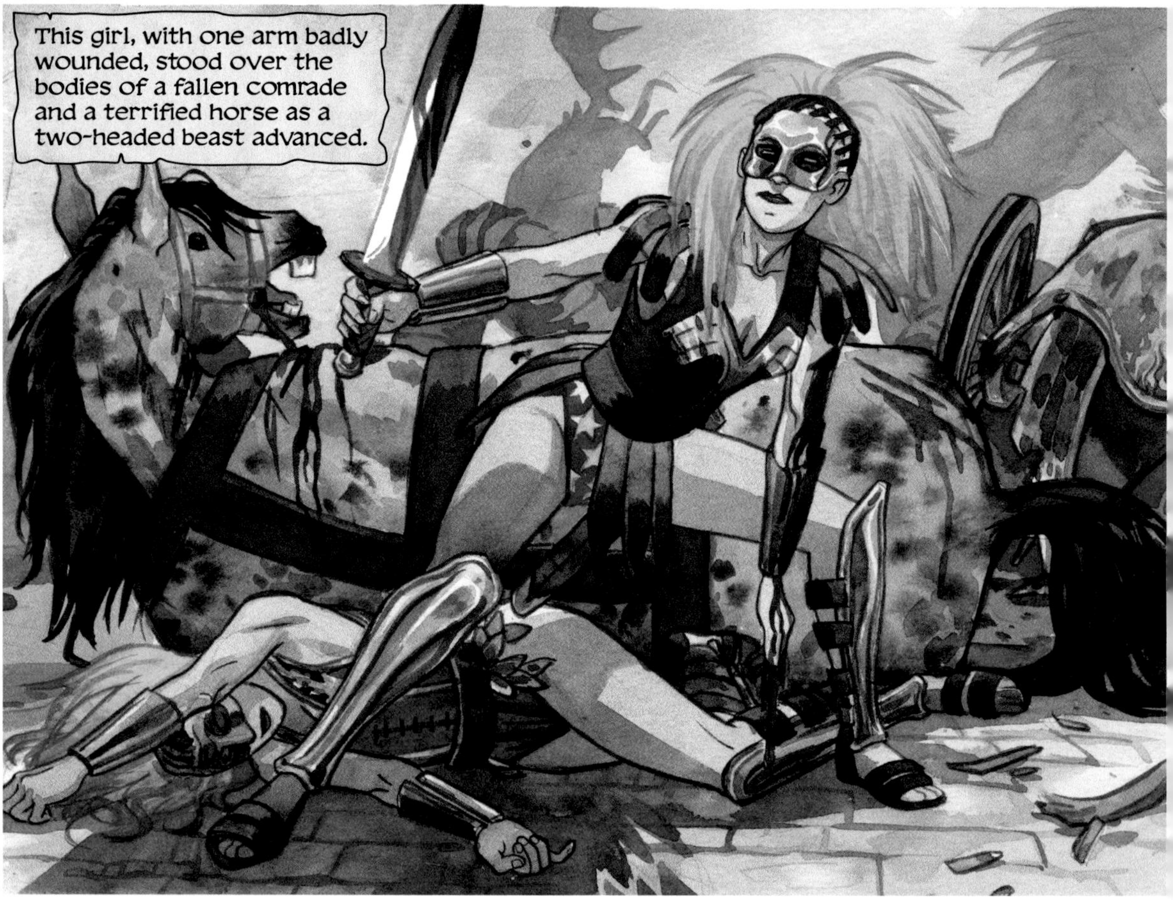
This girl, with one arm badly wounded, stood over the bodies of a fallen comrade and a terrified horse as a two-headed beast advanced.

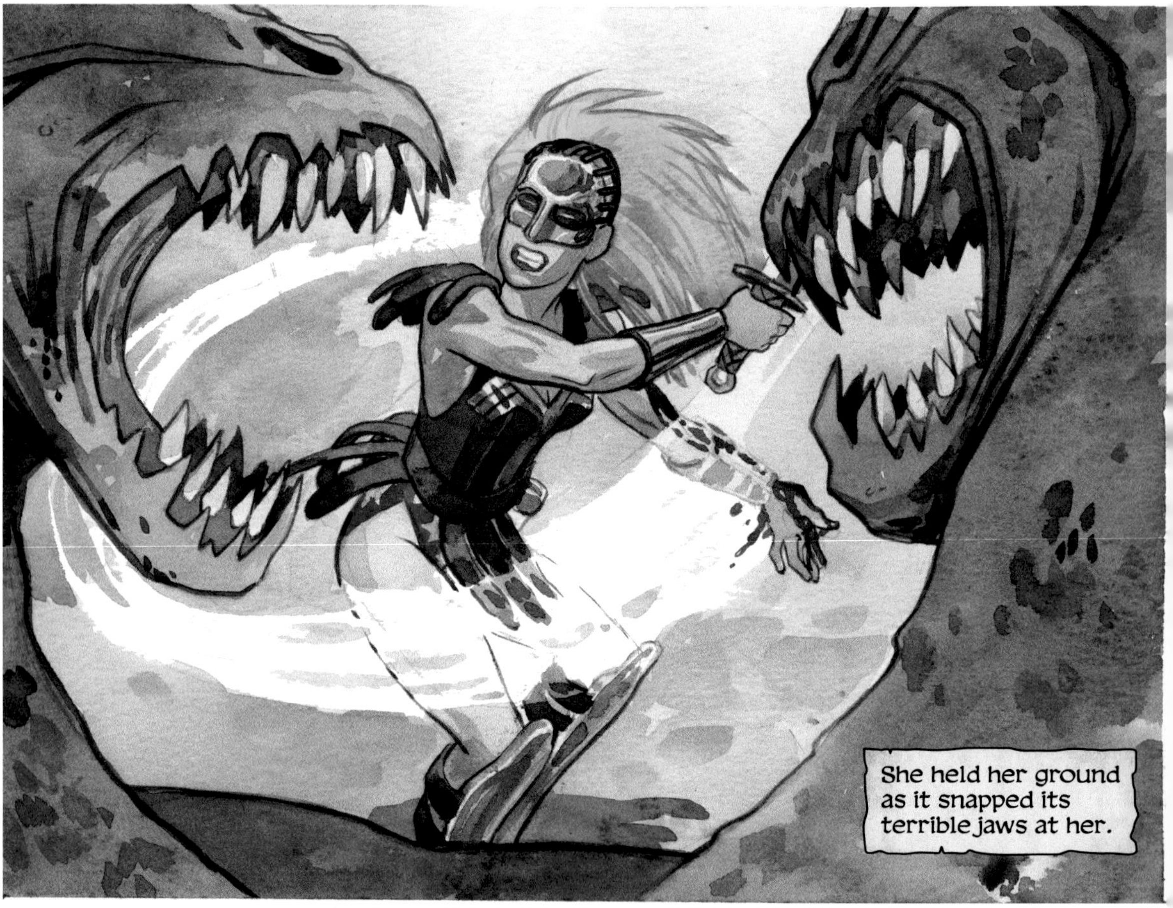
She held her ground as it snapped its terrible jaws at her.

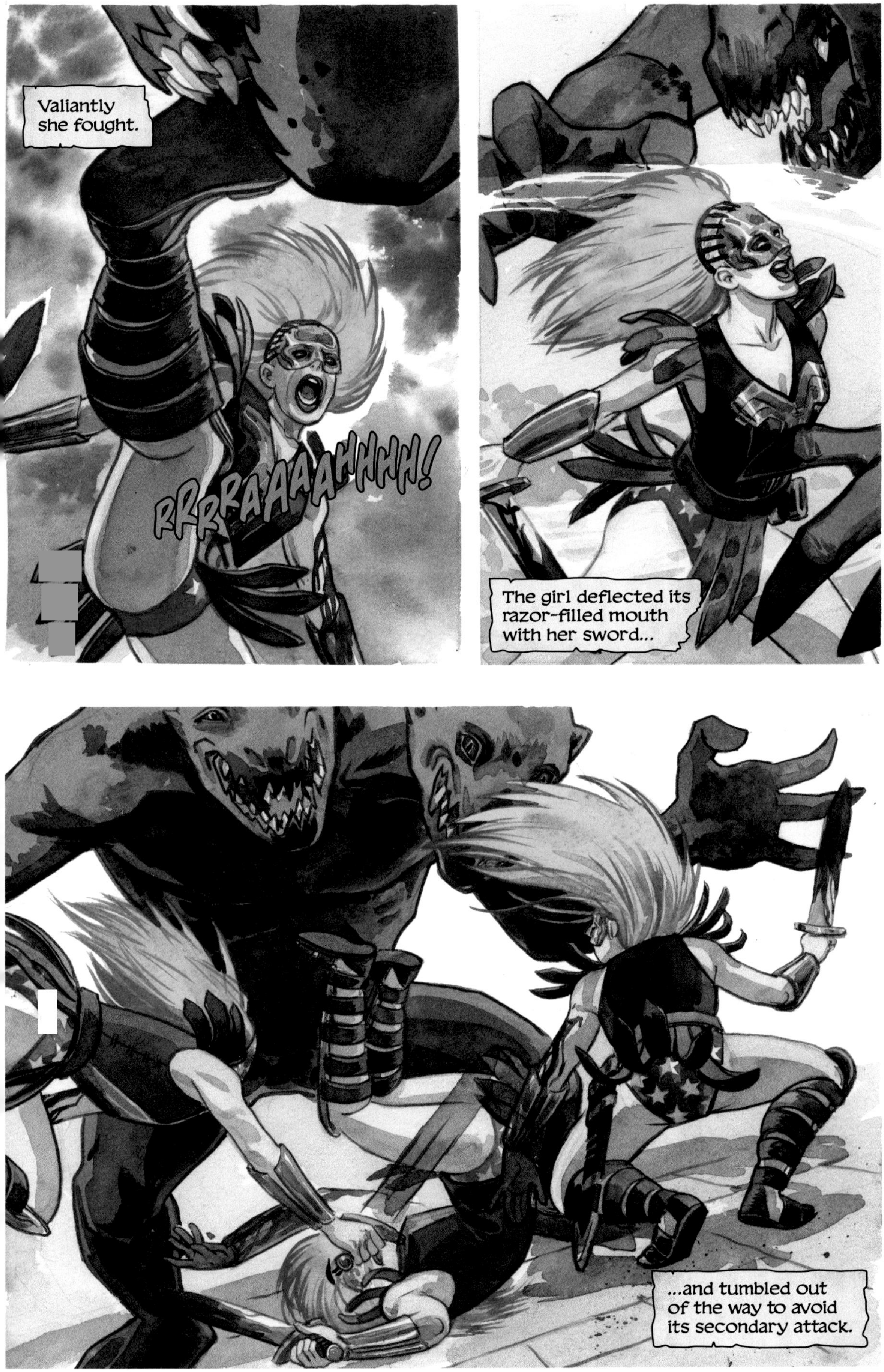
Valiantly she fought.
RRRRAAAAHHHH!
The girl deflected its razor-filled mouth with her sword...
...and tumbled out of the way to avoid its secondary attack.

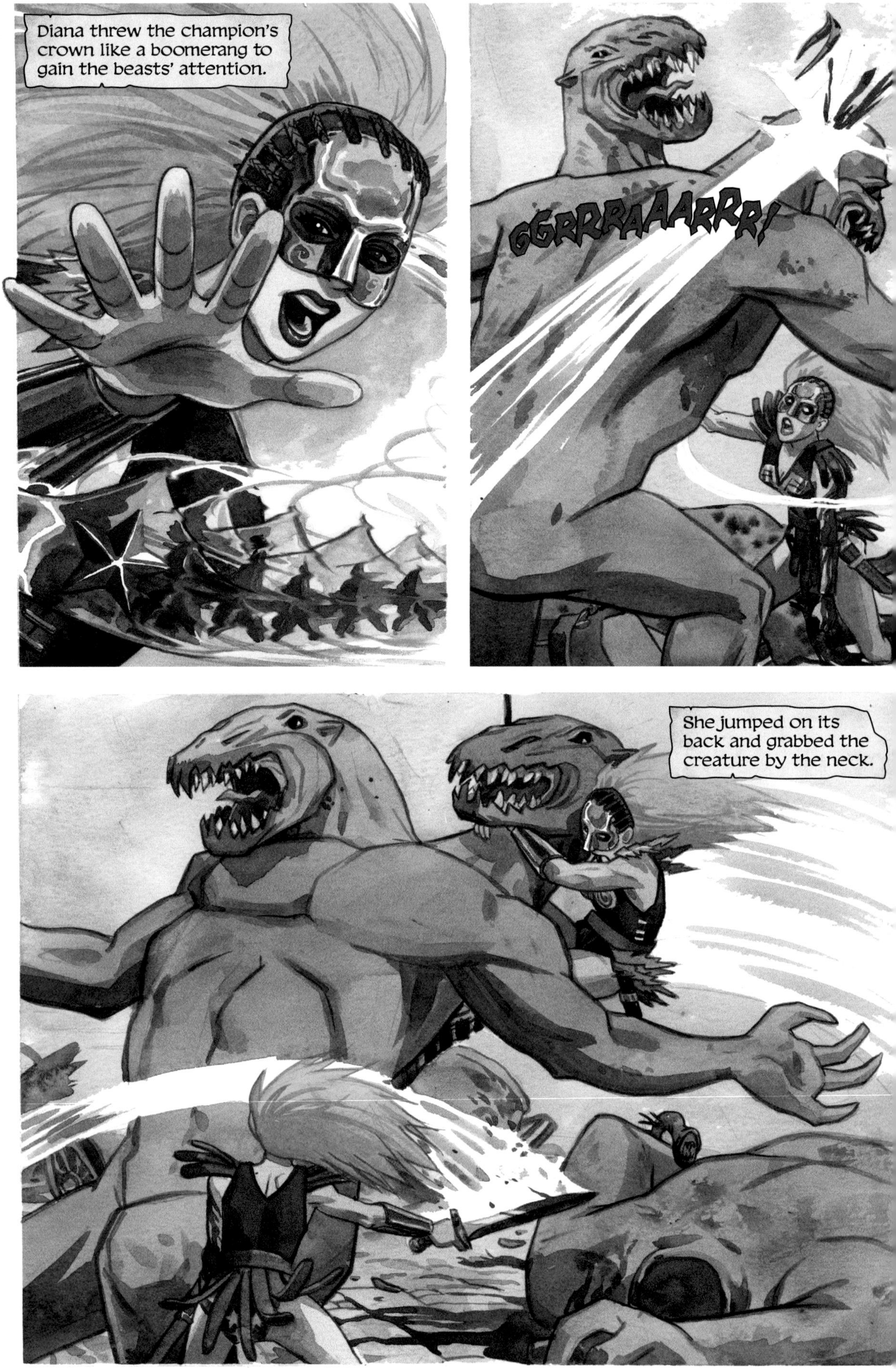
Diana threw the champion's crown like a boomerang to gain the beasts' attention.
GGRRRAAARRRR!
She jumped on its back and grabbed the creature by the neck.

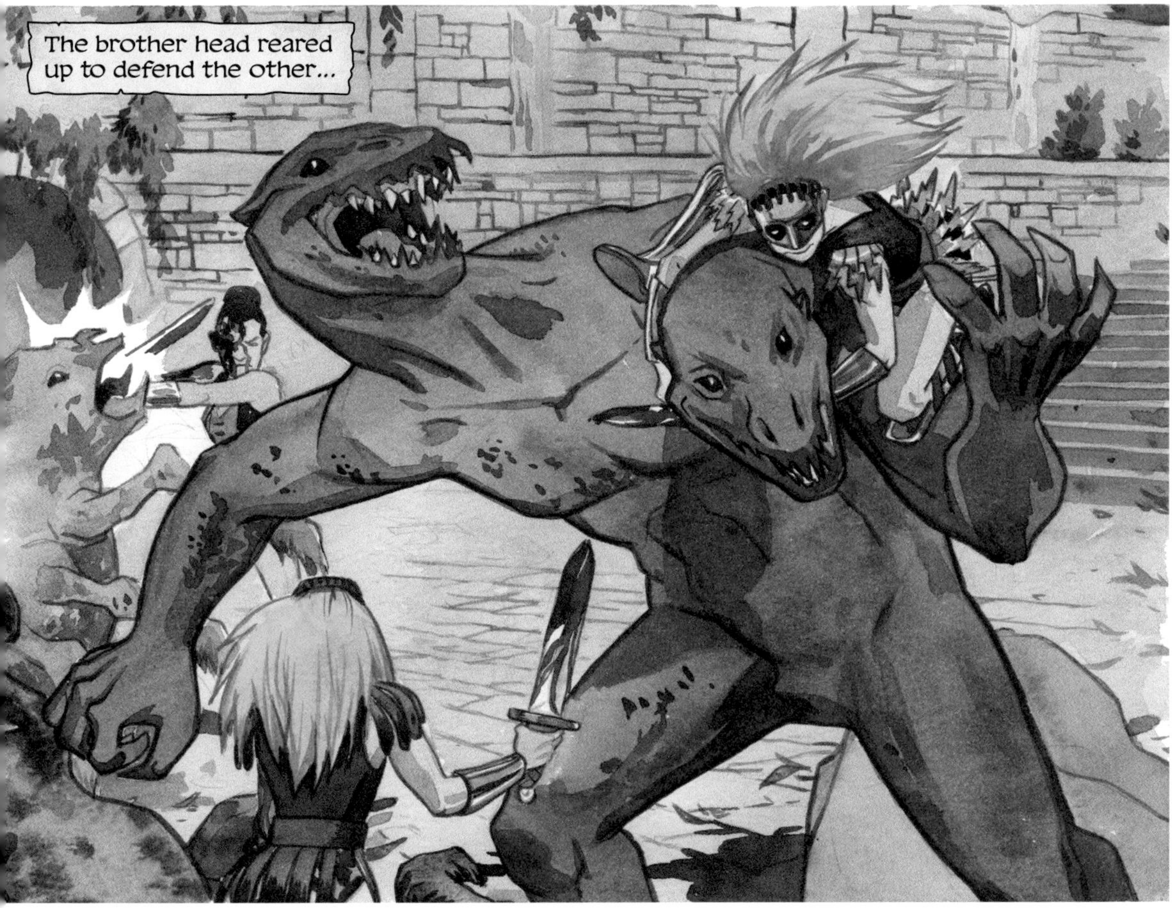
The brother head reared up to defend the other...

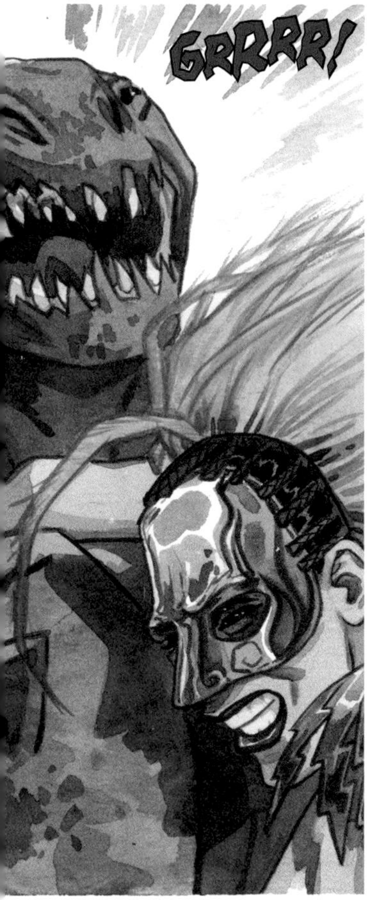
GRRRR!

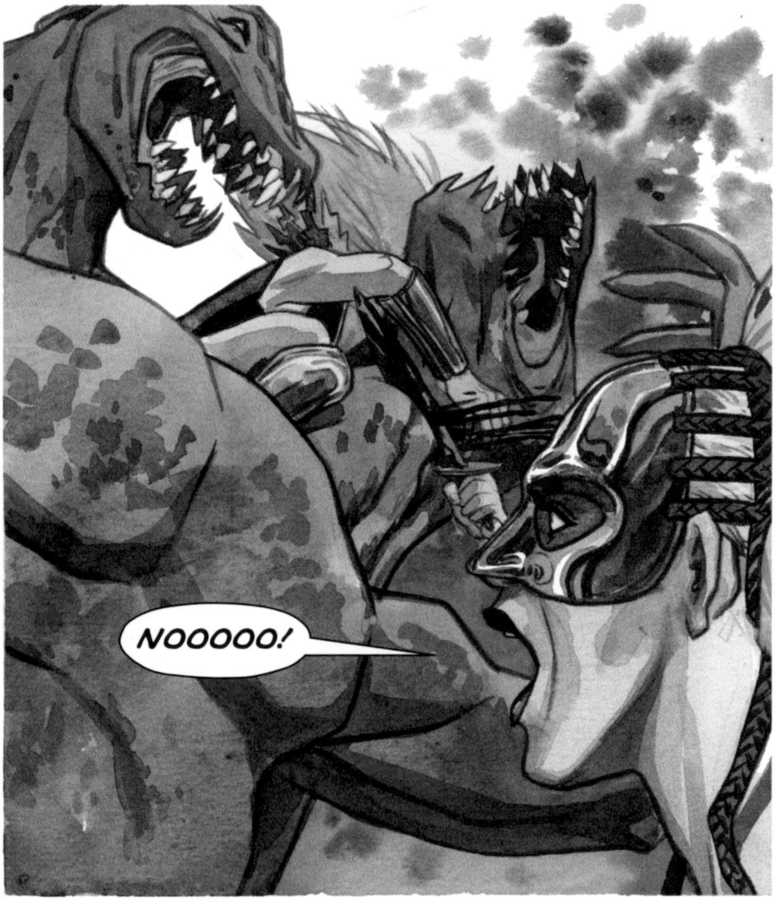
NOOOOO!

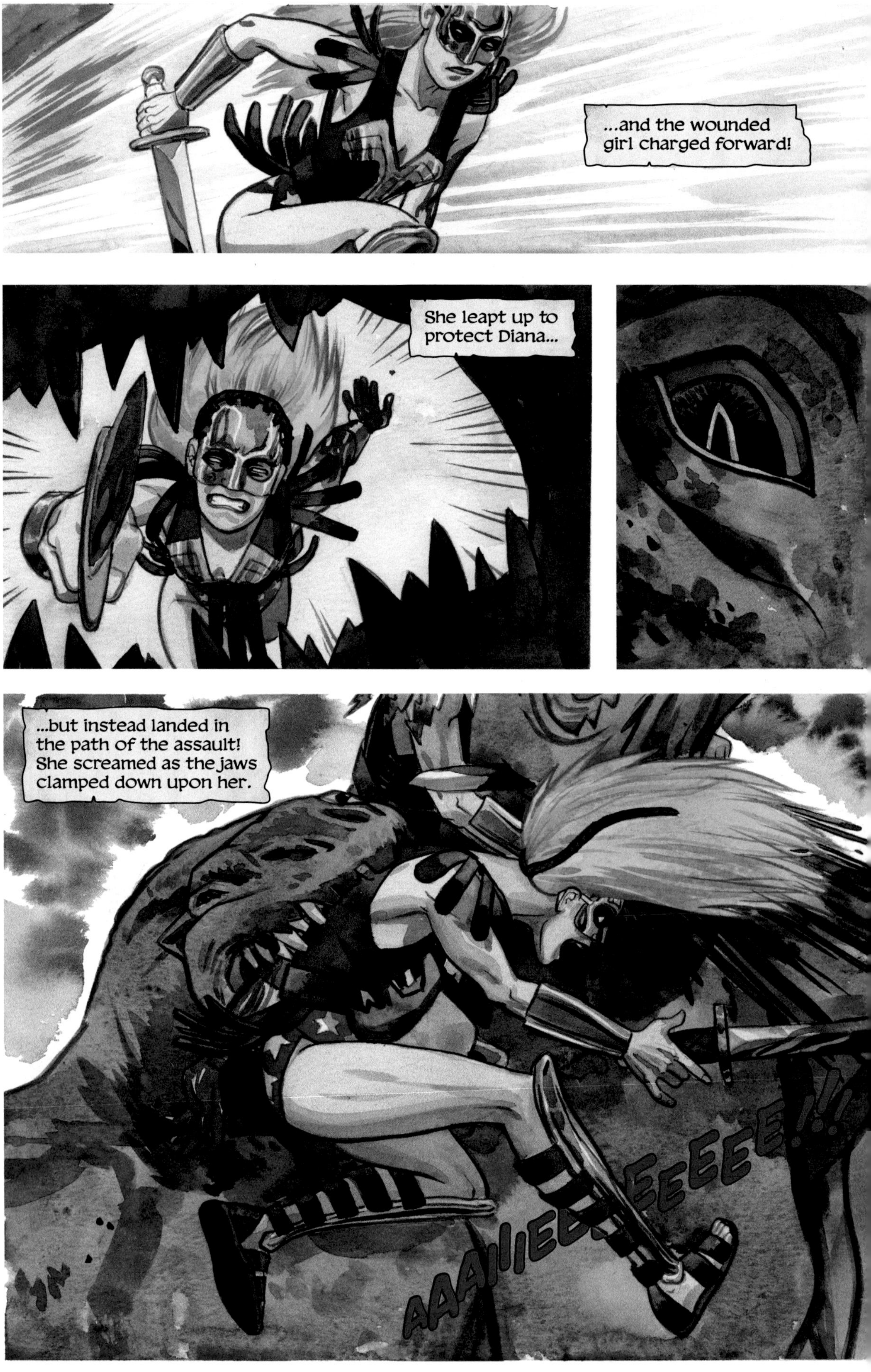
...and the wounded girl charged forward!
She leapt up to protect Diana...
...but instead landed in the path of the assault! She screamed as the jaws clamped down upon her.
AAAIIIEEEEEEEE!!!

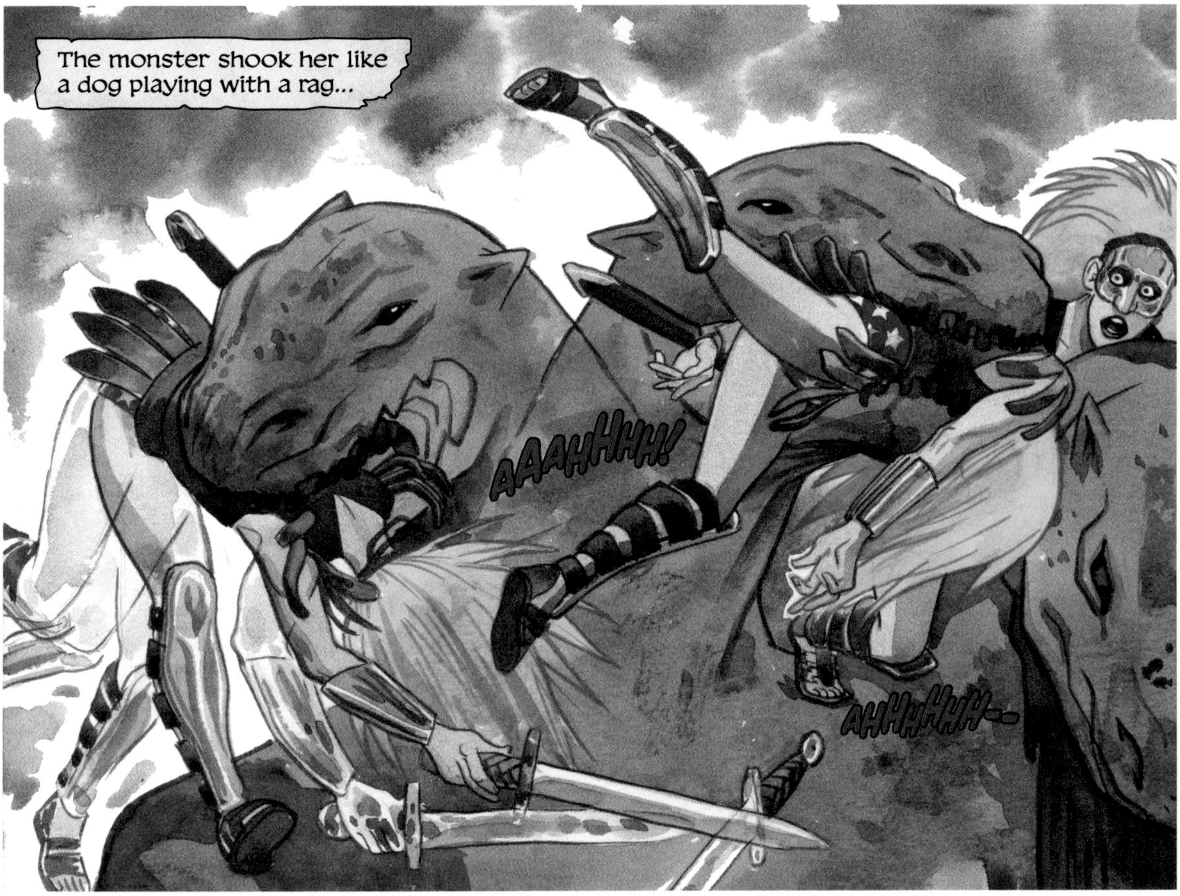
The monster shook her like a dog playing with a rag...
AAAHHHH!
AHHHHHH--

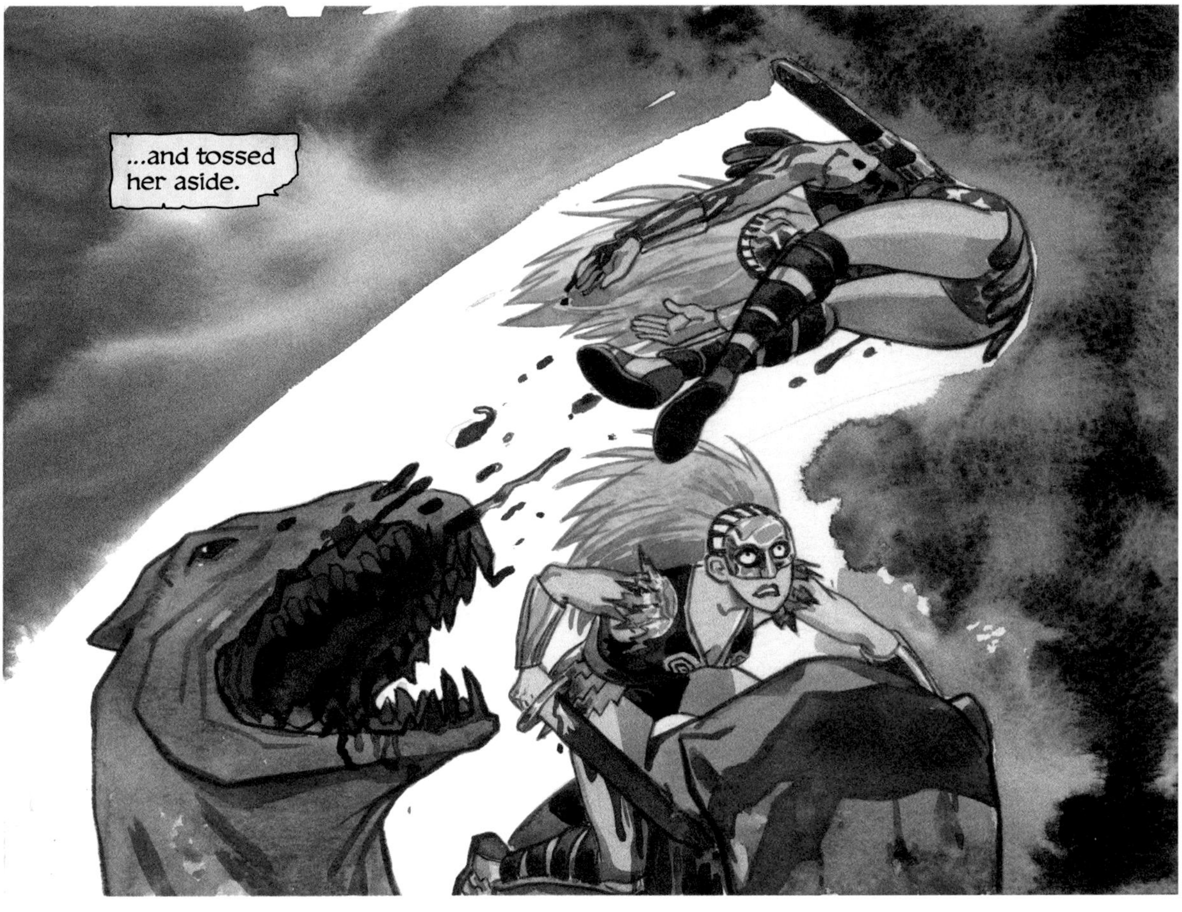
...and tossed her aside.

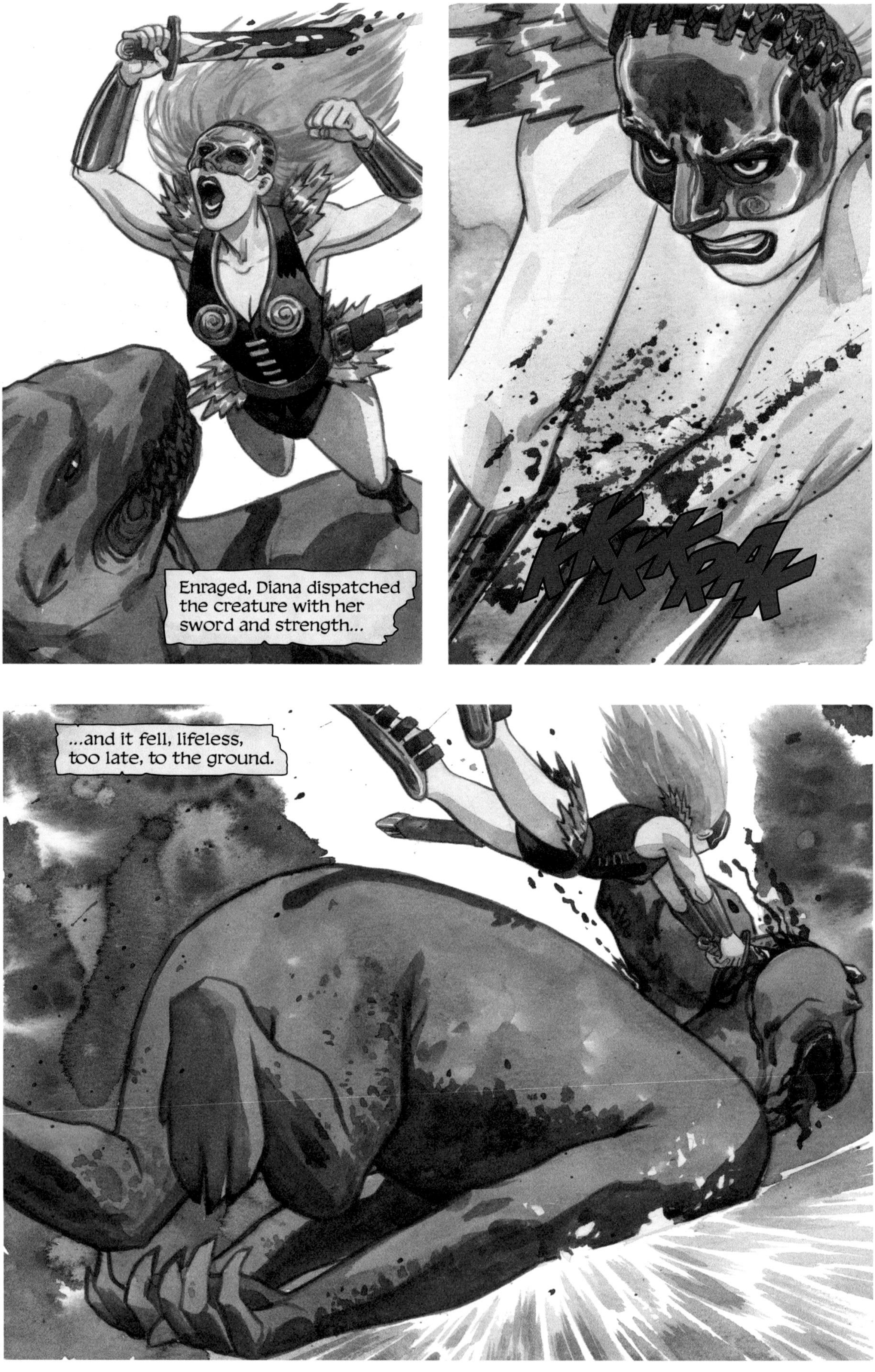
Enraged, Diana dispatched the creature with her sword and strength...
KKKRAK
...and it fell, lifeless, too late, to the ground.

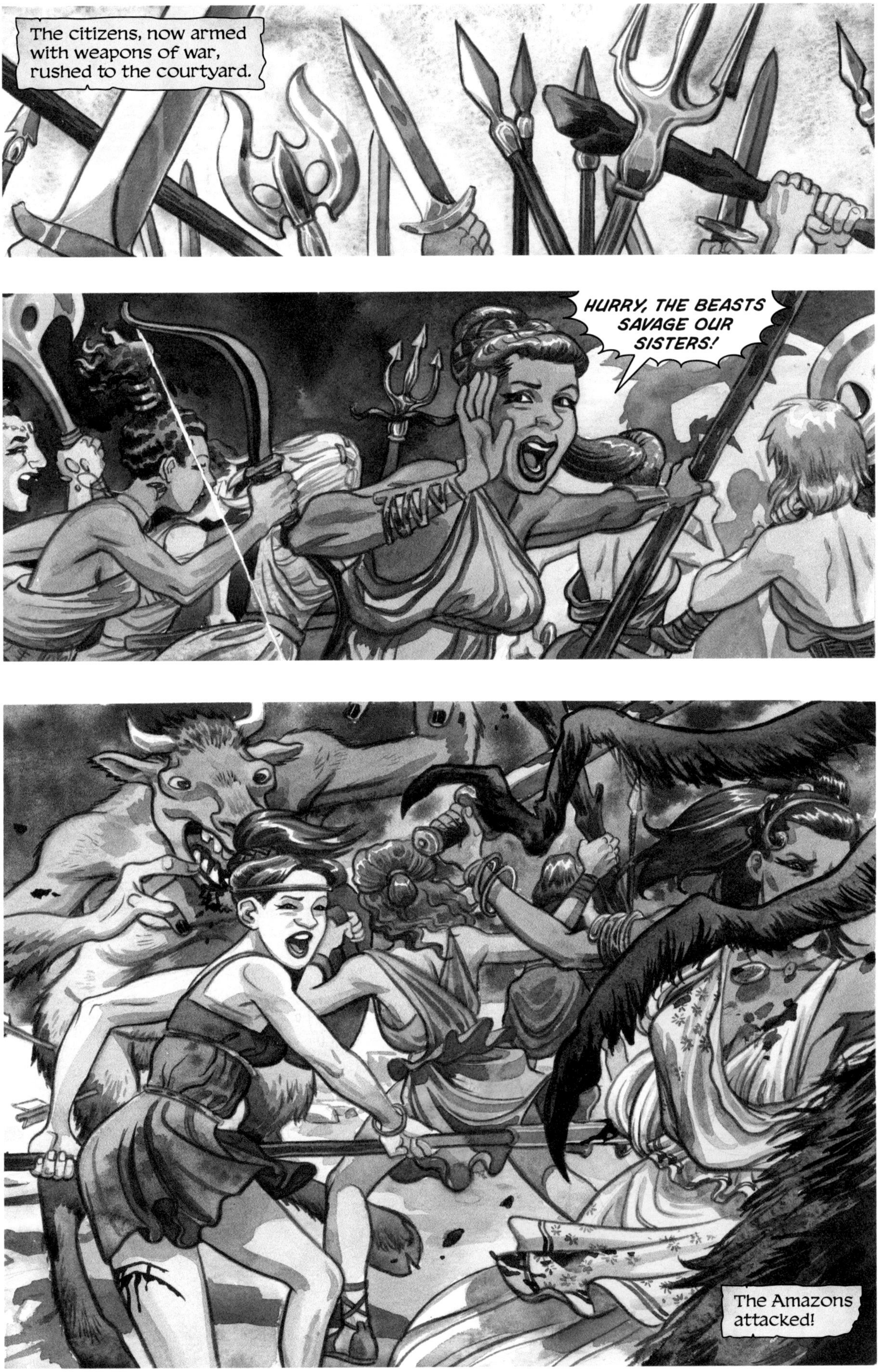
The citizens, now armed with weapons of war, rushed to the courtyard.
HURRY, THE BEASTS SAVAGE OUR SISTERS!
The Amazons attacked!

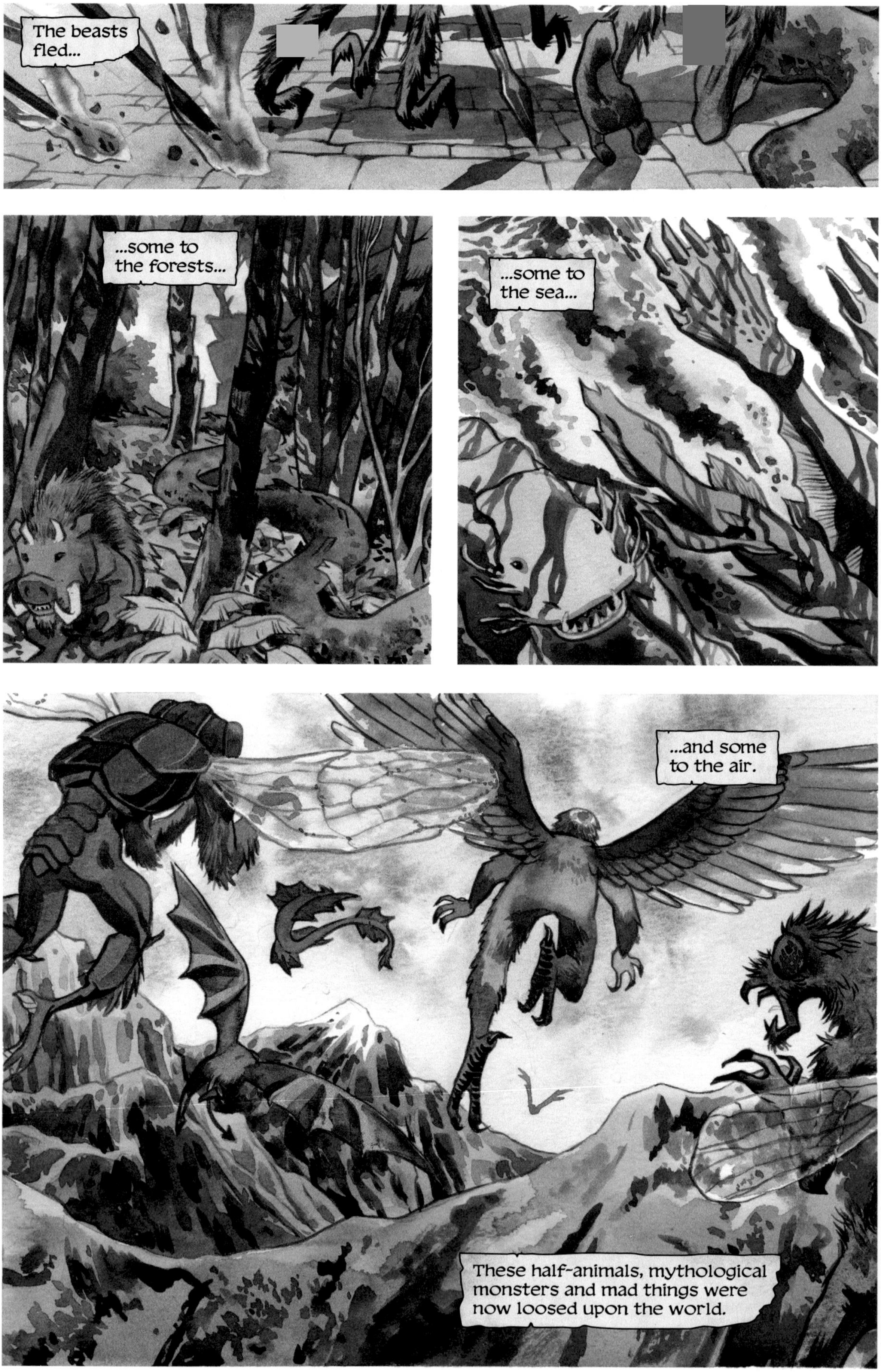
The beasts fled...
...some to the forests...
...some to the sea...
...and some to the air.
These half-animals, mythological monsters and mad things were now loosed upon the world.

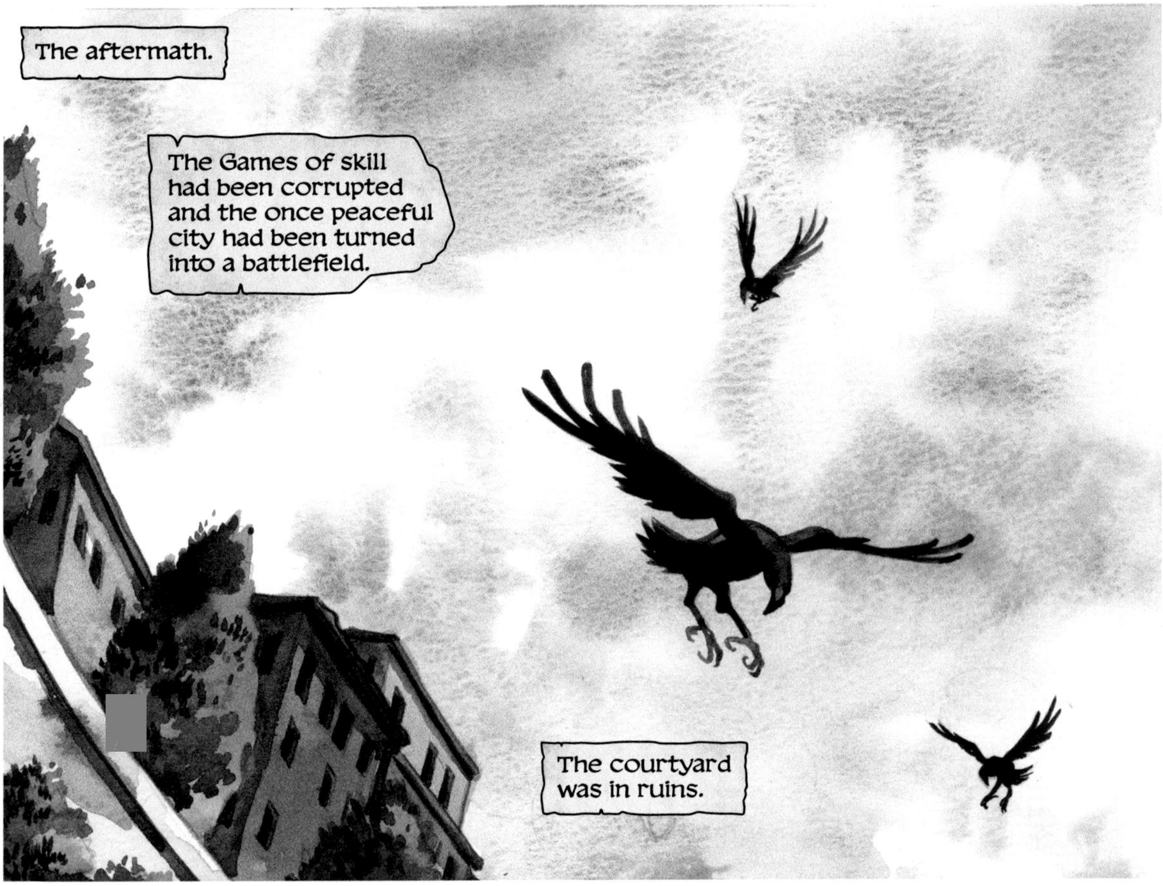
The aftermath.
The Games of skill had been corrupted and the once peaceful city had been turned into a battlefield.
The courtyard was in ruins.

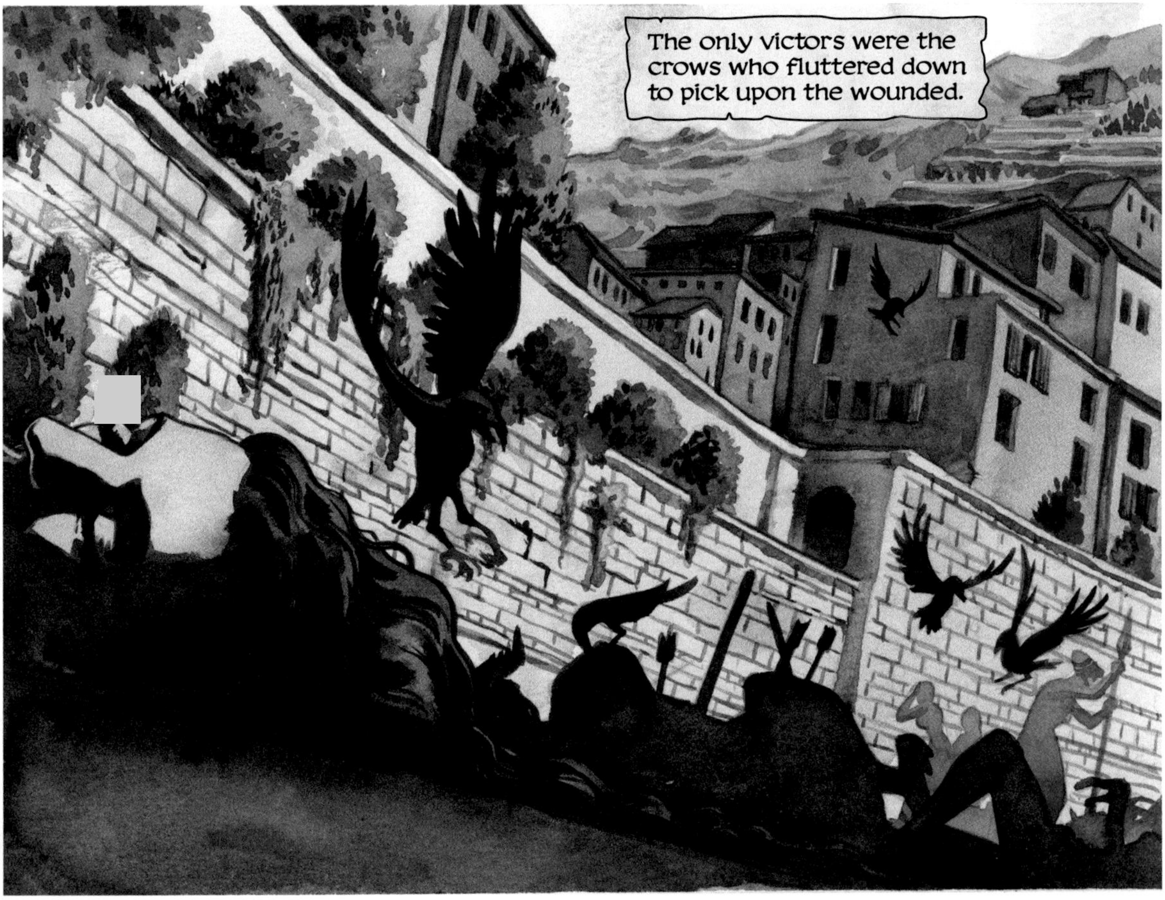
The only victors were the crows who fluttered down to pick upon the wounded.

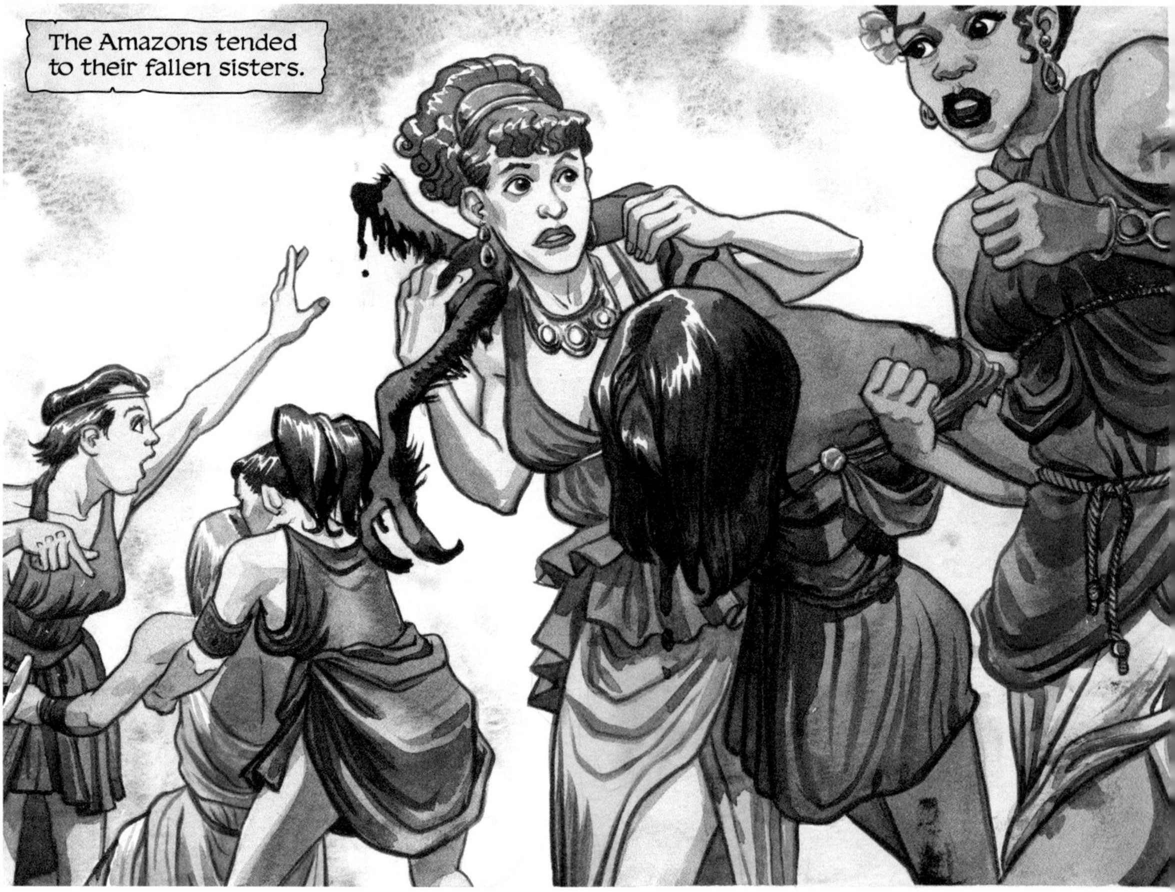
The Amazons tended
to their fallen sisters.

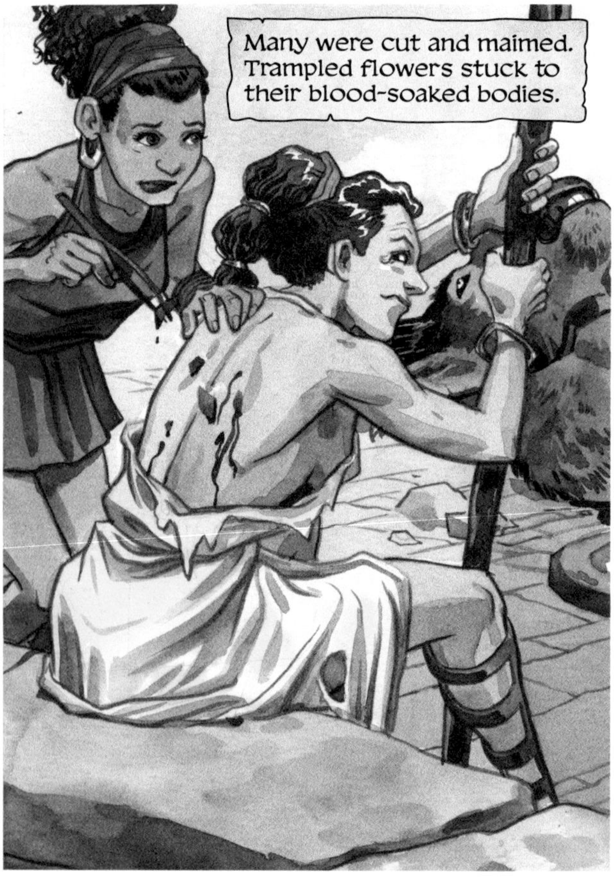
Many were cut and maimed.
Trampled flowers stuck to
their blood-soaked bodies.

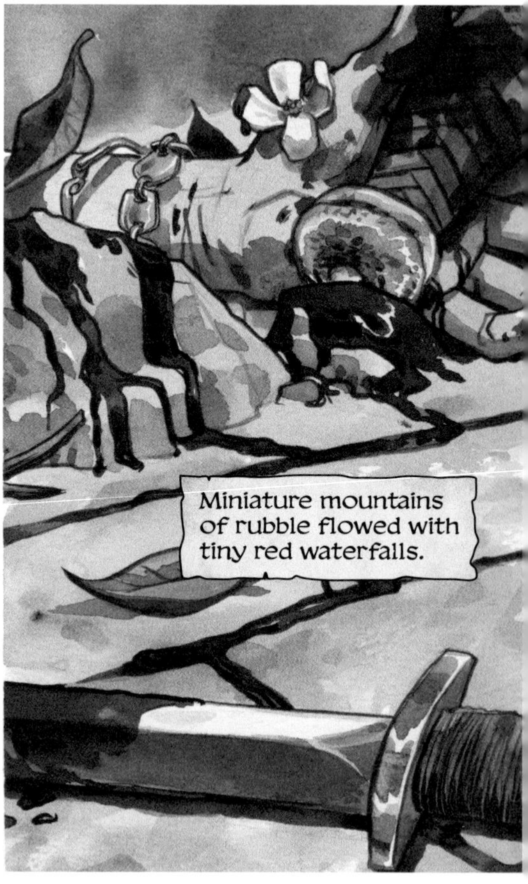
Miniature mountains
of rubble flowed with
tiny red waterfalls.

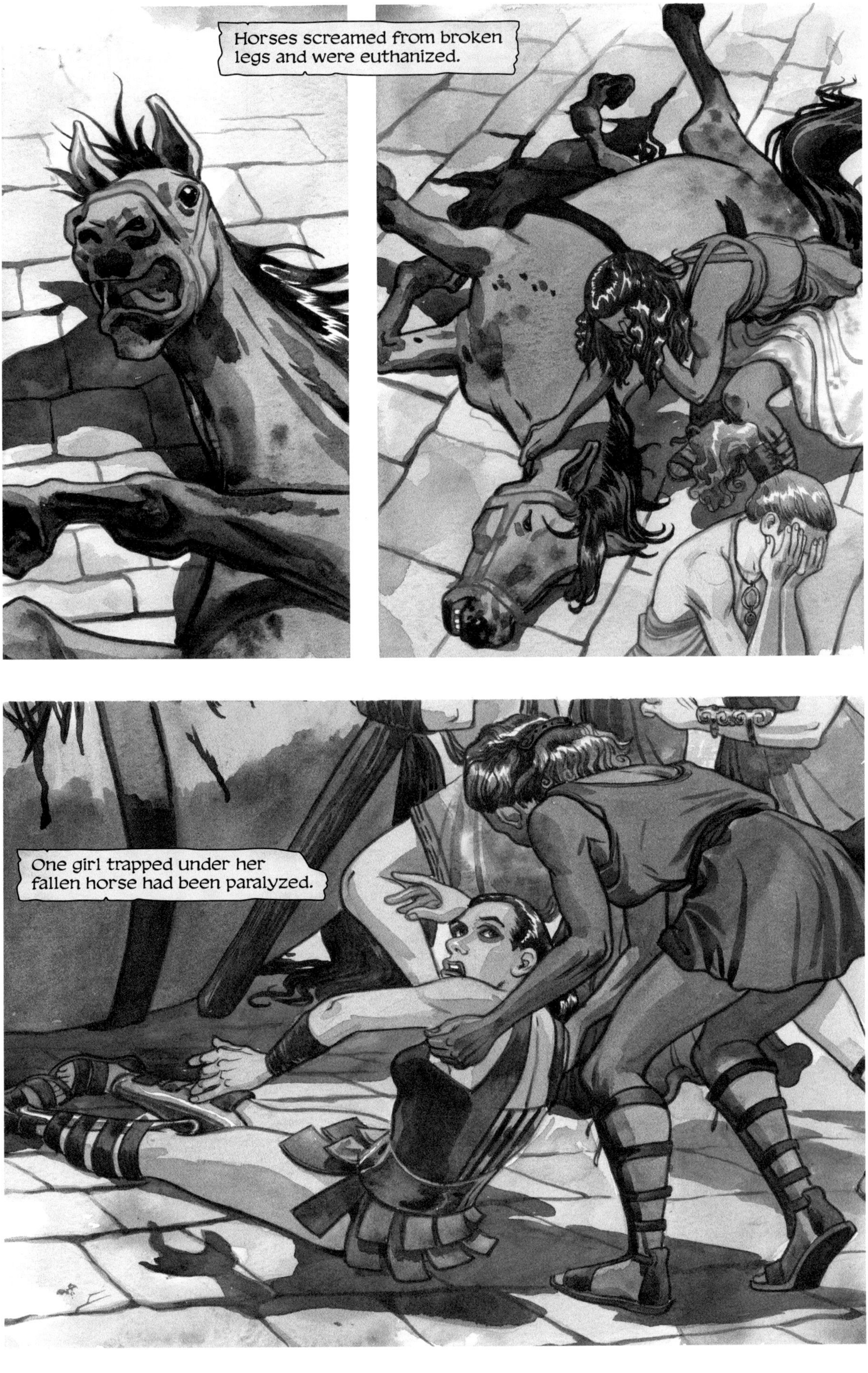
Horses screamed from broken legs and were euthanized.
One girl trapped under her fallen horse had been paralyzed.

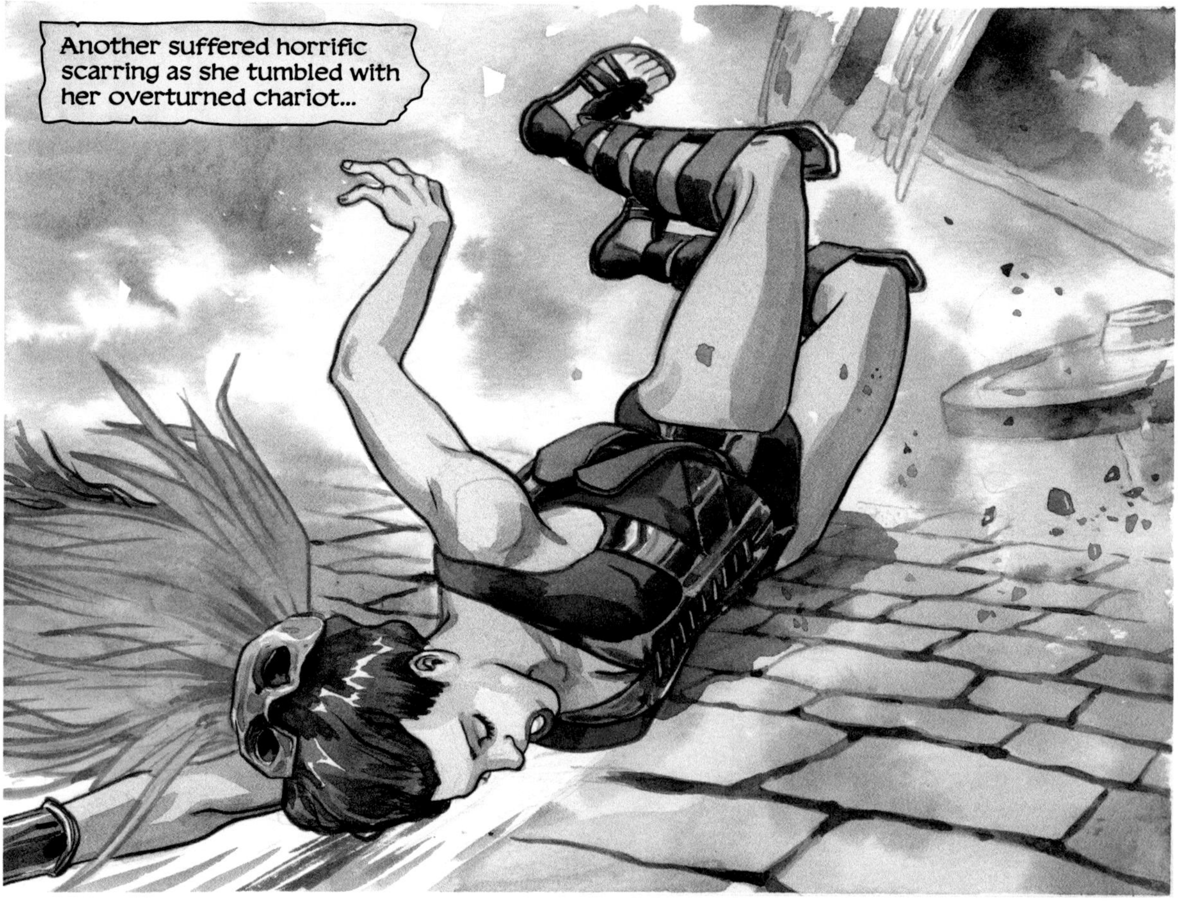
Another suffered horrific scarring as she tumbled with her overturned chariot...

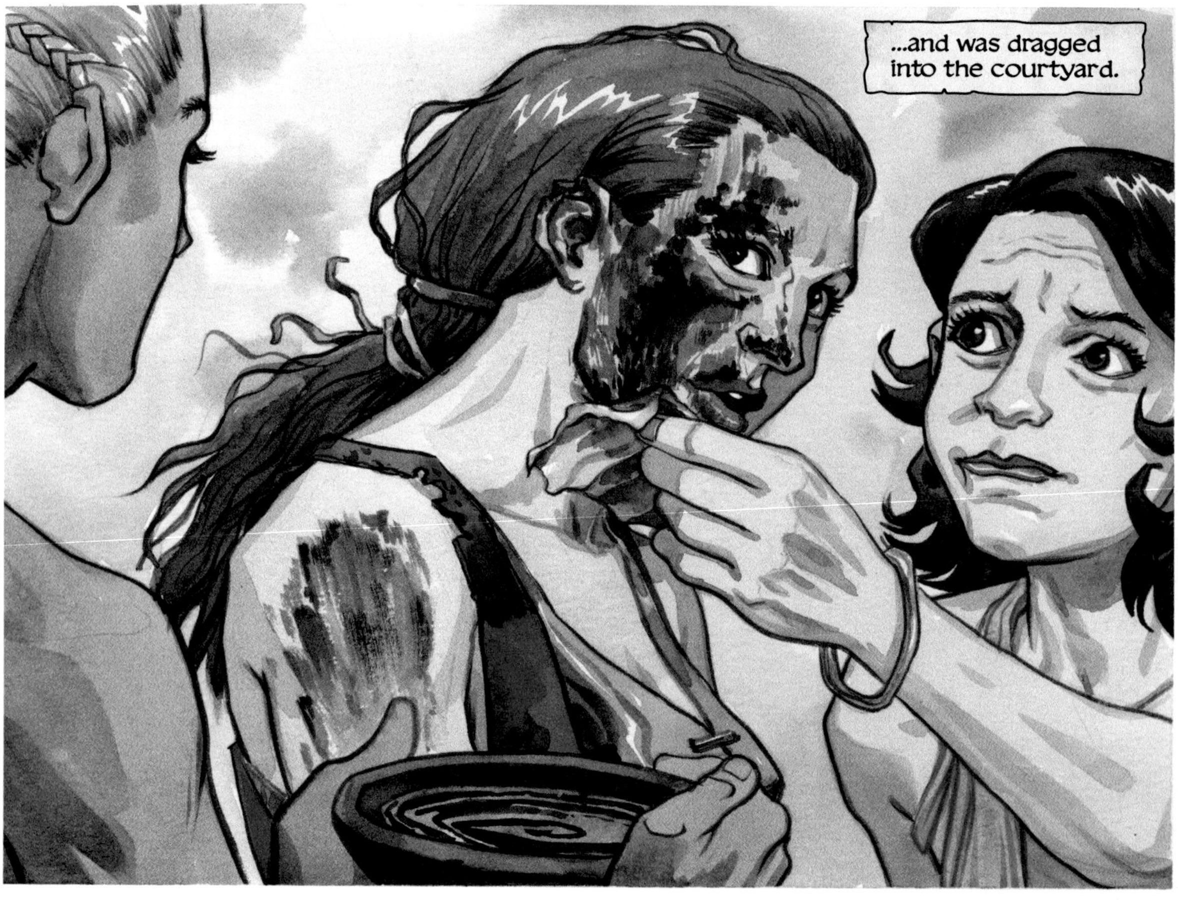
...and was dragged into the courtyard.

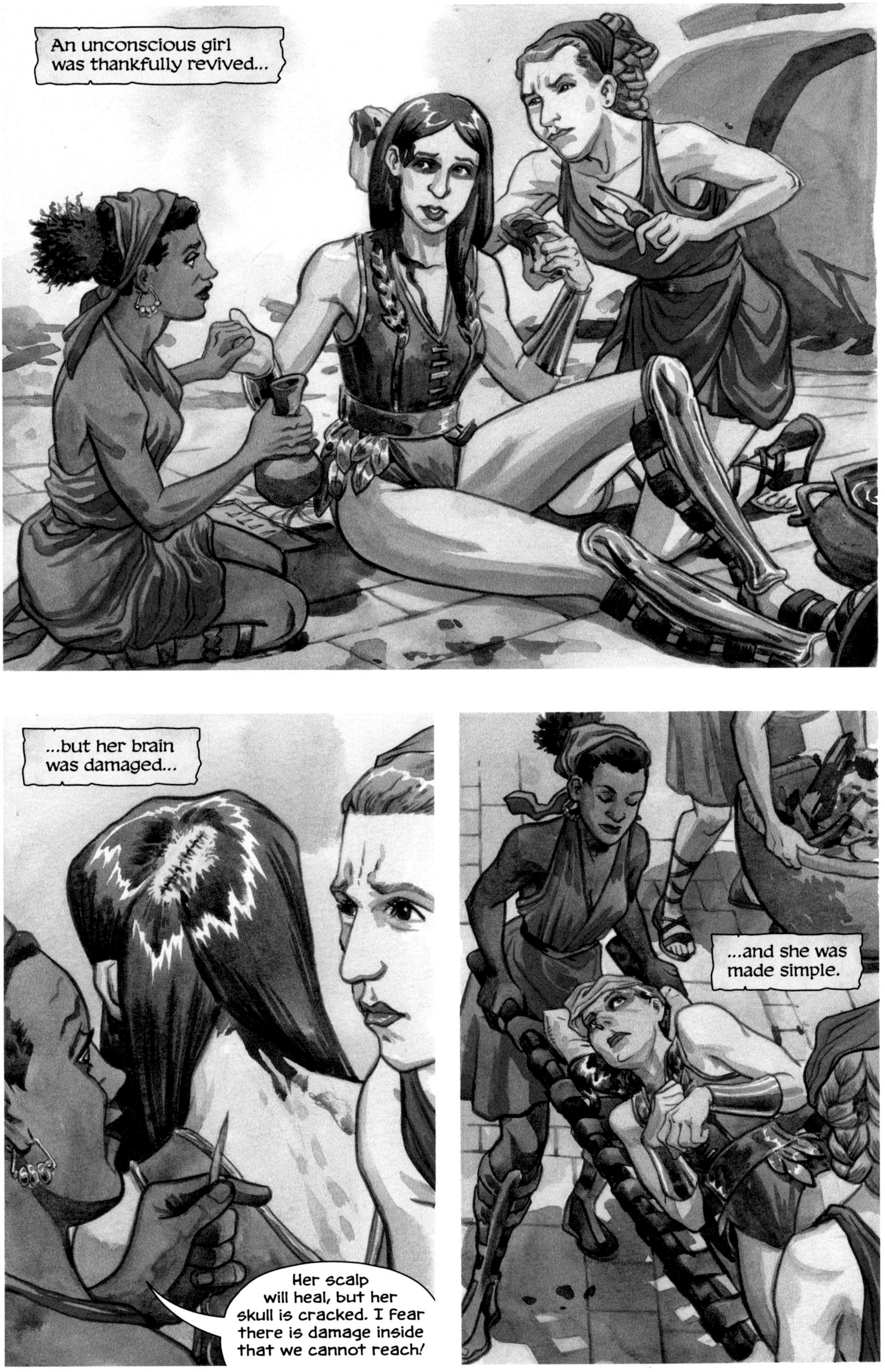
An unconscious girl
was thankfully revived...
...but her brain
was damaged...
Her scalp
will heal, but her
skull is cracked. I fear
there is damage inside
that we cannot reach!
...and she was
made simple.

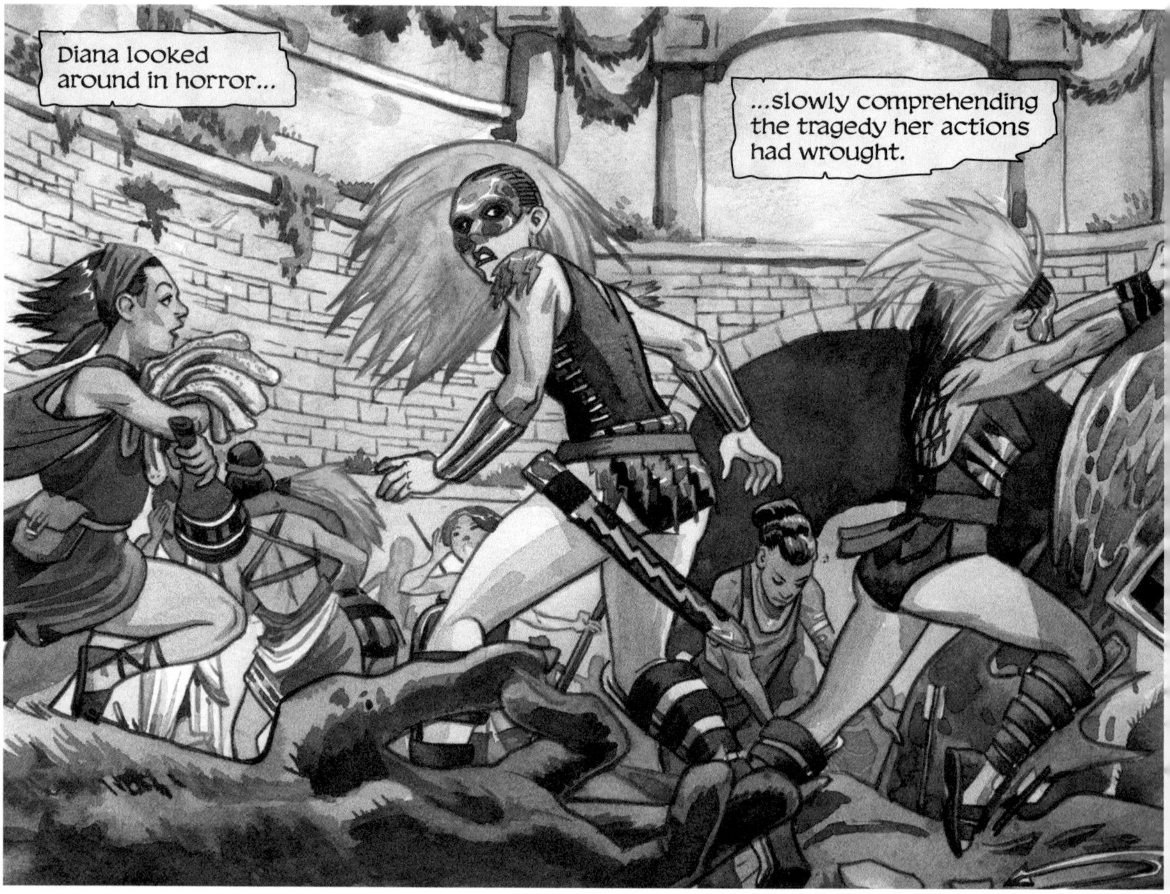
Diana looked around in horror...
...slowly comprehending the tragedy her actions had wrought.

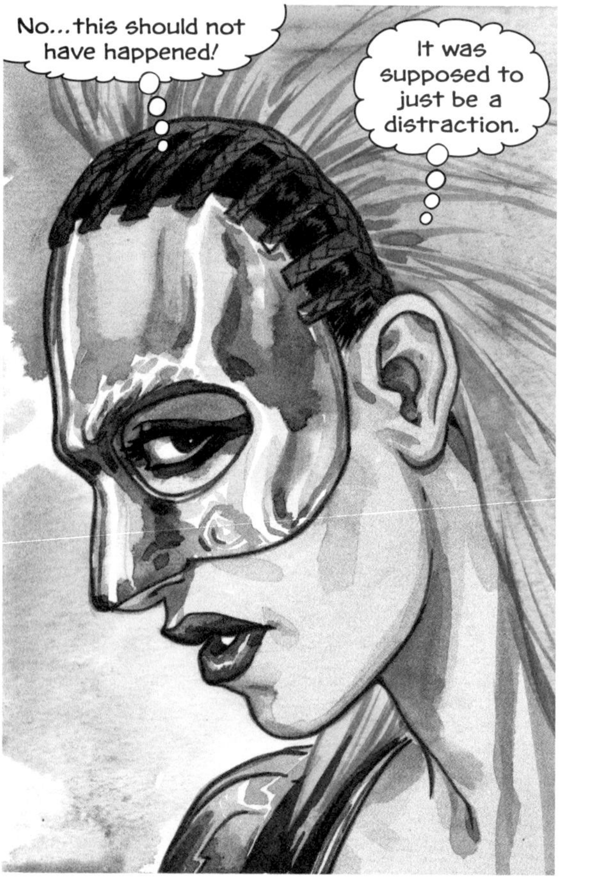
No...this should not have happened!
It was supposed to just be a distraction.

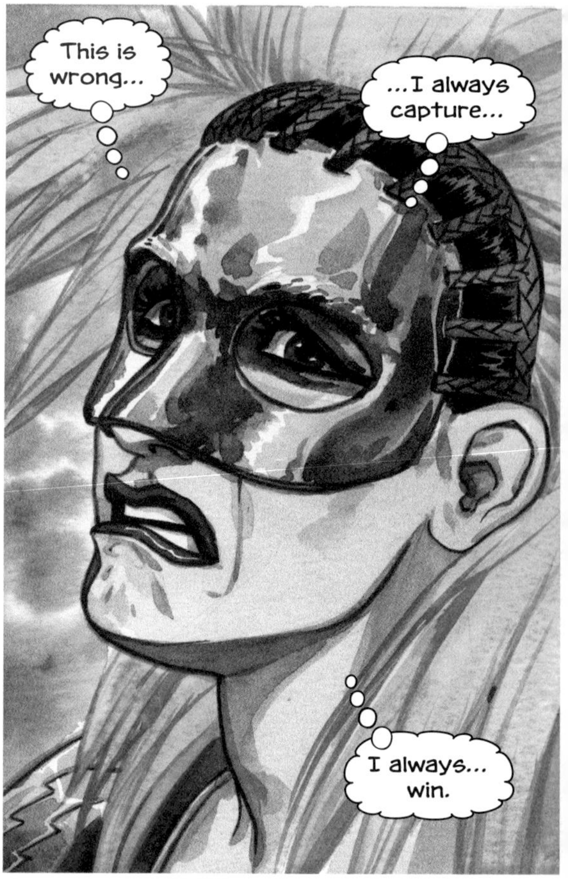
This is wrong...
...I always capture...
I always... win.

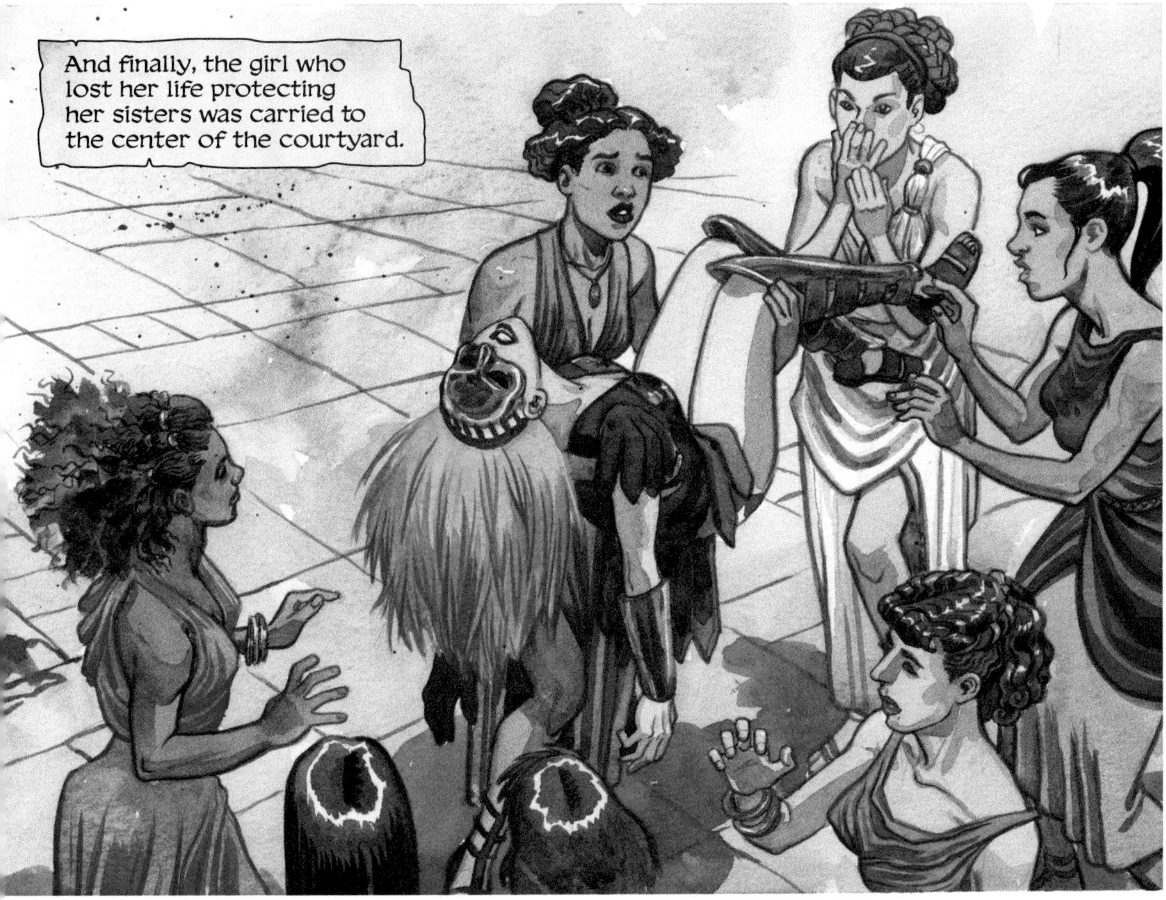
And finally, the girl who lost her life protecting her sisters was carried to the center of the courtyard.

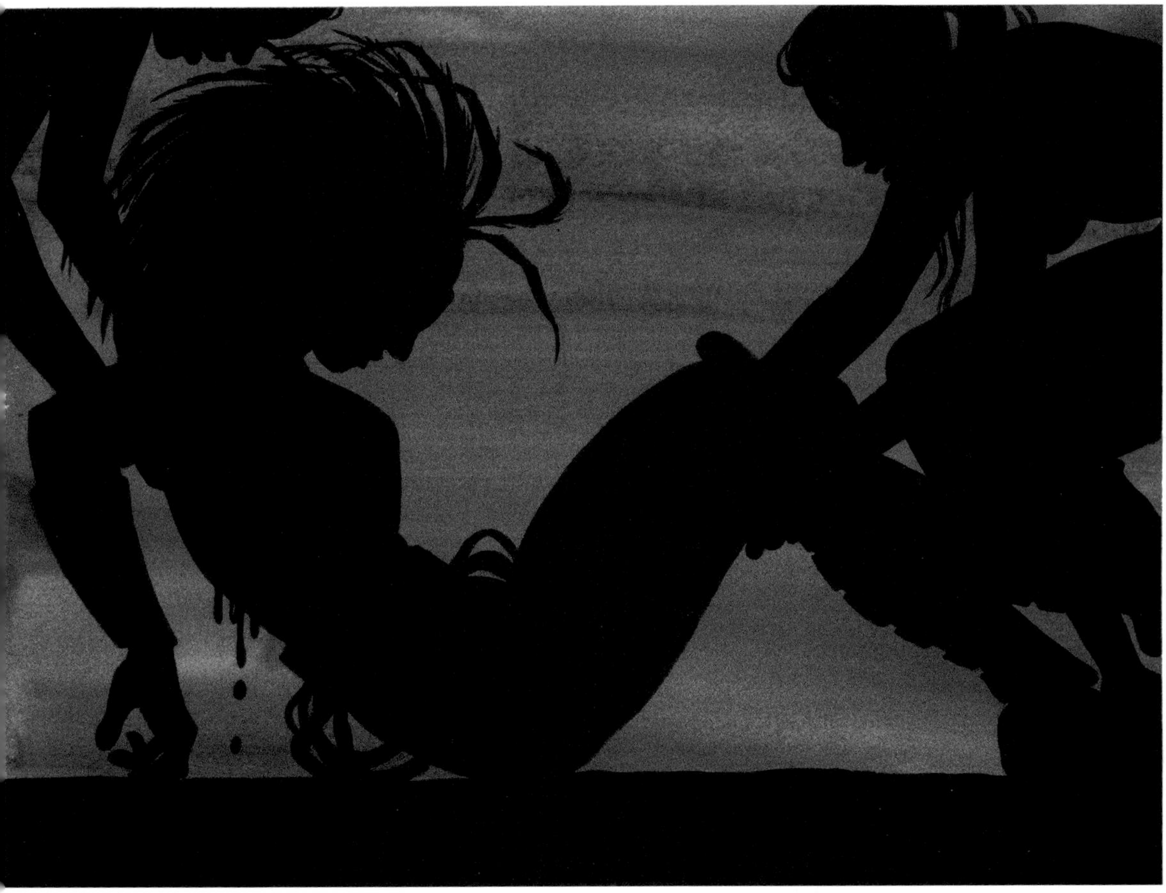

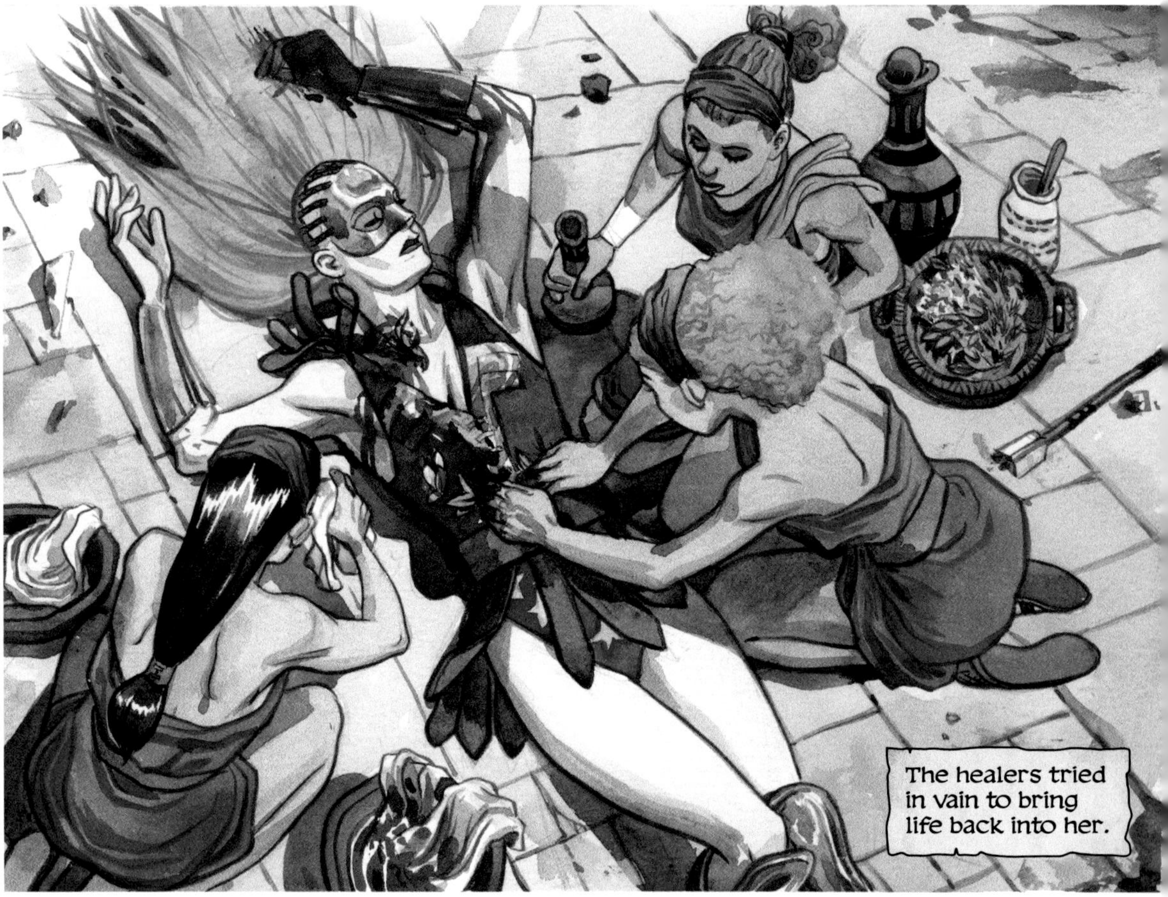
The healers tried in vain to bring life back into her.

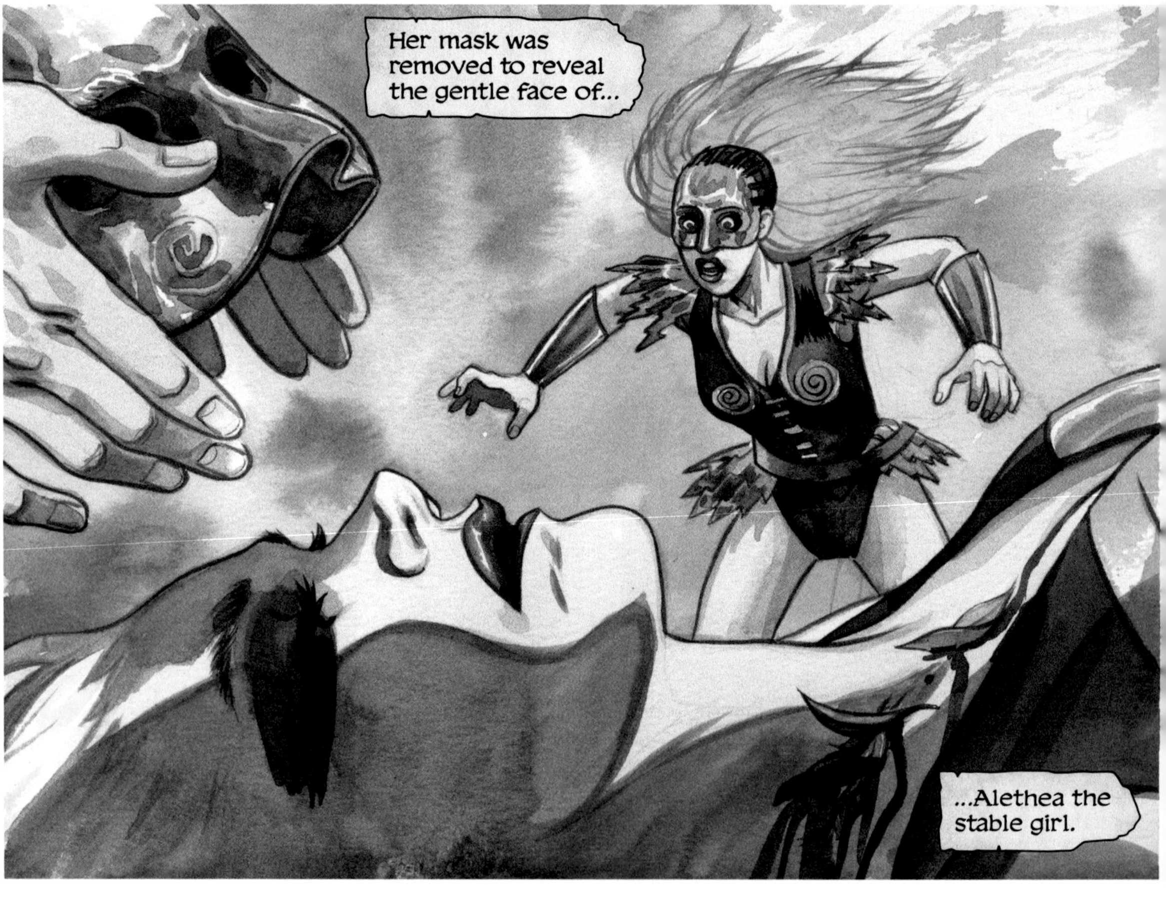
Her mask was removed to reveal the gentle face of...
...Alethea the stable girl.

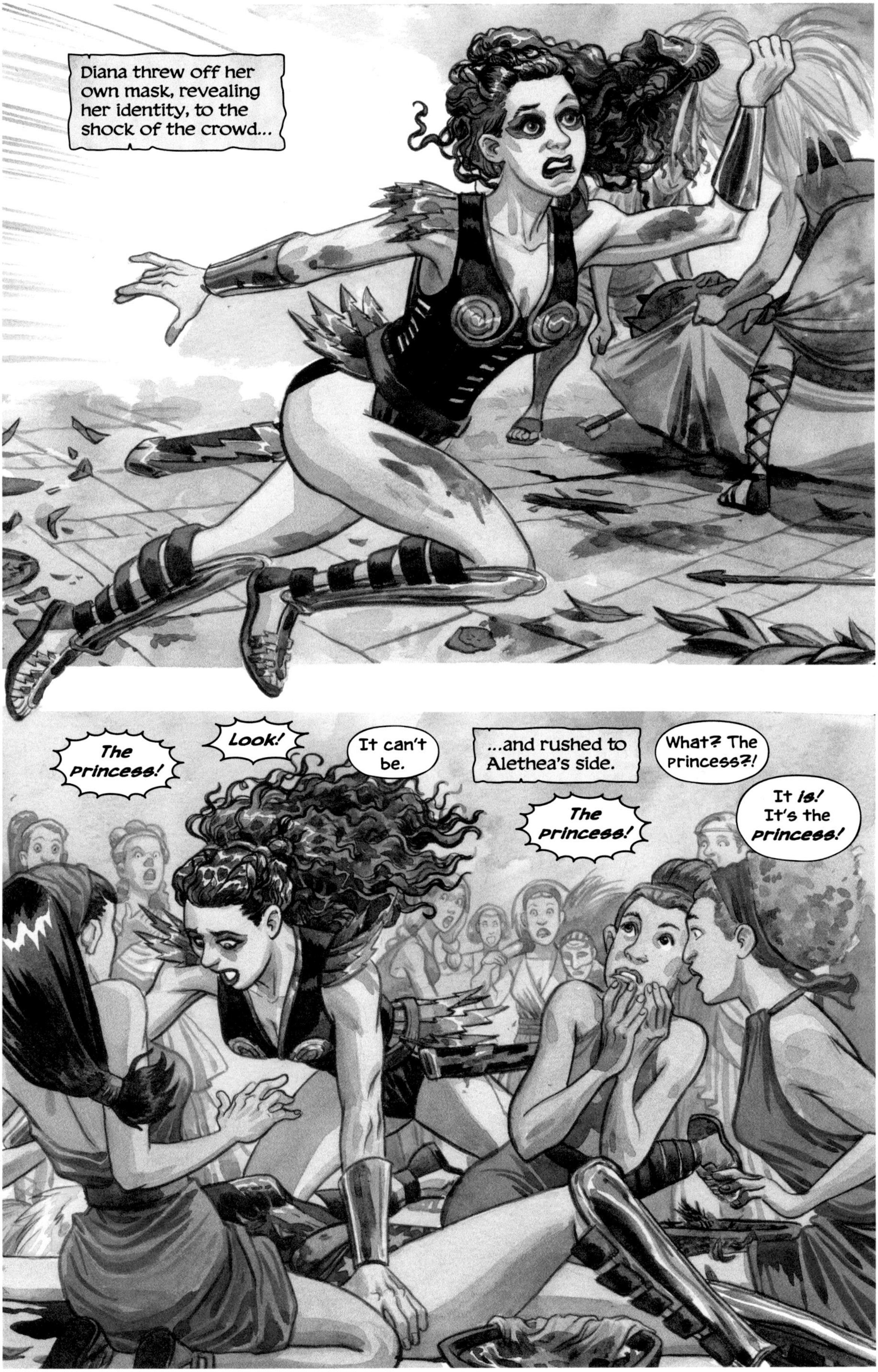
Diana threw off her own mask, revealing her identity, to the shock of the crowd...
The princess!
Look!
It can't be.
...and rushed to Alethea's side.
What? The princess?!
The princess!
It is! It's the princess!

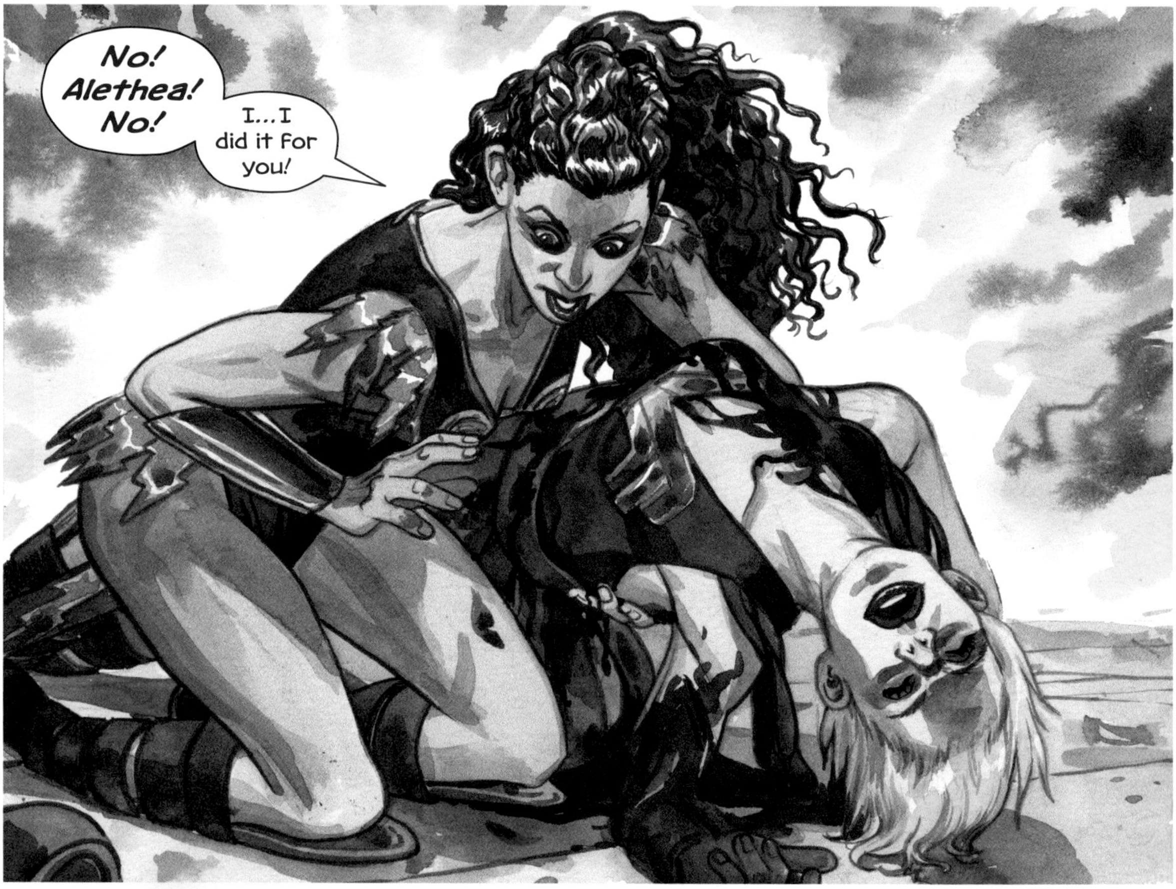
No! Alethea! No!
I...I did it for you!

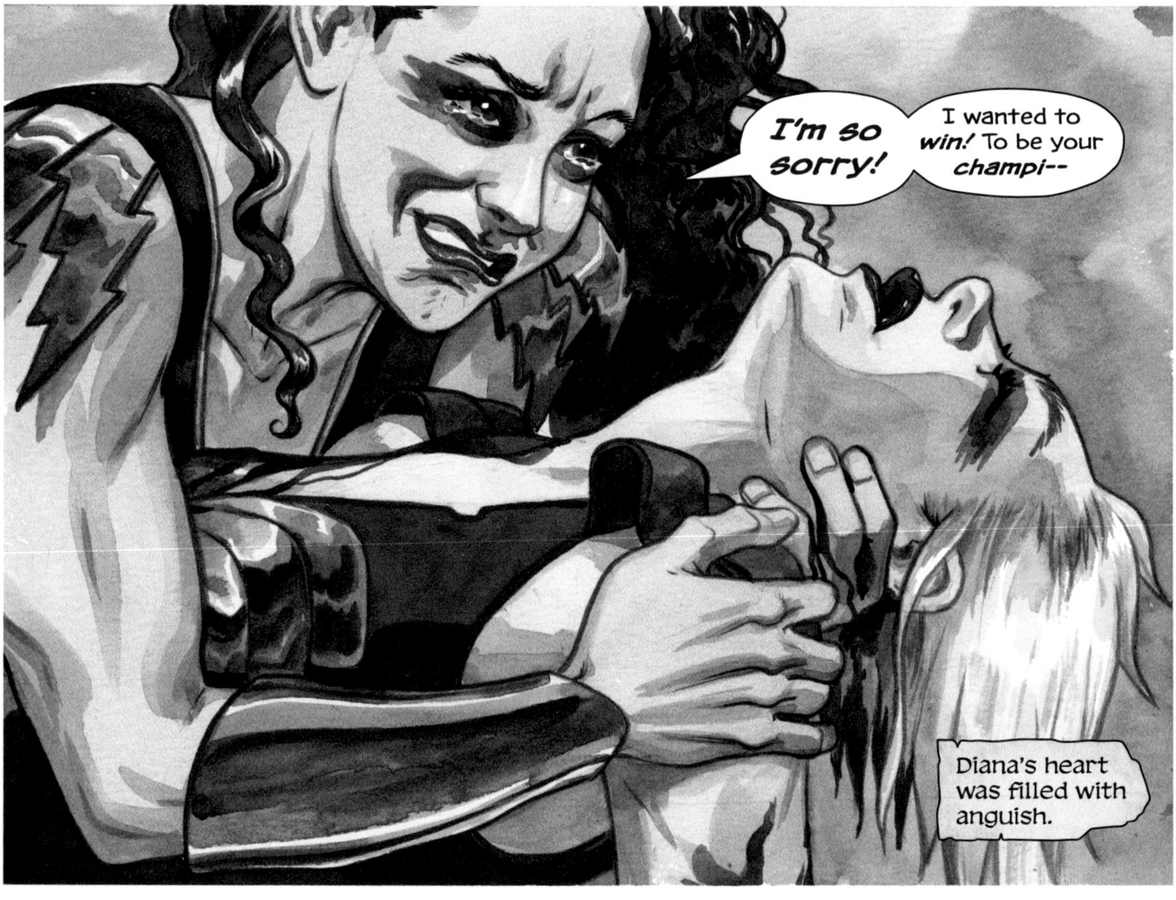
I'm so sorry!
I wanted to win! To be your champi--
Diana's heart was filled with anguish.

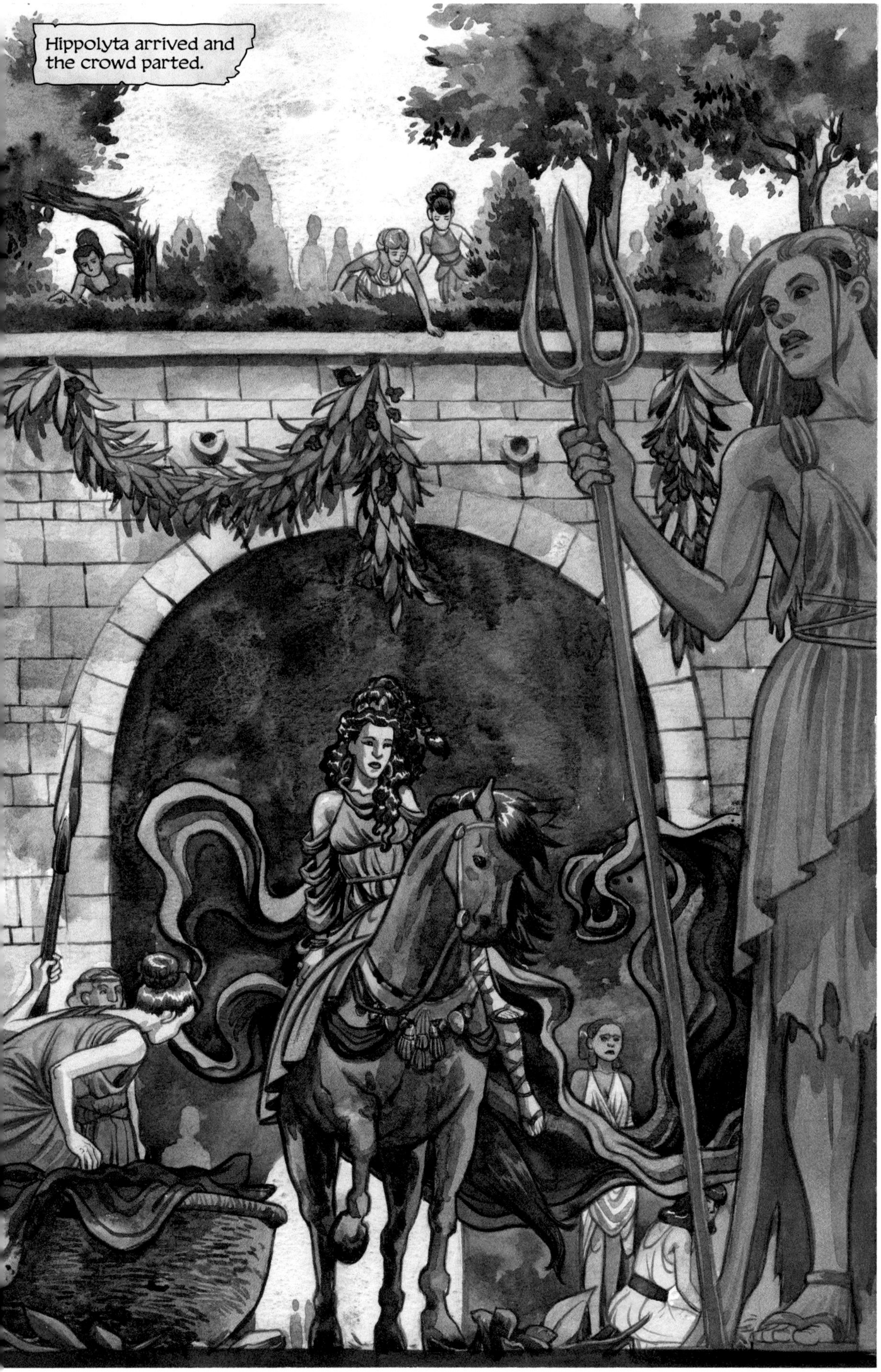
Hippolyta arrived and the crowd parted.

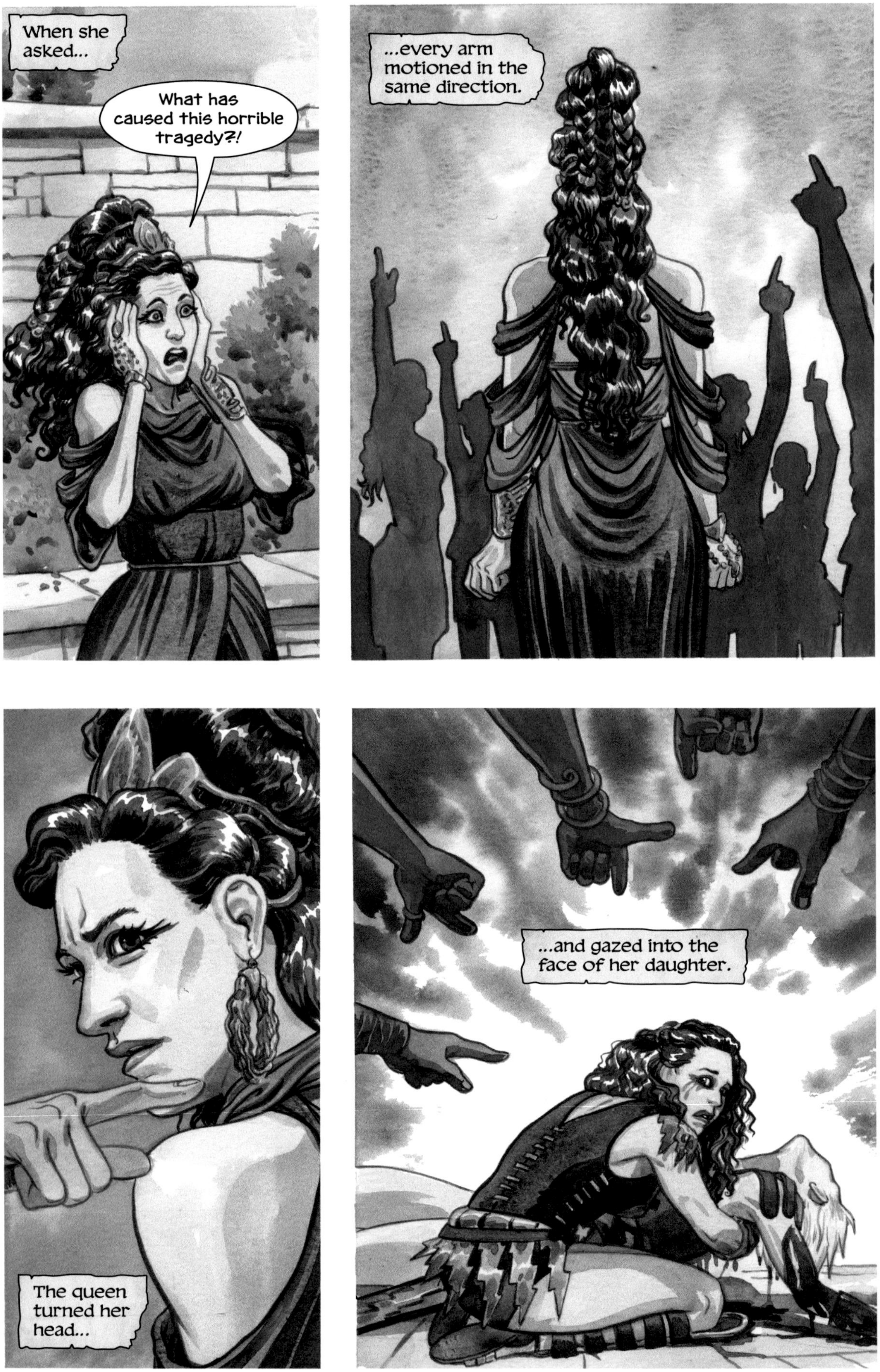
When she asked...
What has caused this horrible tragedy?!
...every arm motioned in the same direction.
The queen turned her head...
...and gazed into the face of her daughter.

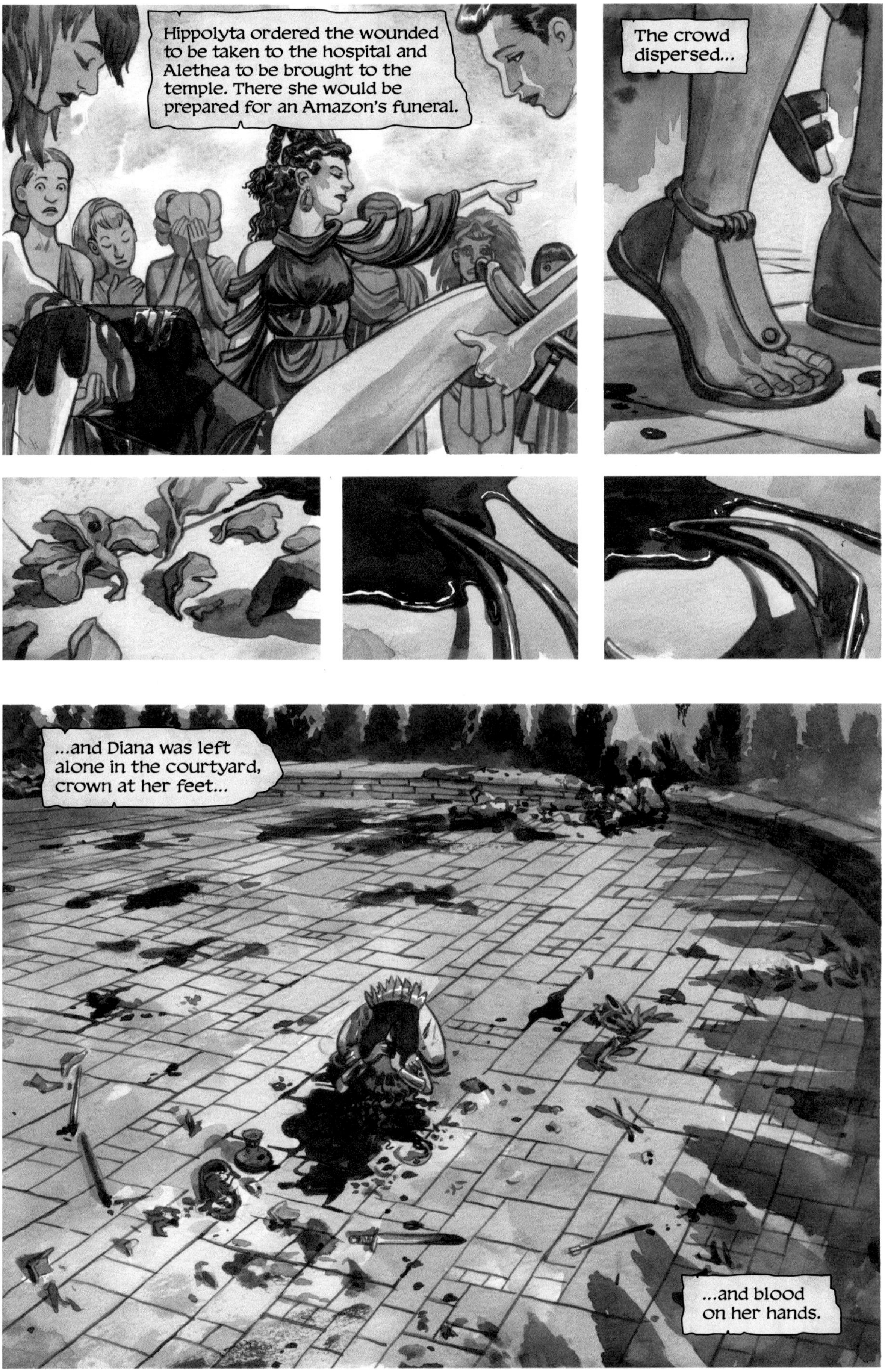
Hippolyta ordered the wounded to be taken to the hospital and Alethea to be brought to the temple. There she would be prepared for an Amazon's funeral.
The crowd dispersed...
...and Diana was left alone in the courtyard, crown at her feet...
...and blood on her hands.

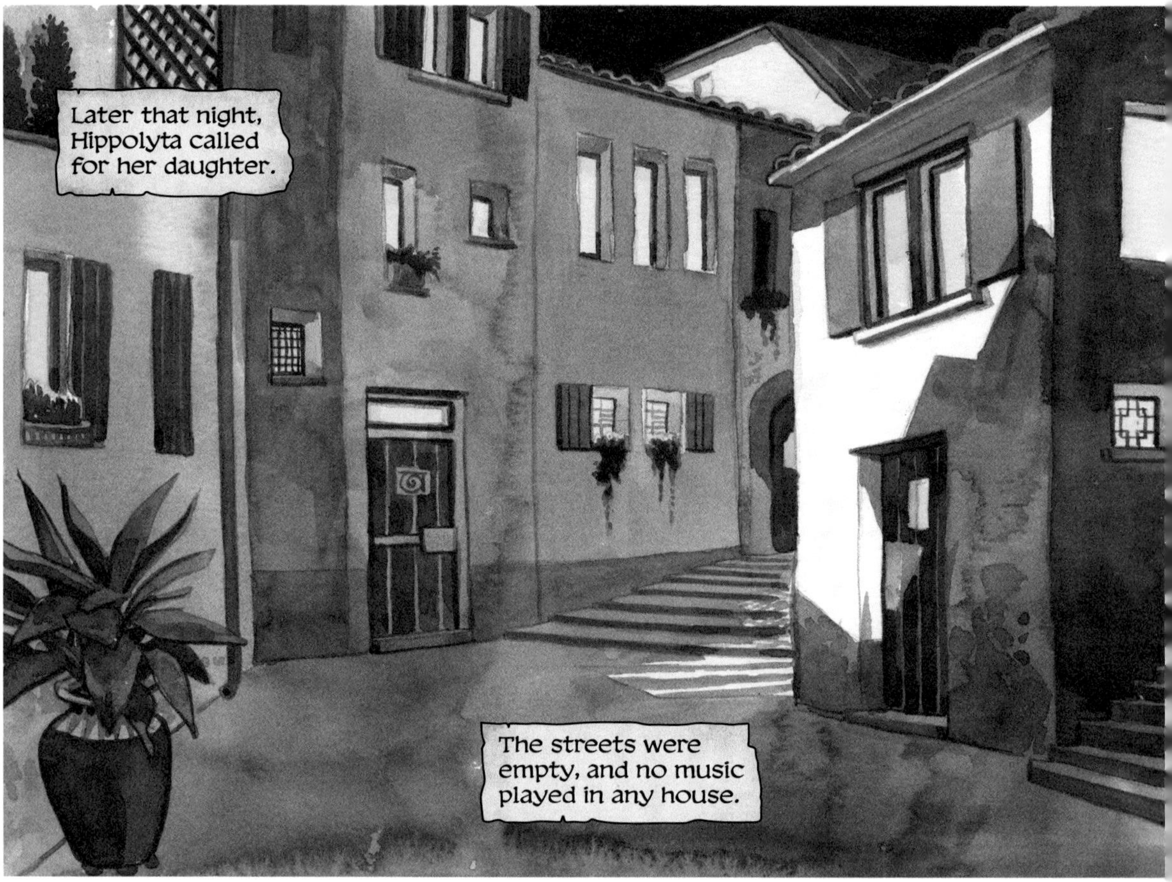
Later that night, Hippolyta called for her daughter.
The streets were empty, and no music played in any house.

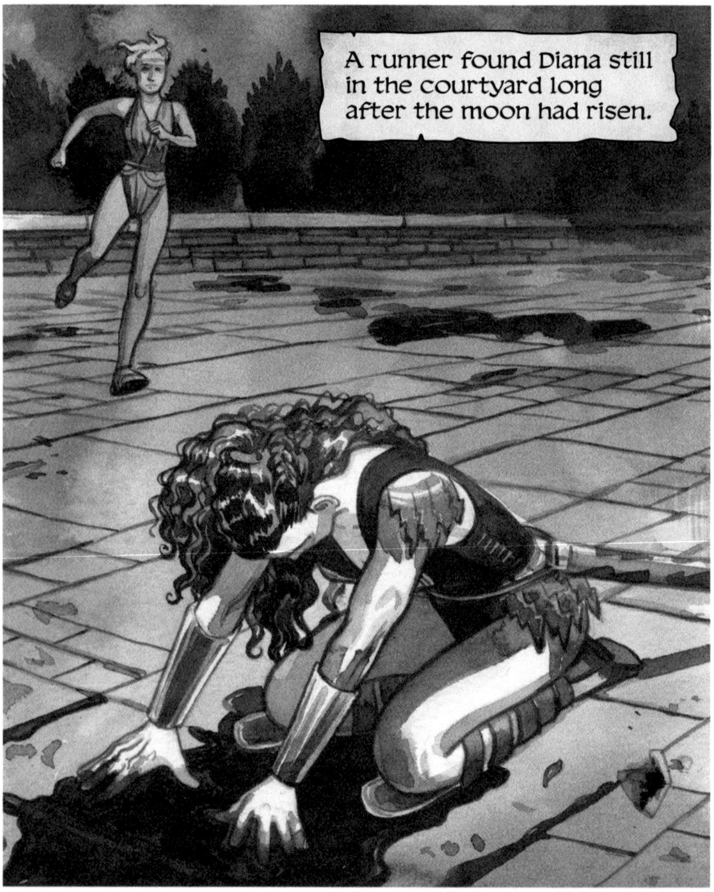
A runner found Diana still in the courtyard long after the moon had risen.

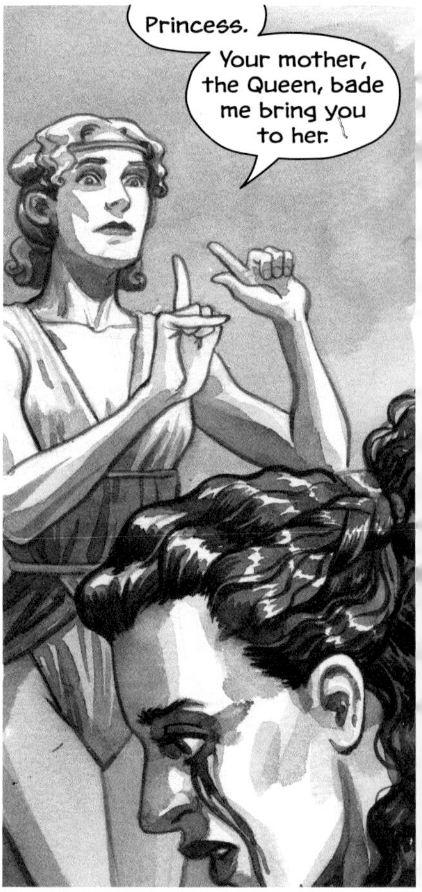
Princess.
Your mother, the Queen, bade me bring you to her.

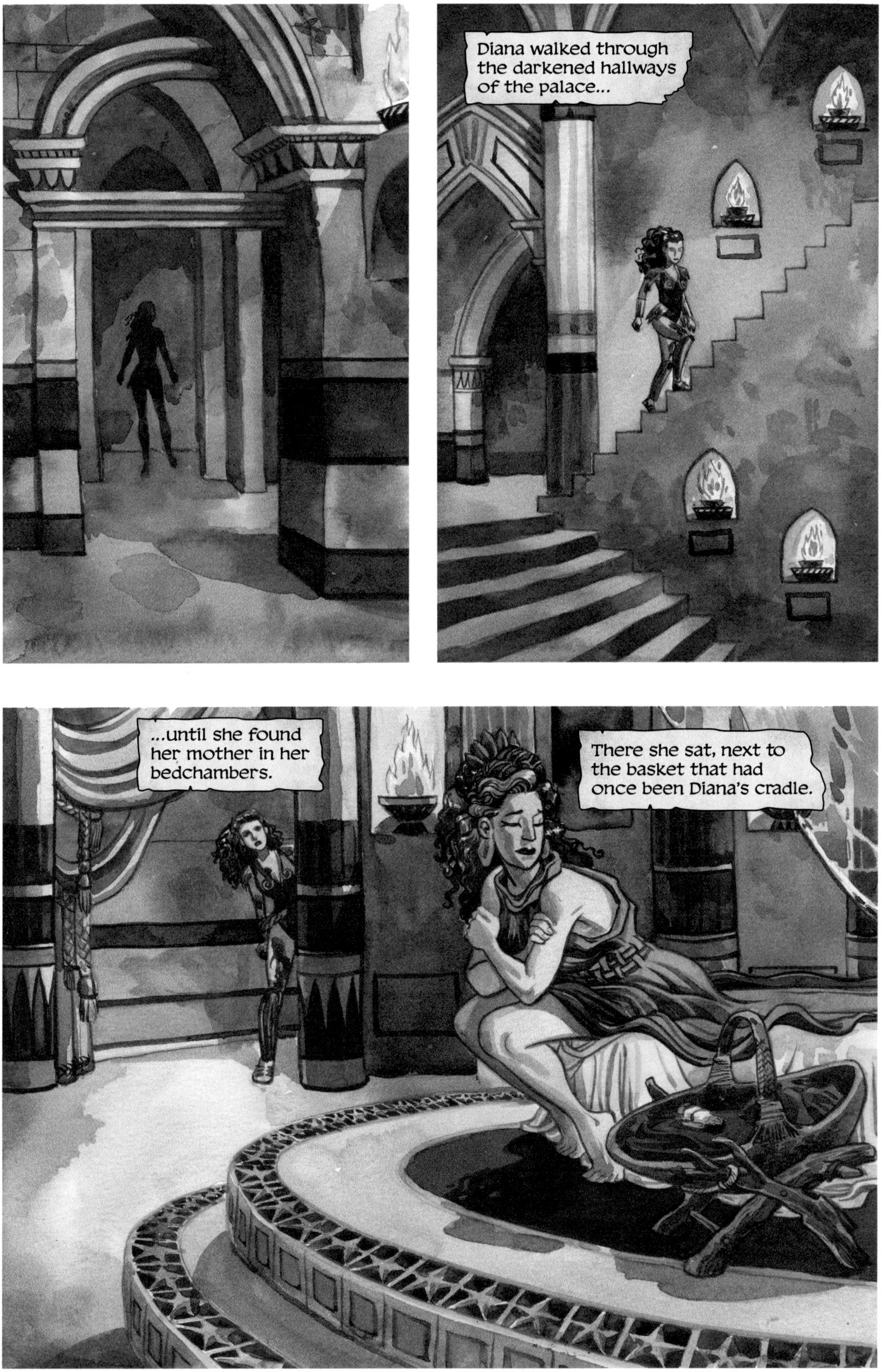
Diana walked through the darkened hallways of the palace...
...until she found her mother in her bedchambers.
There she sat, next to the basket that had once been Diana's cradle.

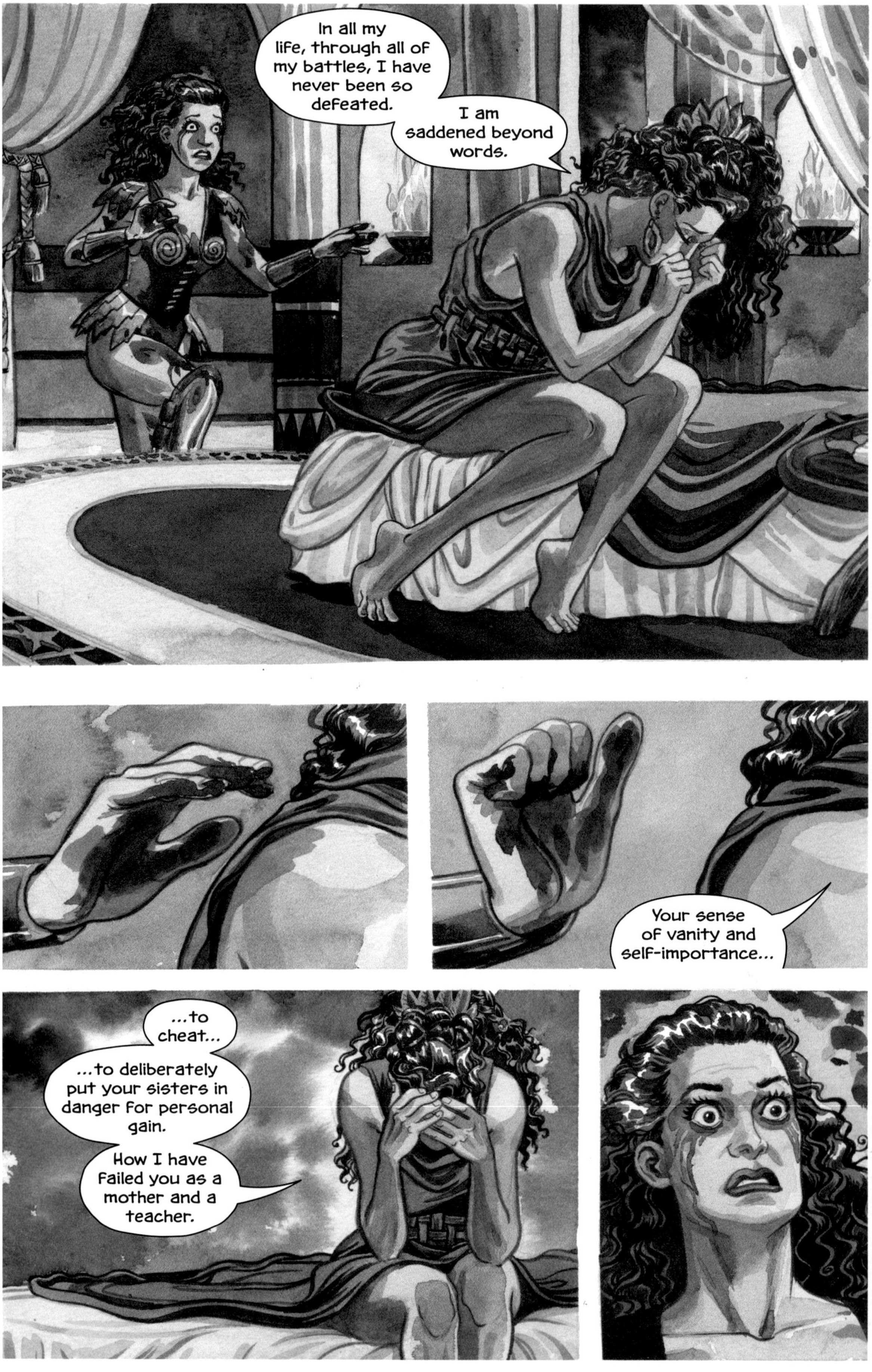
In all my life, through all of my battles, I have never been so defeated.
I am saddened beyond words.
Your sense of vanity and self-importance...
...to cheat...
...to deliberately put your sisters in danger for personal gain.
How I have failed you as a mother and a teacher.

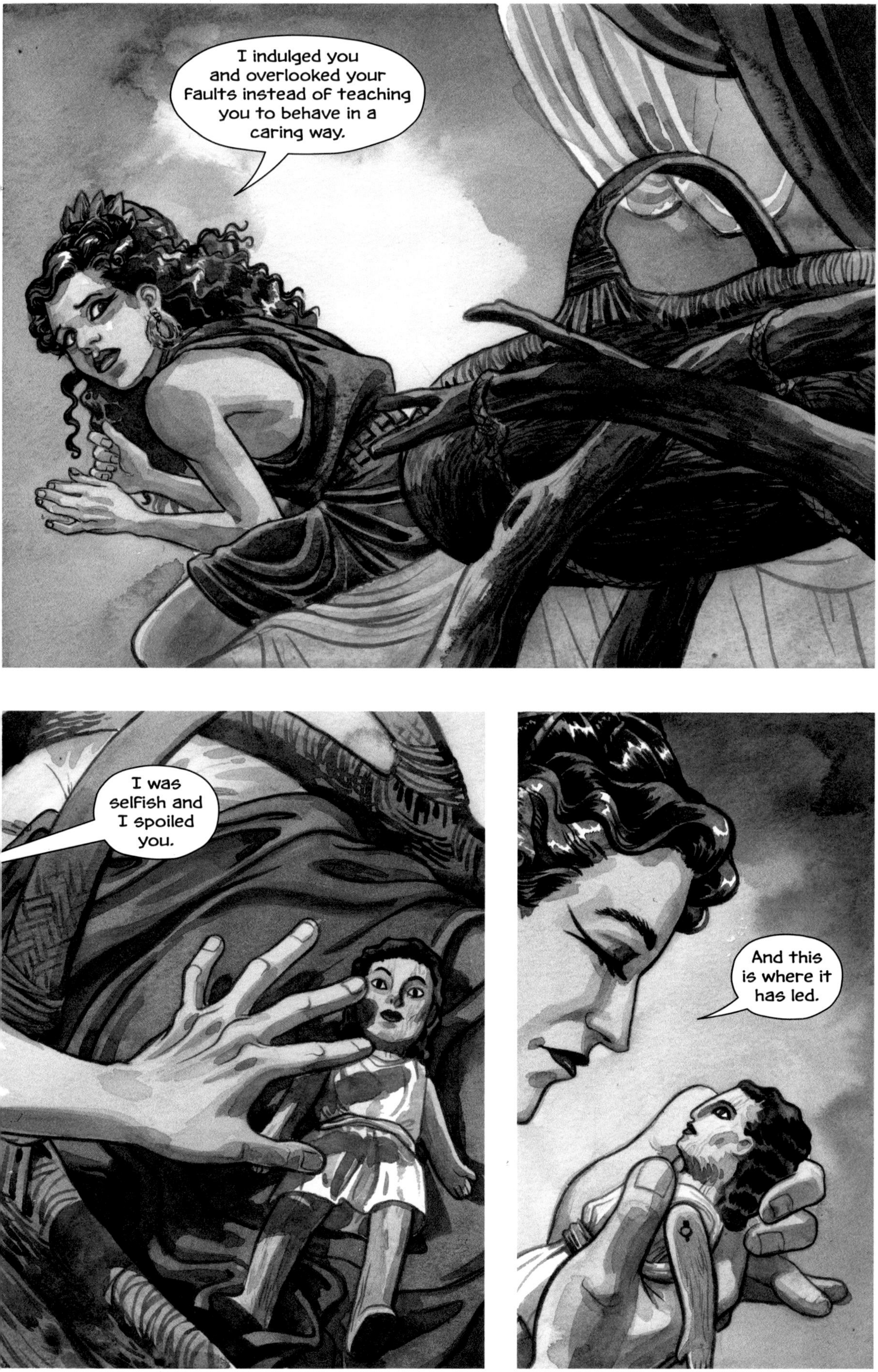
I indulged you and overlooked your faults instead of teaching you to behave in a caring way.
I was selfish and I spoiled you.
And this is where it has led.

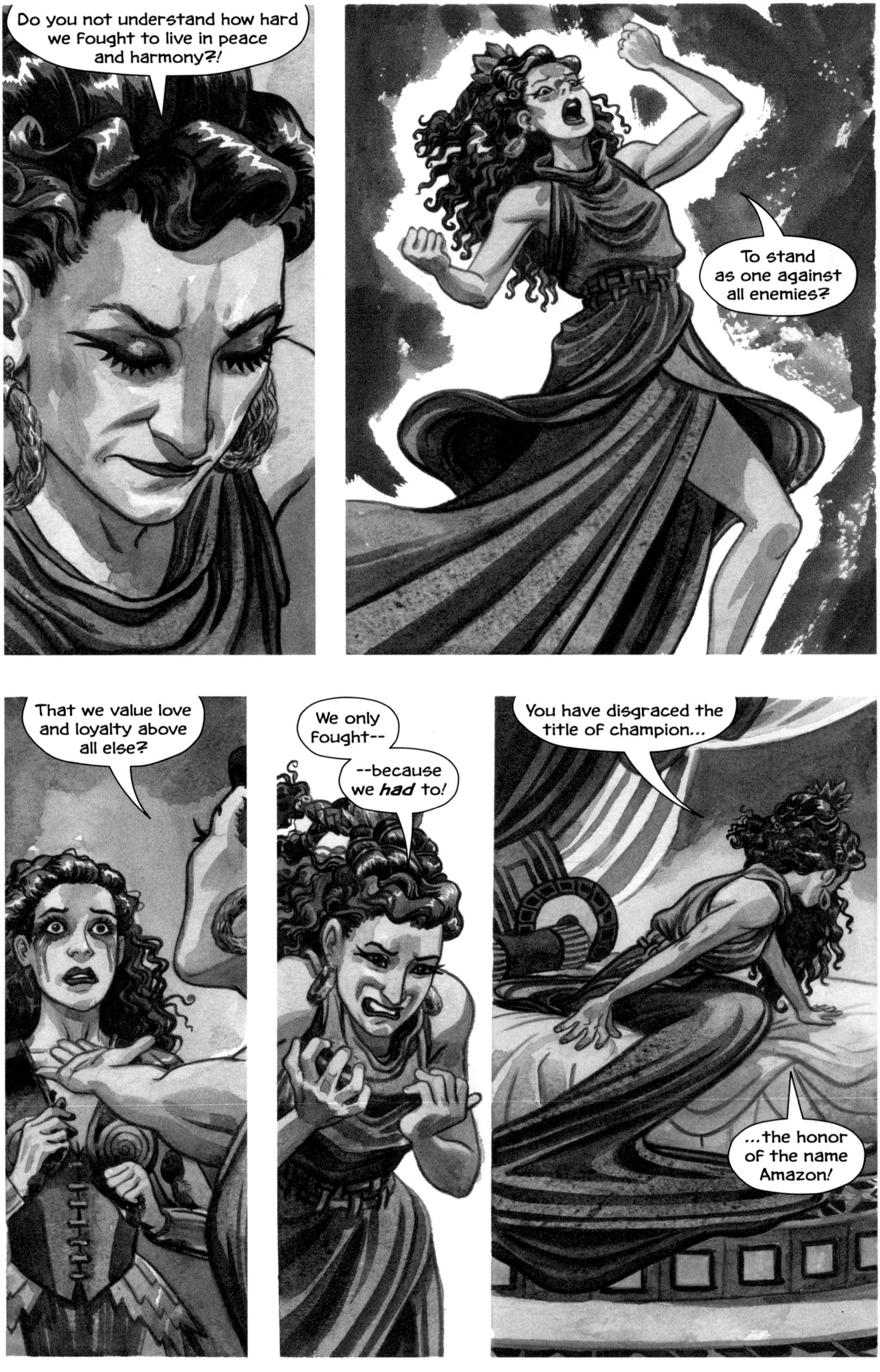
Do you not understand how hard we fought to live in peace and harmony?!
To stand as one against all enemies?
That we value love and loyalty above all else?
We only fought--
--because we *had* to!
You have disgraced the title of champion...
...the honor of the name Amazon!

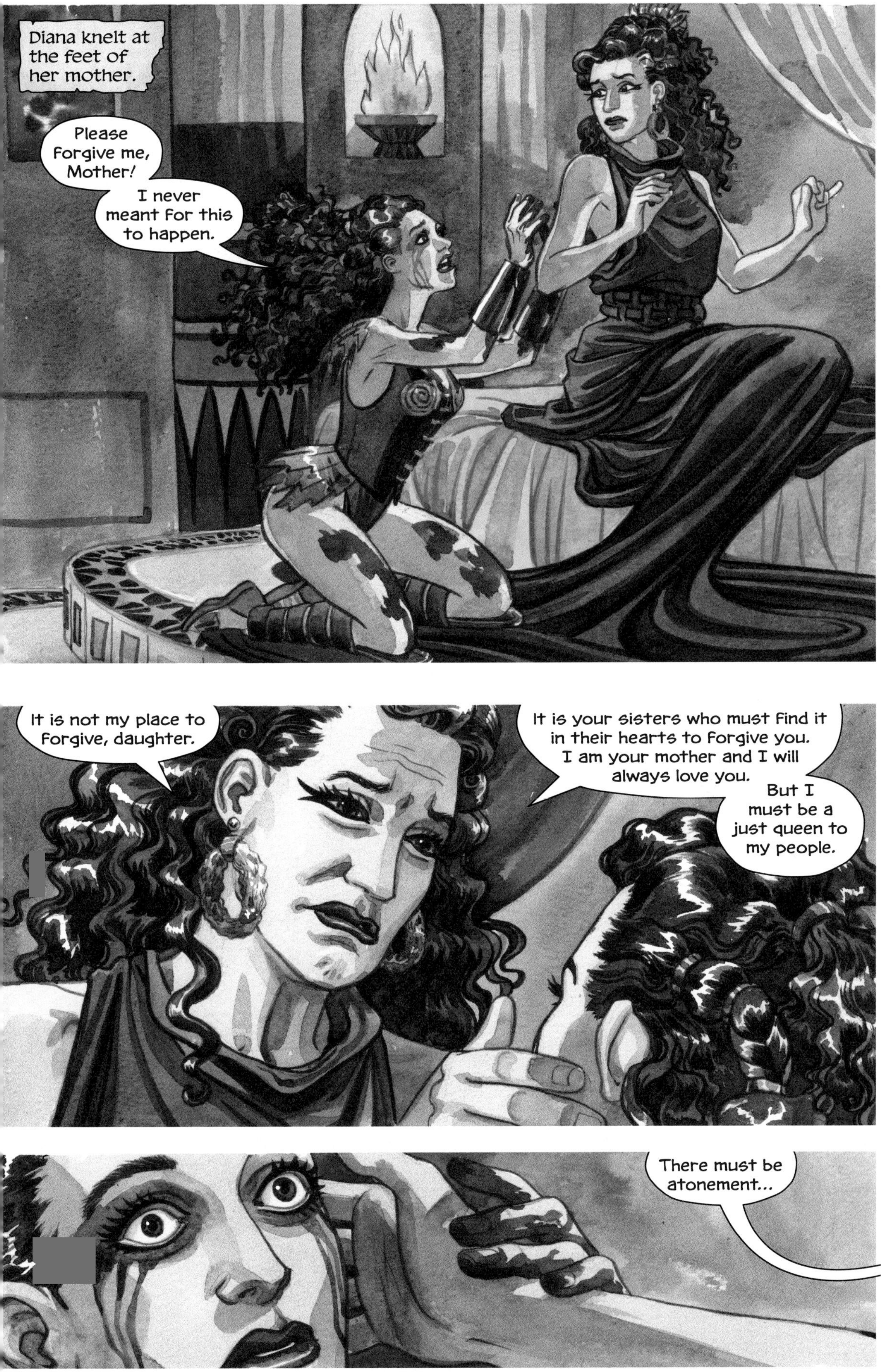
Diana knelt at the feet of her mother.
Please forgive me, Mother!
I never meant for this to happen.
It is not my place to forgive, daughter.
It is your sisters who must find it in their hearts to forgive you. I am your mother and I will always love you.
But I must be a just queen to my people.
There must be atonement...

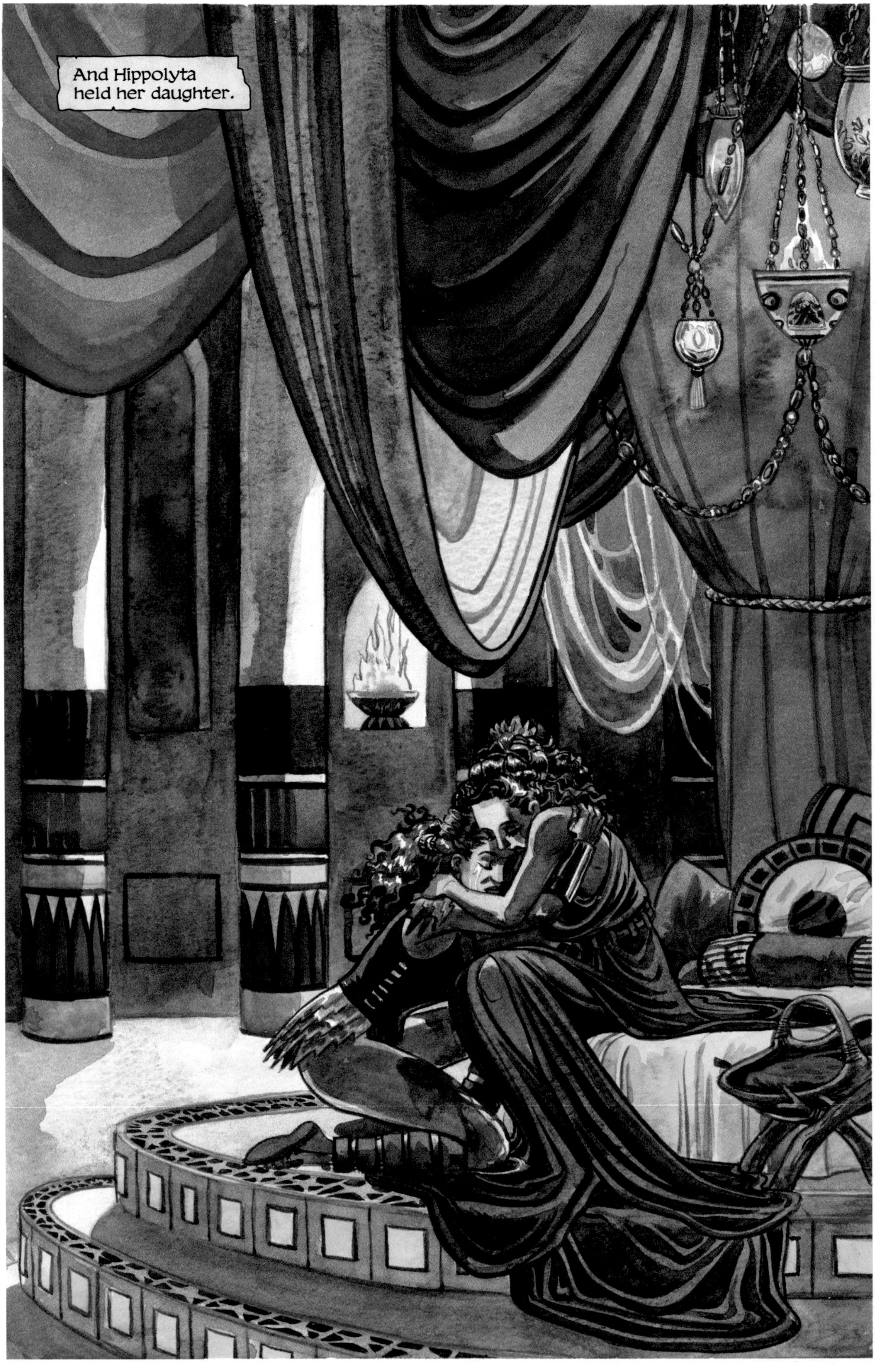
And Hippolyta held her daughter.

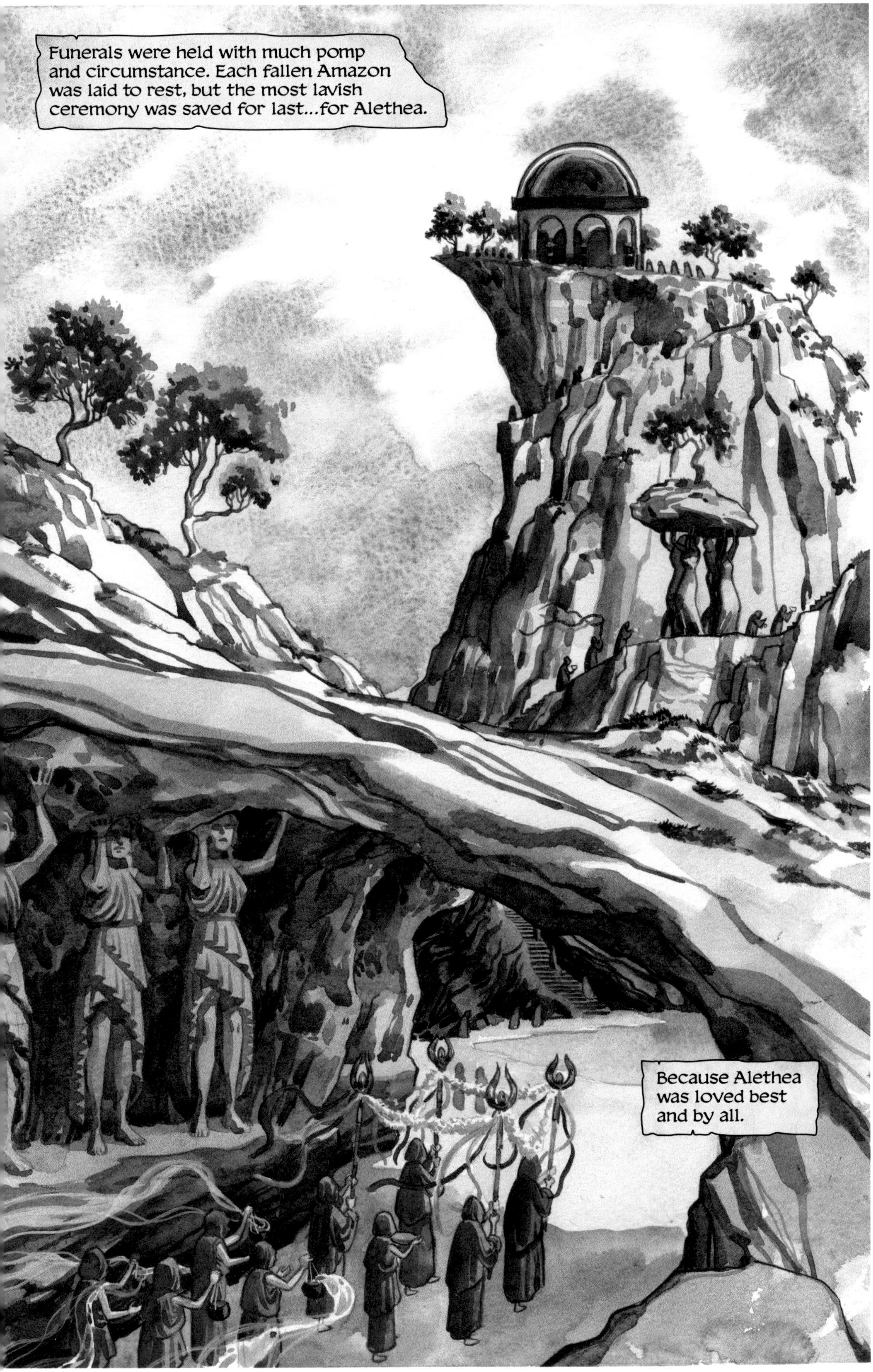
Funerals were held with much pomp and circumstance. Each fallen Amazon was laid to rest, but the most lavish ceremony was saved for last...for Alethea.
Because Alethea was loved best and by all.

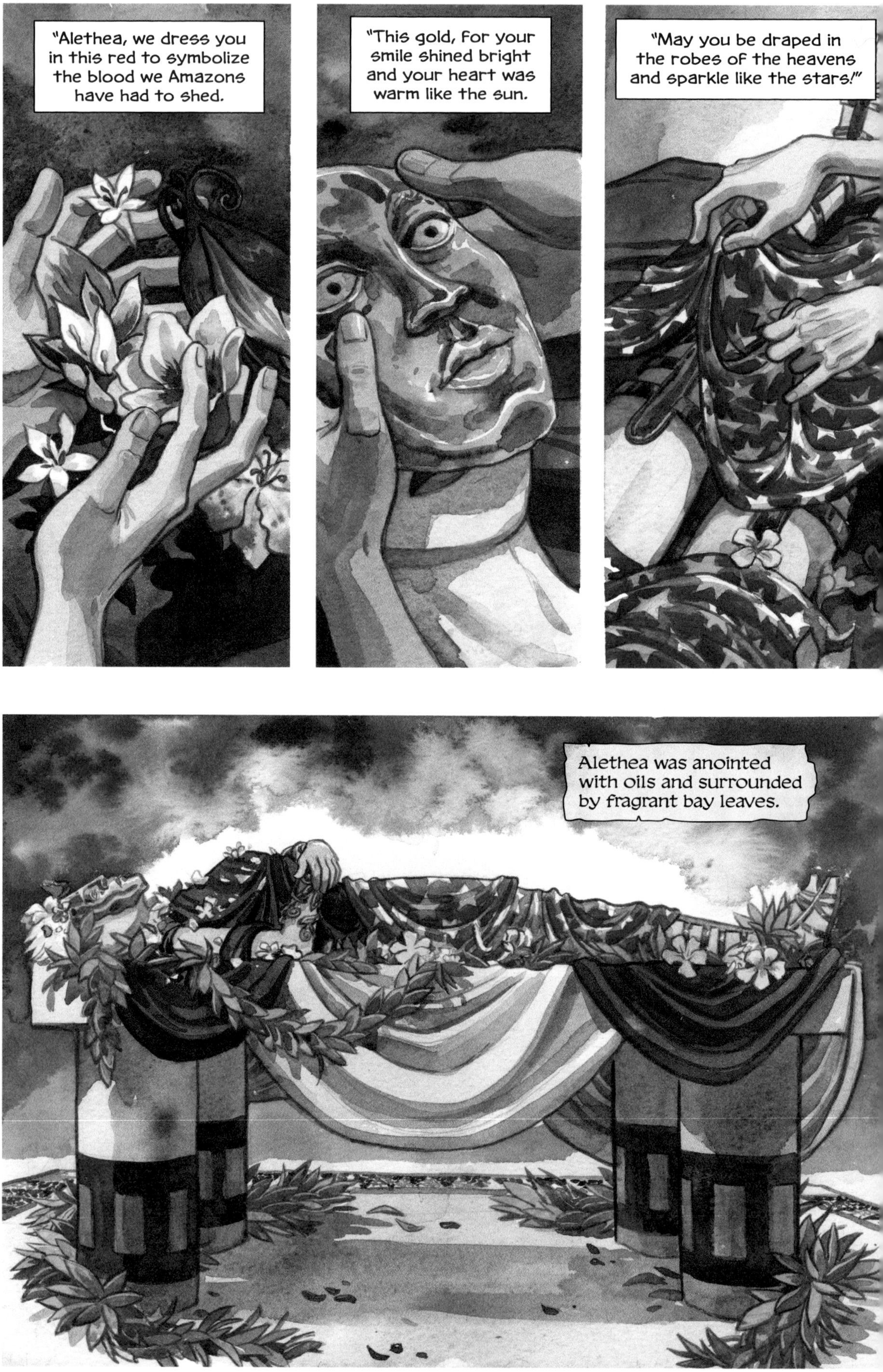
"Alethea, we dress you in this red to symbolize the blood we Amazons have had to shed.
"This gold, for your smile shined bright and your heart was warm like the sun.
"May you be draped in the robes of the heavens and sparkle like the stars!"
Alethea was anointed with oils and surrounded by fragrant bay leaves.

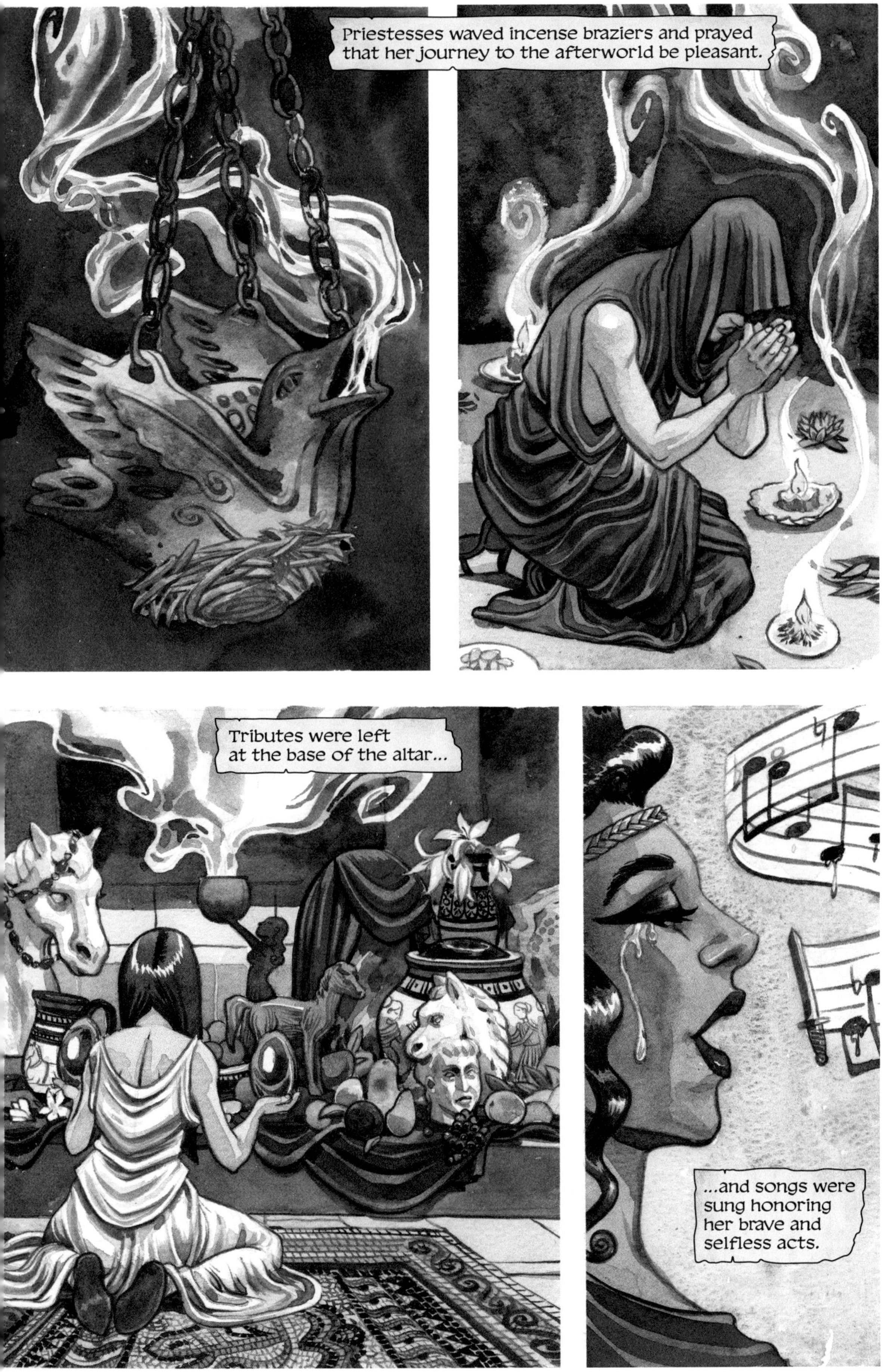
Priestesses waved incense braziers and prayed
that her journey to the afterworld be pleasant.
Tributes were left
at the base of the altar...
...and songs were
sung honoring
her brave and
selfless acts.

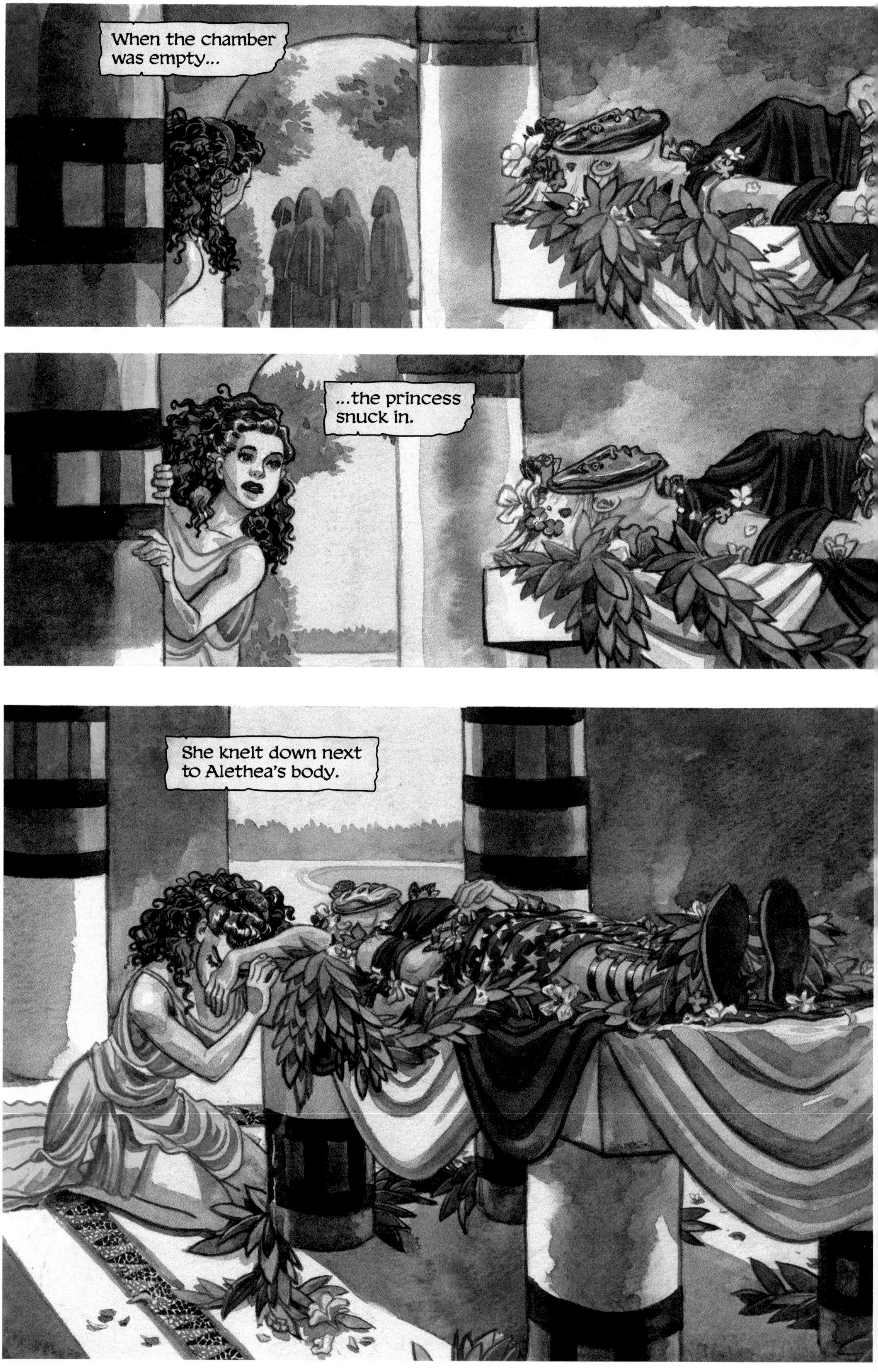
When the chamber was empty...
...the princess snuck in.
She knelt down next to Alethea's body.

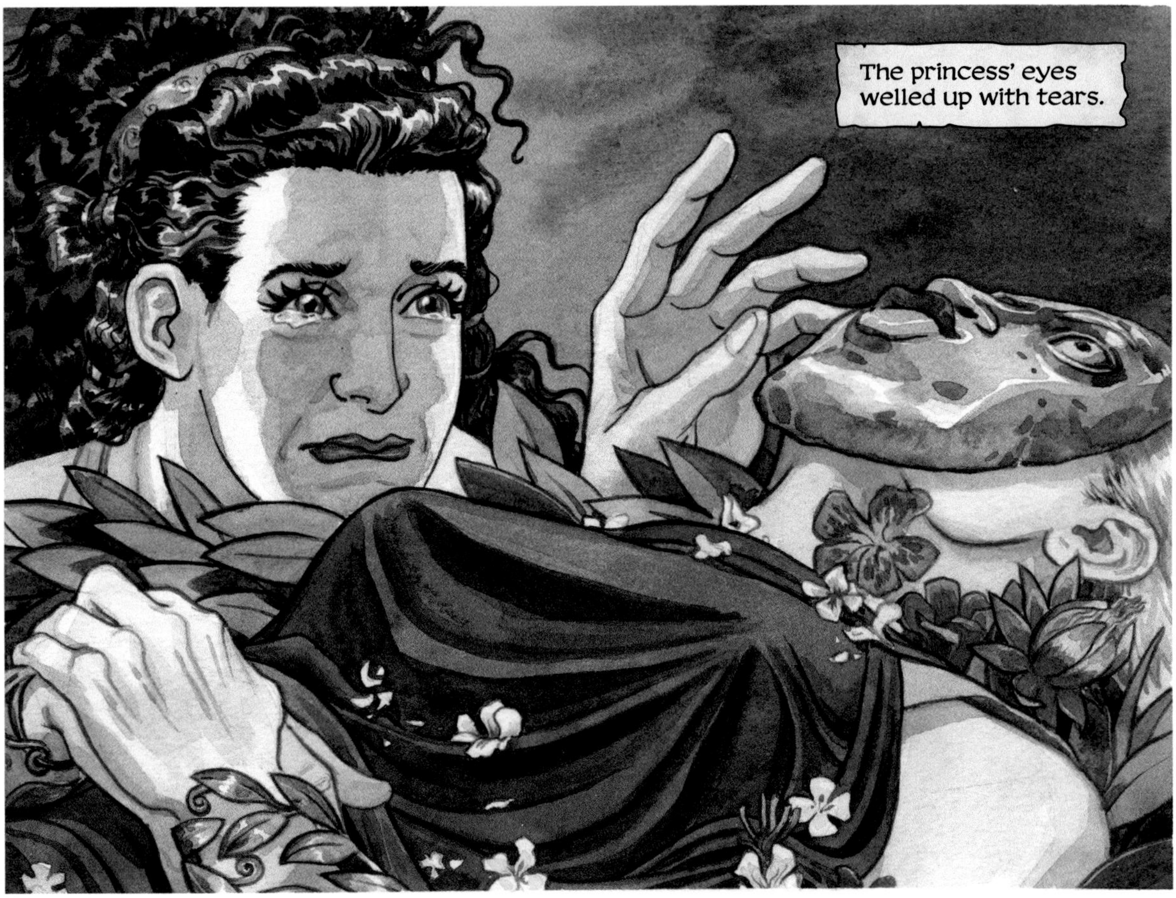
The princess' eyes welled up with tears.

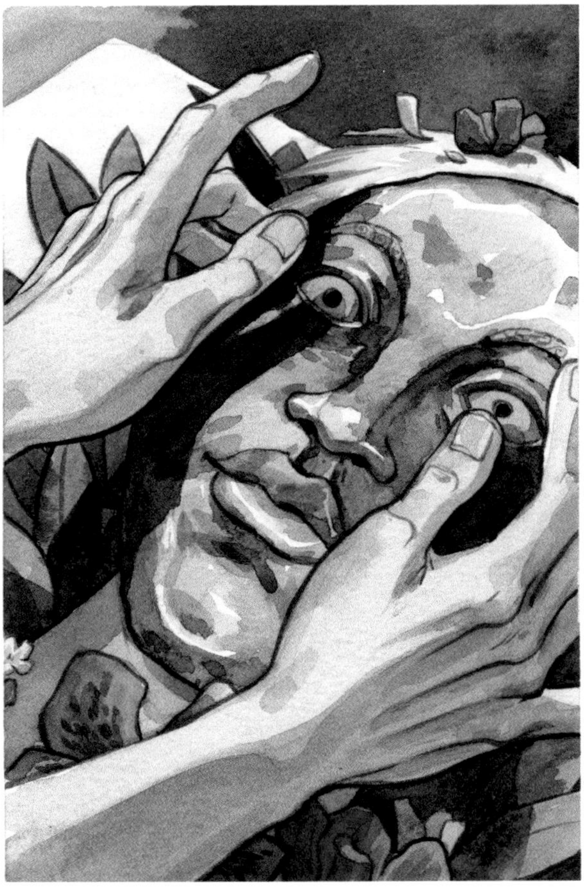

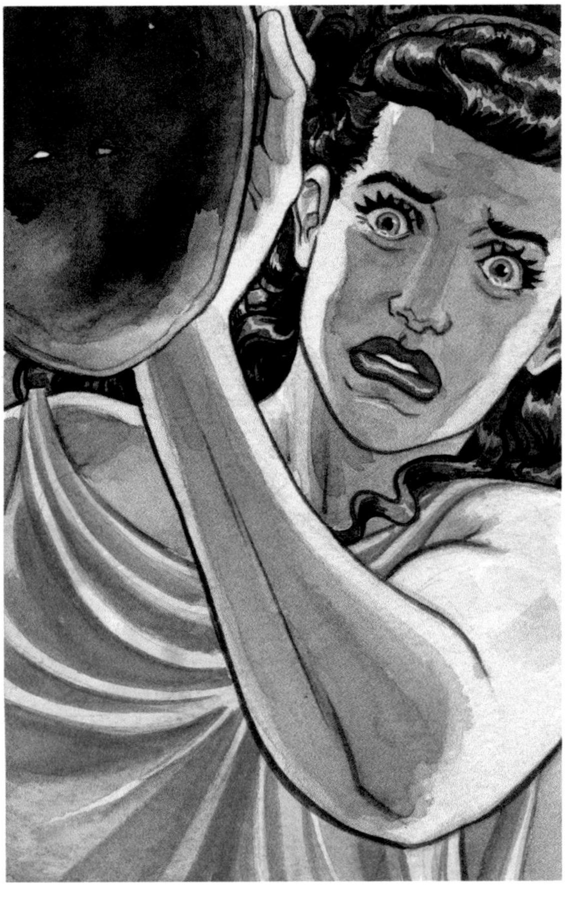

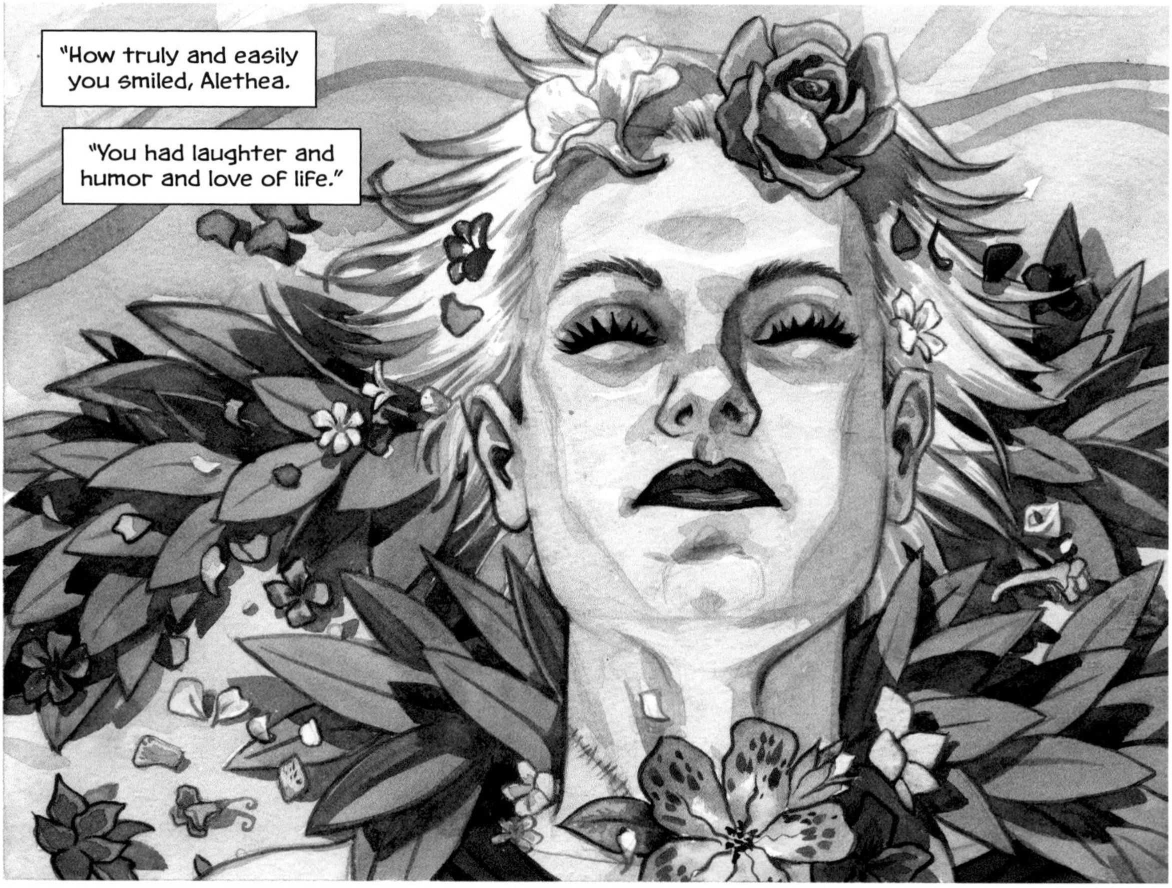
"How truly and easily you smiled, Alethea.
"You had laughter and humor and love of life."

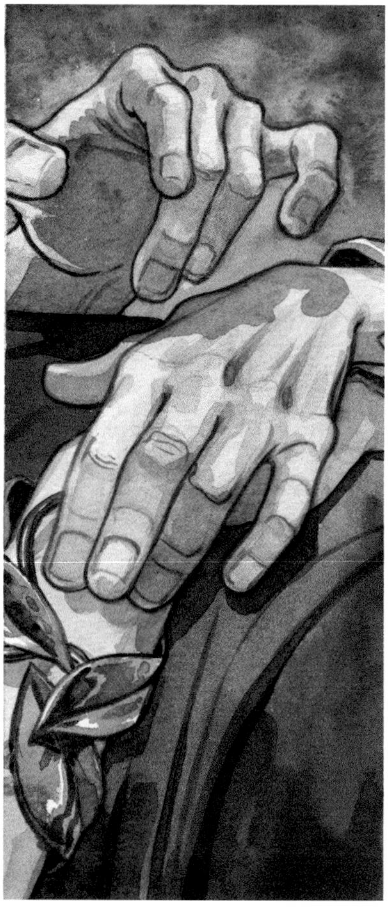

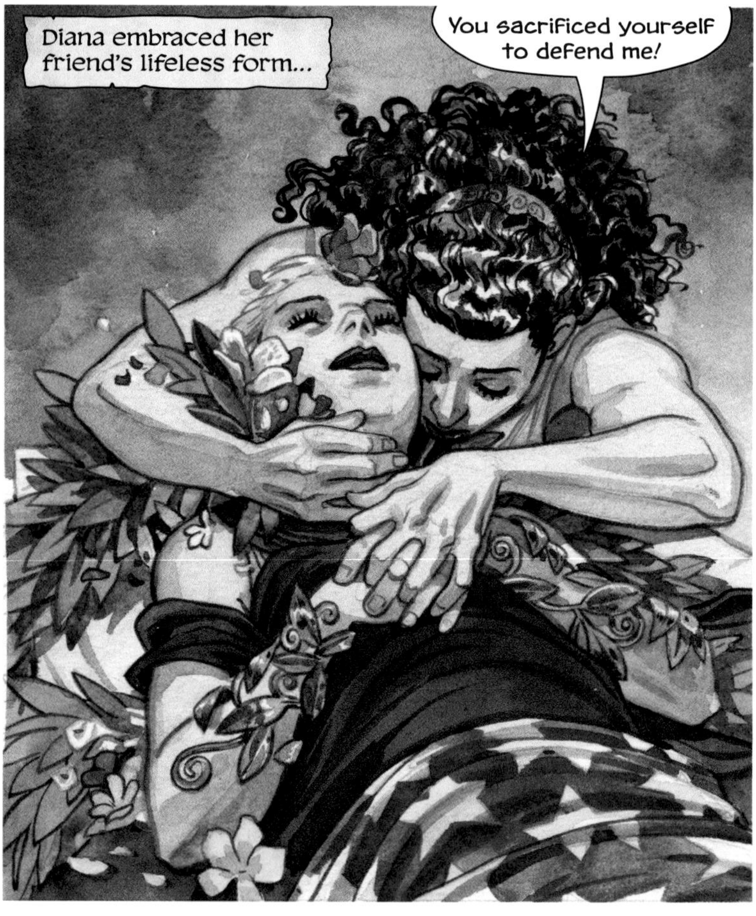
Diana embraced her friend's lifeless form...
You sacrificed yourself to defend me!

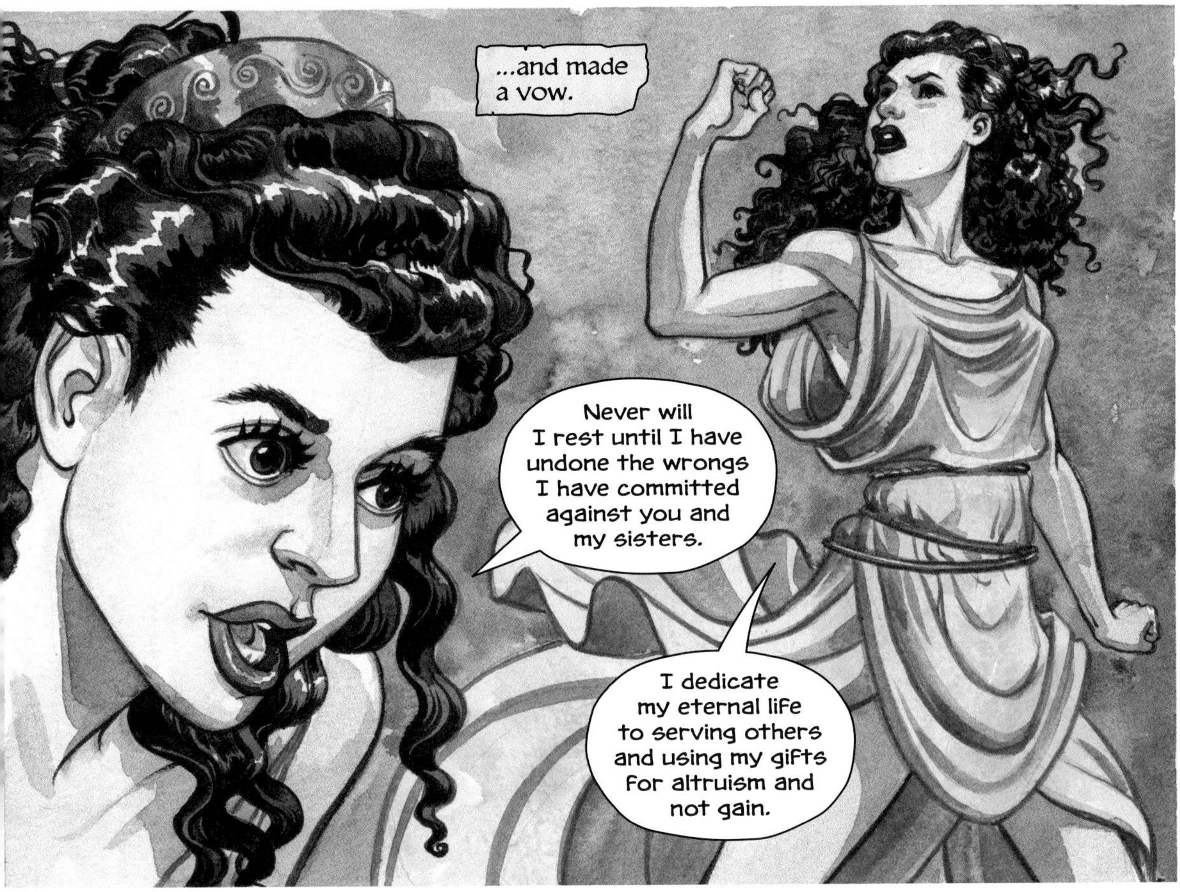
...and made a vow.
Never will I rest until I have undone the wrongs I have committed against you and my sisters.
I dedicate my eternal life to serving others and using my gifts for altruism and not gain.

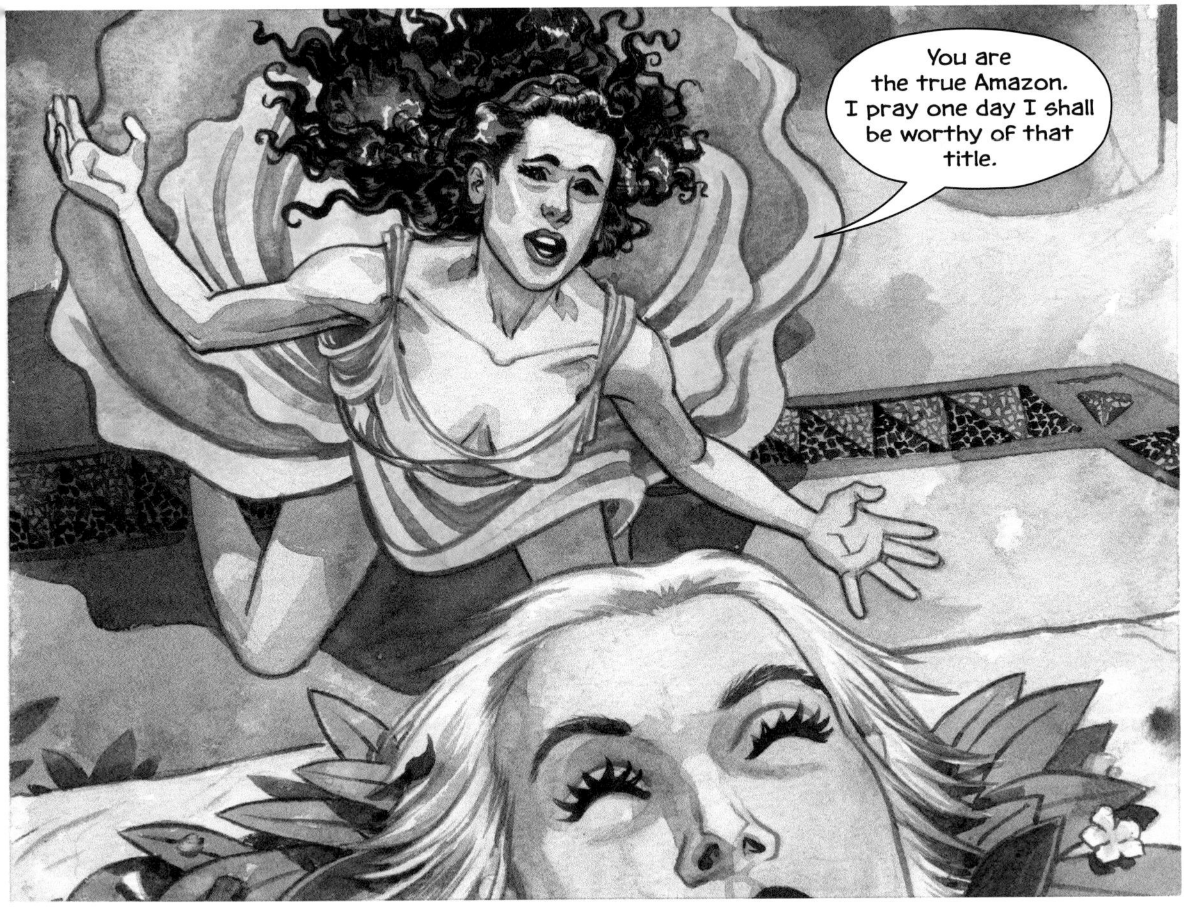
You are the true Amazon. I pray one day I shall be worthy of that title.

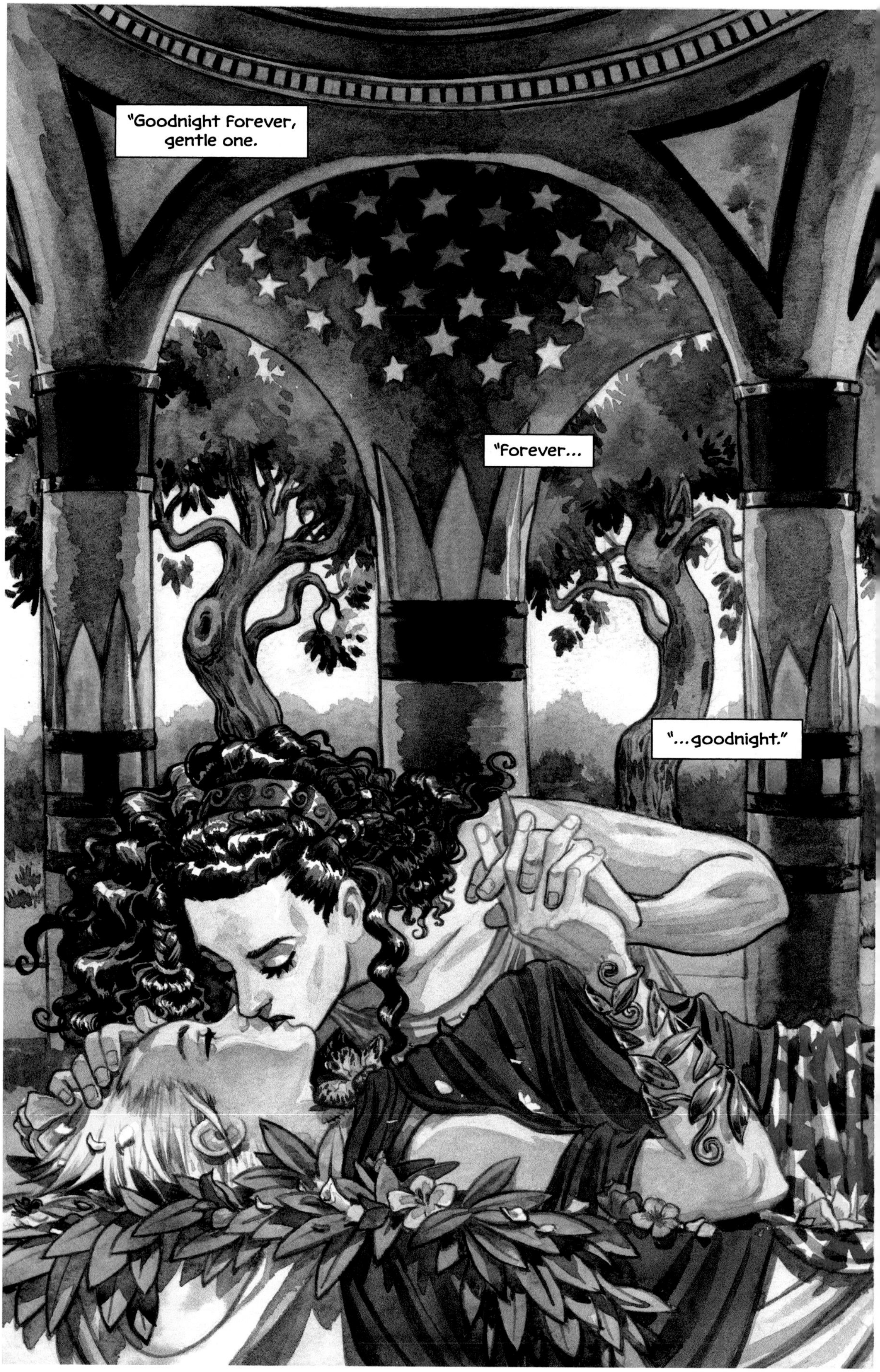
"Goodnight forever, gentle one.
"Forever...
"...goodnight."

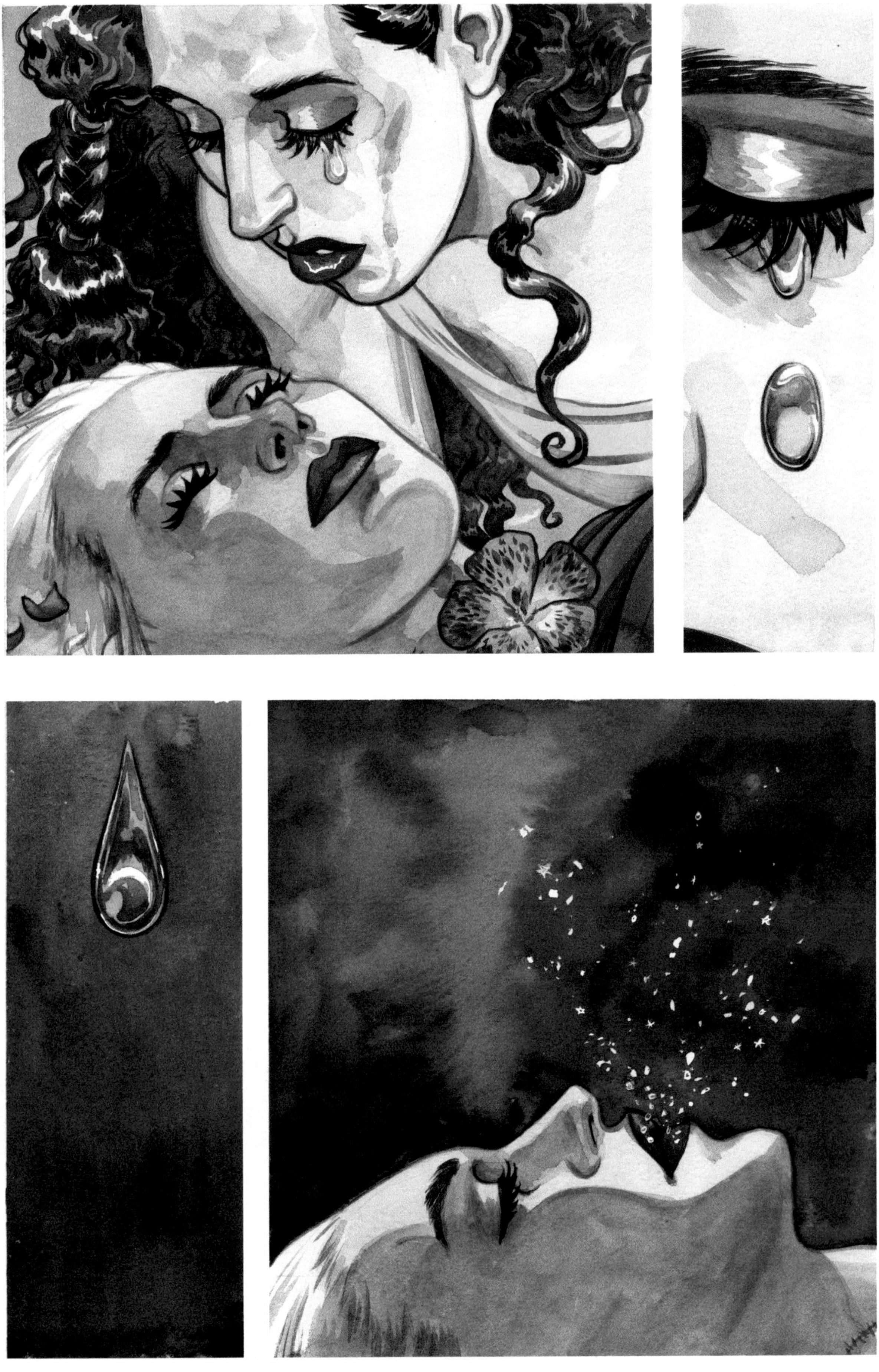

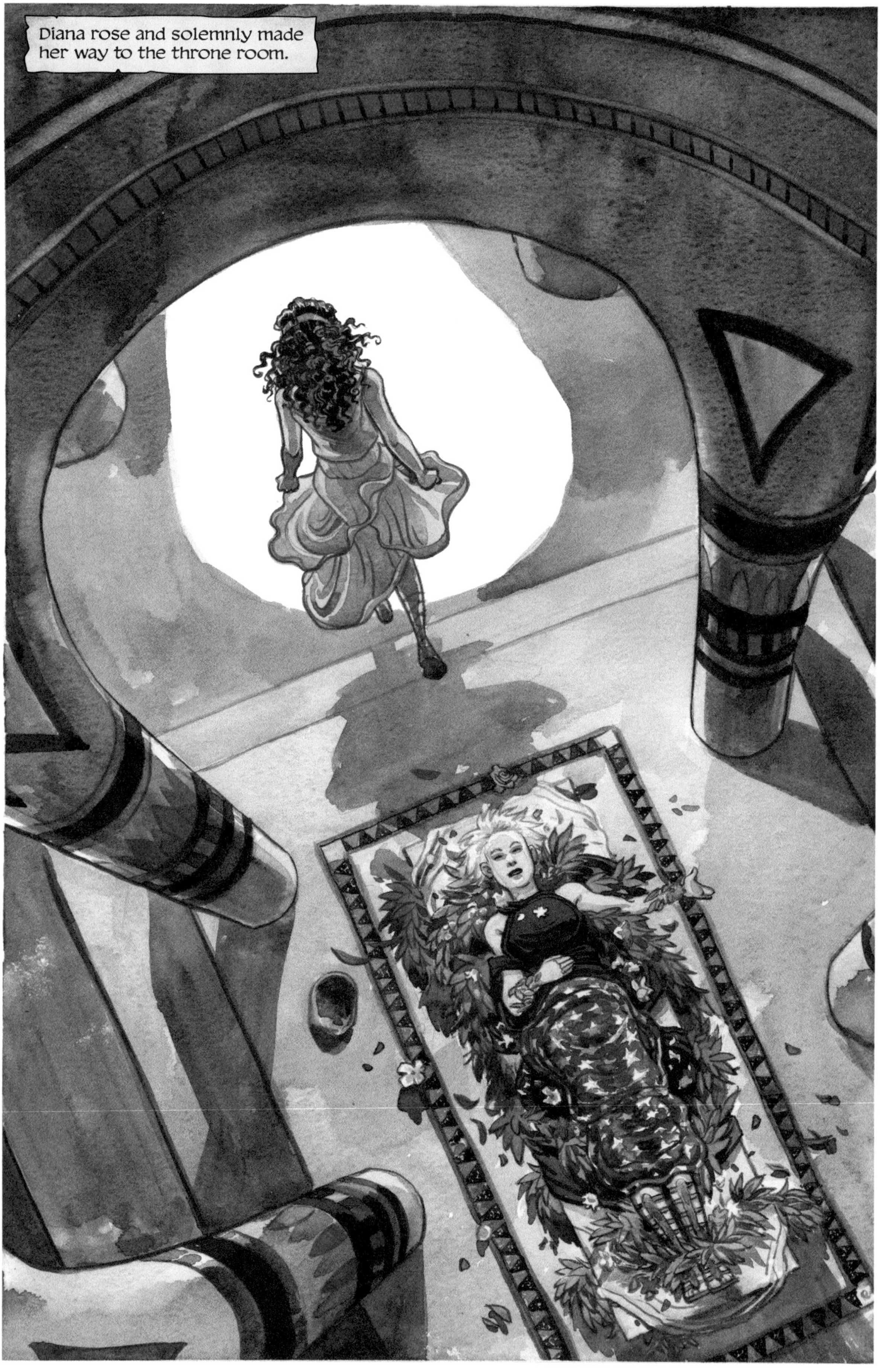
Diana rose and solemnly made her way to the throne room.

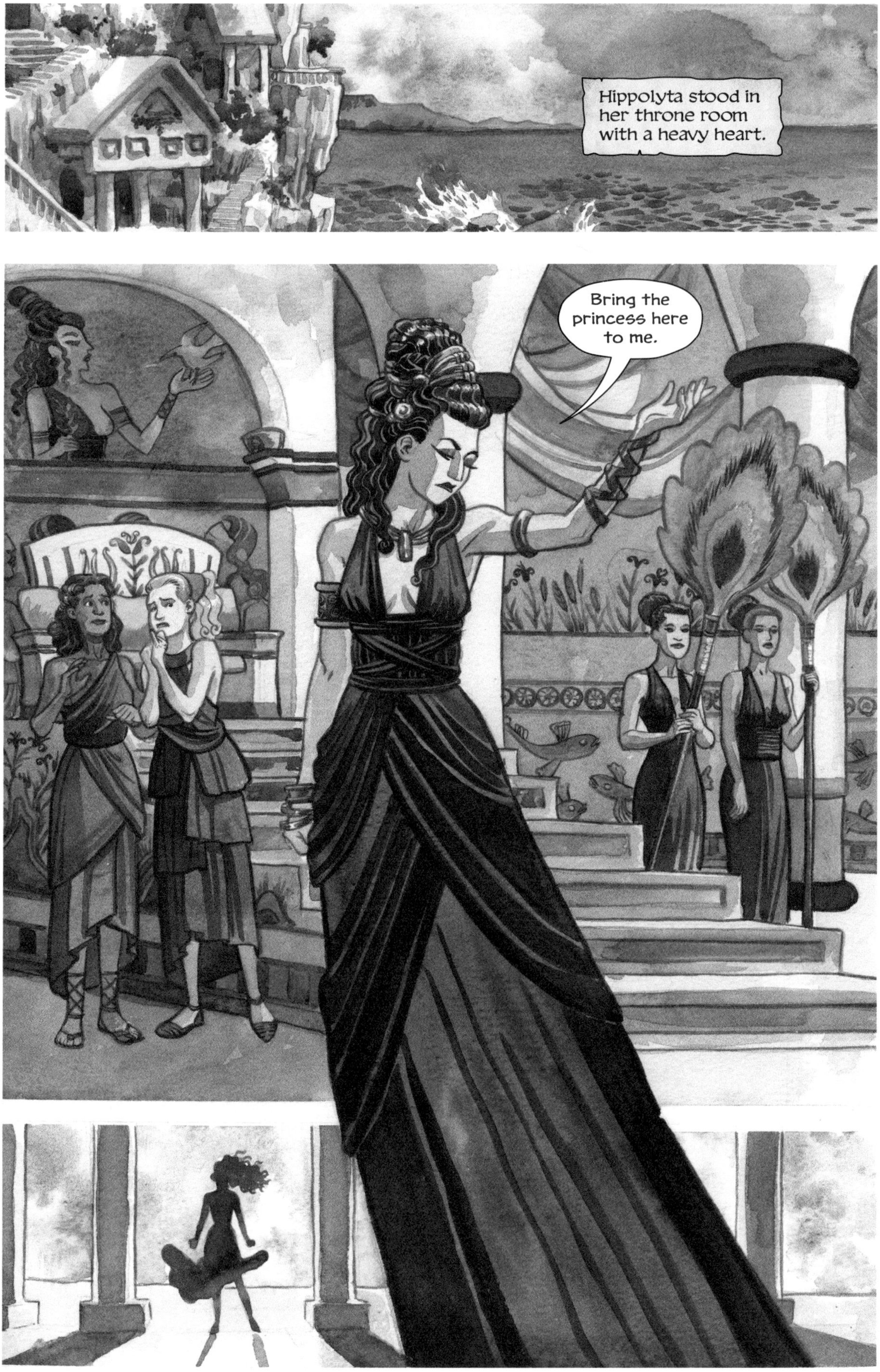
Hippolyta stood in her throne room with a heavy heart.
Bring the princess here to me.

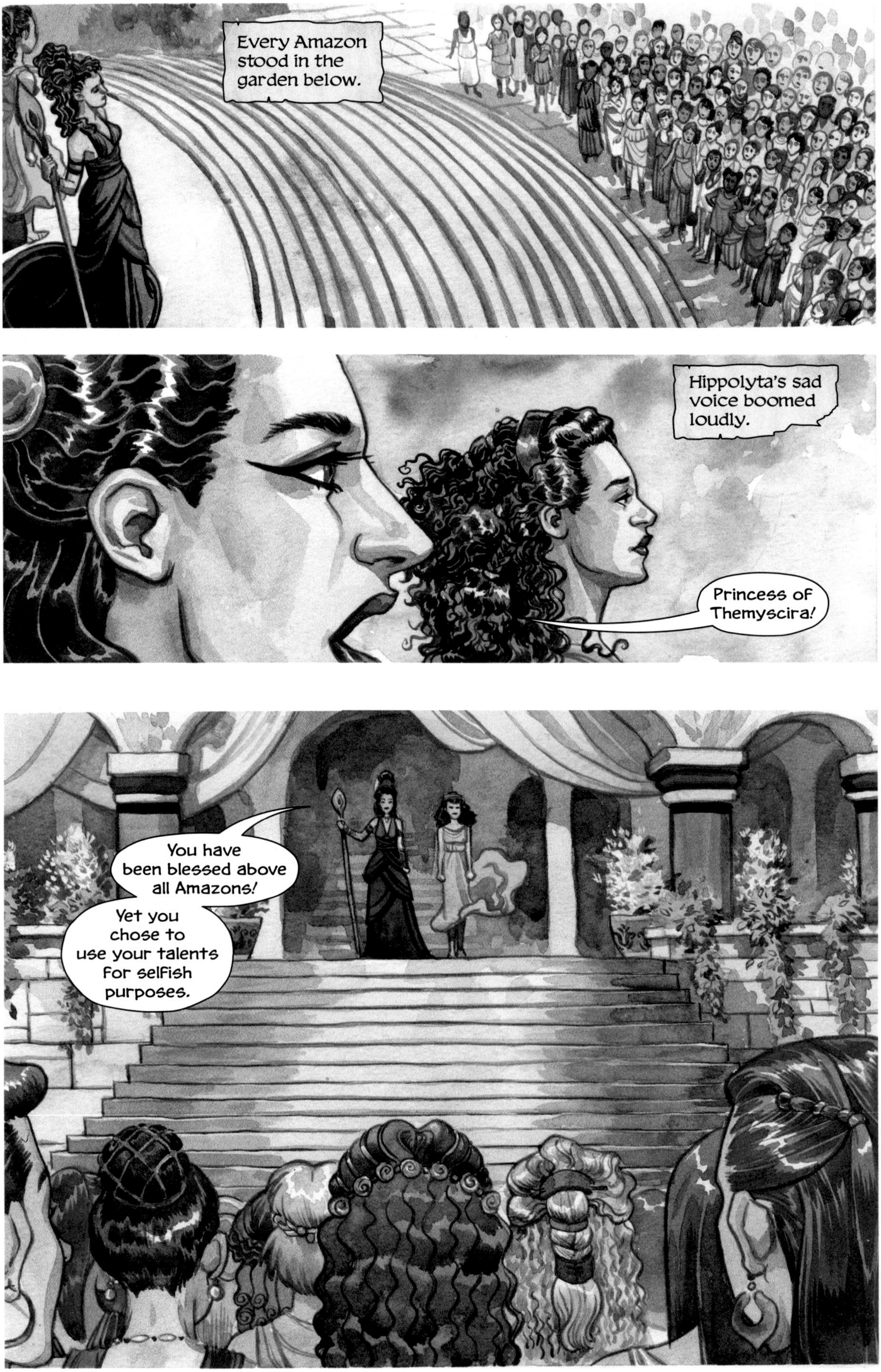
Every Amazon stood in the garden below.
Hippolyta's sad voice boomed loudly.
Princess of Themyscira!
You have been blessed above all Amazons!
Yet you chose to use your talents for selfish purposes.

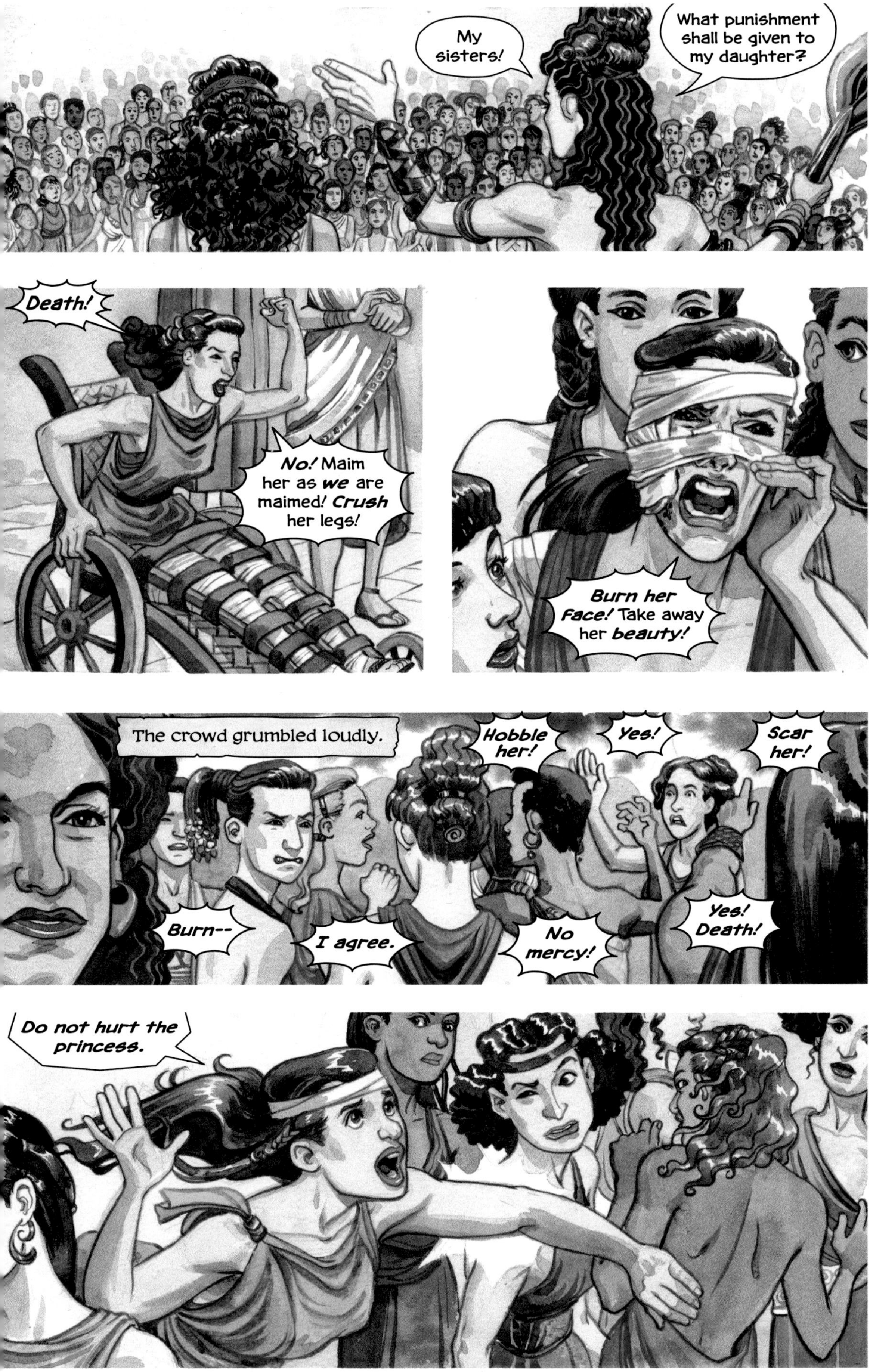
My sisters!
What punishment shall be given to my daughter?
Death!
No! Maim her as we are maimed! Crush her legs!
Burn her face! Take away her beauty!
The crowd grumbled loudly.
Hobble her!
Yes!
Scar her!
Burn--
I agree.
No mercy!
Yes! Death!
Do not hurt the princess.

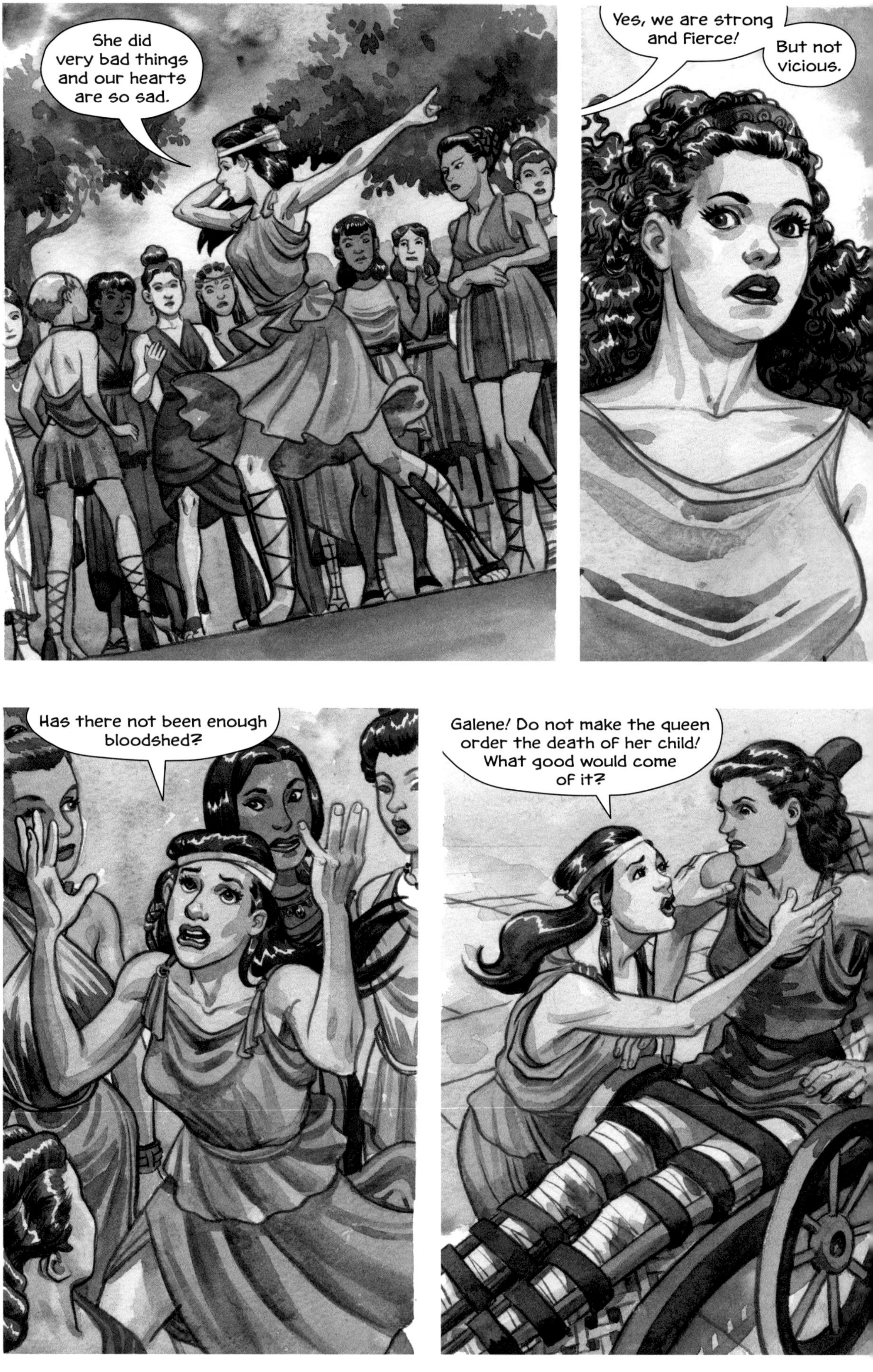
She did very bad things and our hearts are so sad.
Yes, we are strong and fierce!
But not vicious.
Has there not been enough bloodshed?
Galene! Do not make the queen order the death of her child! What good would come of it?

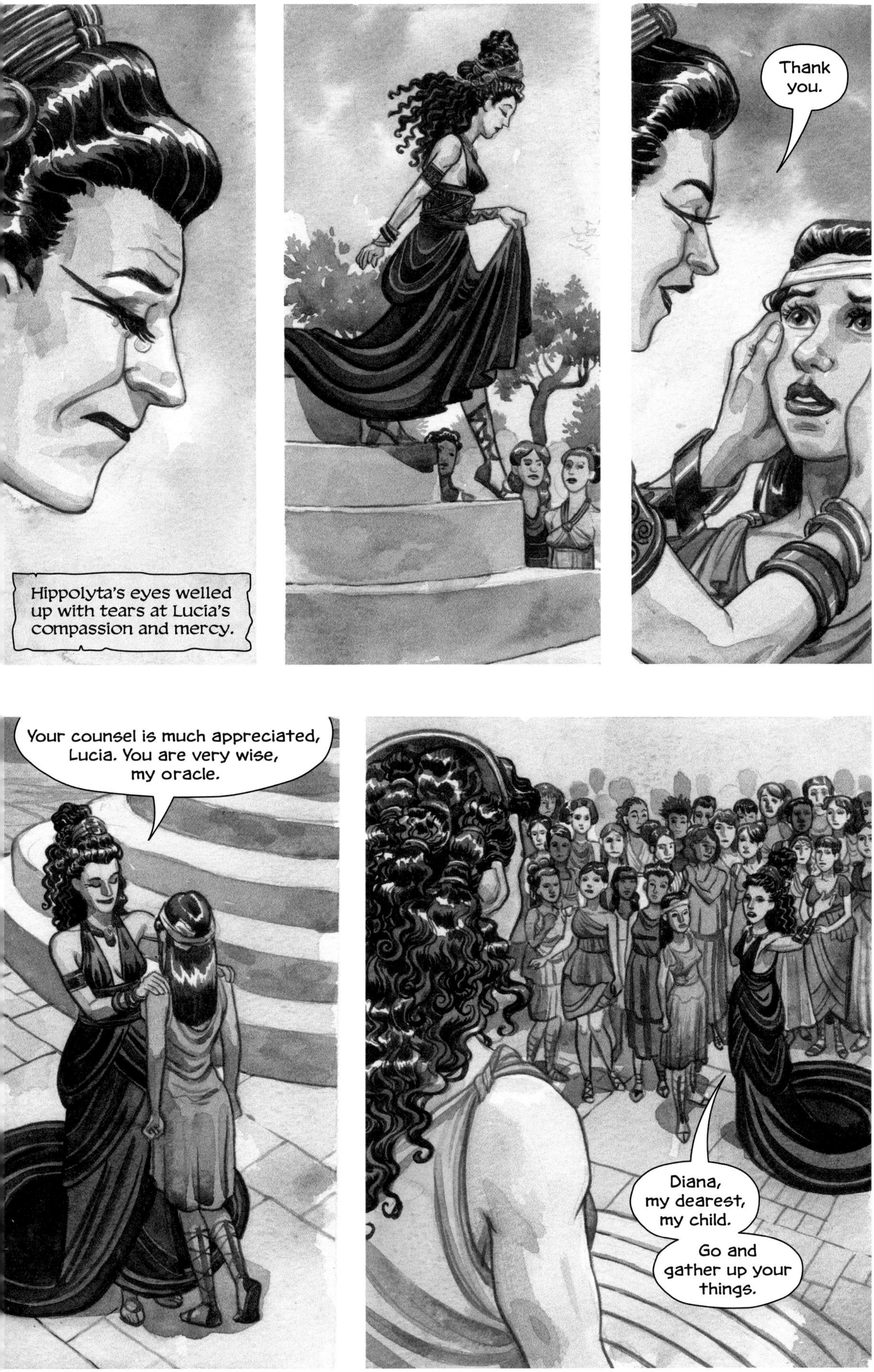
Hippolyta's eyes welled up with tears at Lucia's compassion and mercy.
Thank you.
Your counsel is much appreciated, Lucia. You are very wise, my oracle.
Diana, my dearest, my child.
Go and gather up your things.

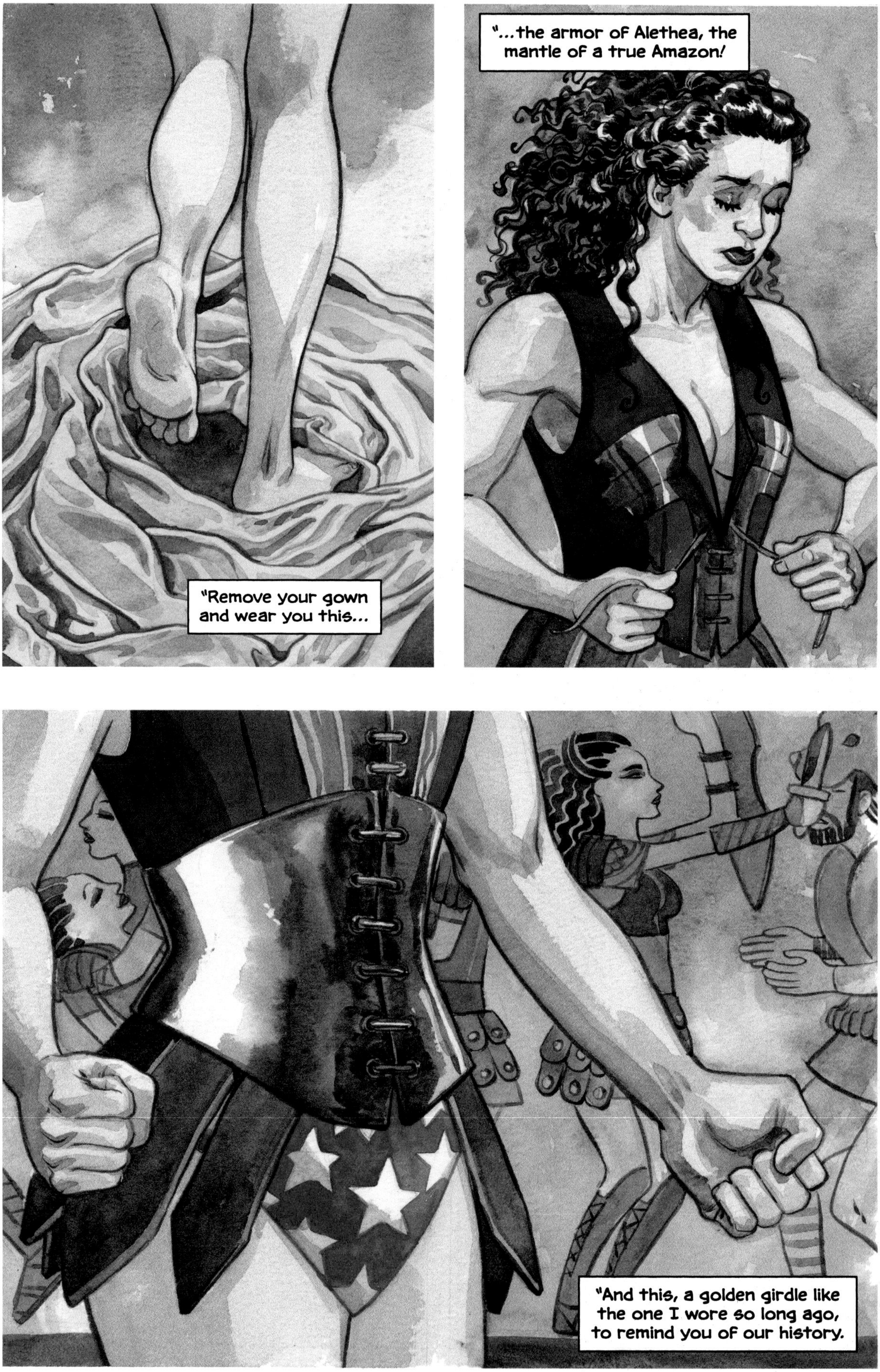
"Remove your gown and wear you this...
"...the armor of Alethea, the mantle of a true Amazon!
"And this, a golden girdle like the one I wore so long ago, to remind you of our history.

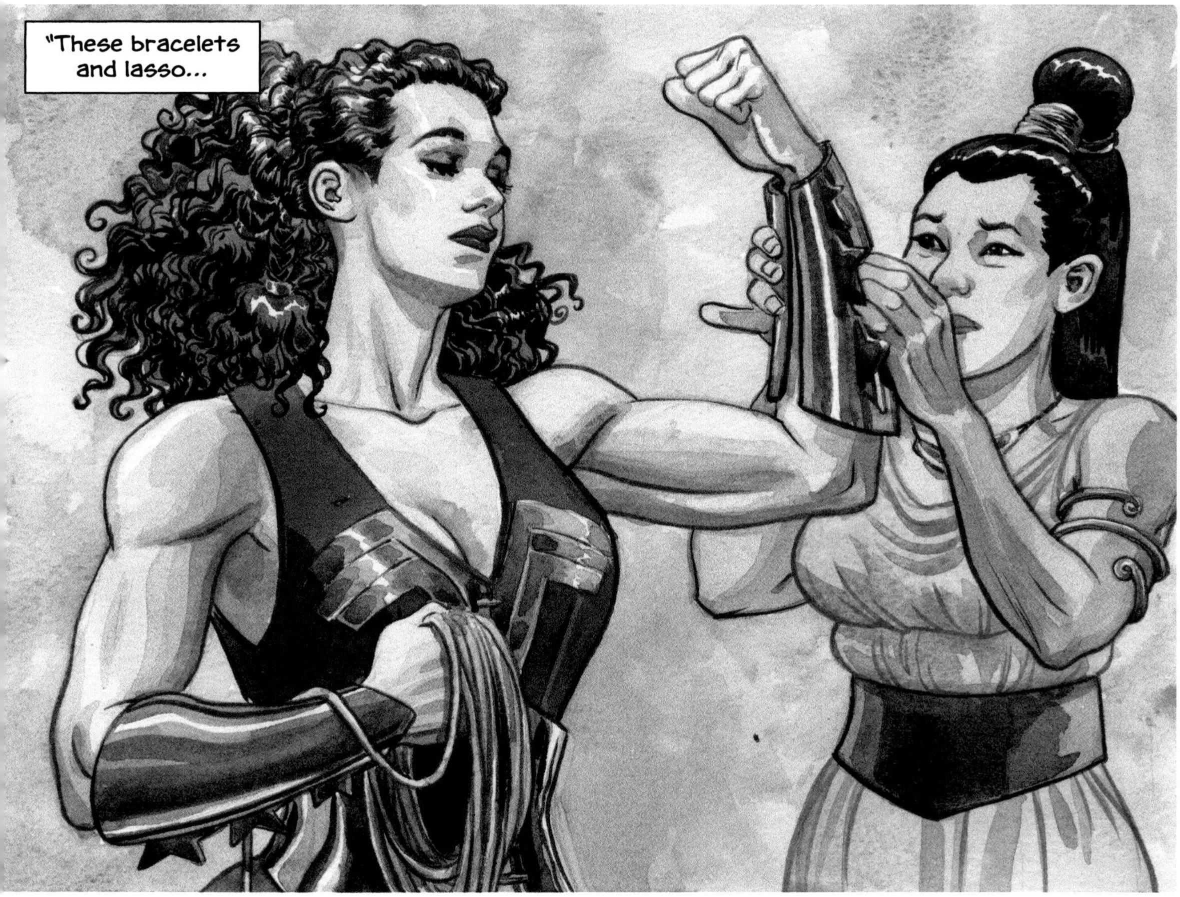
"These bracelets and lasso...

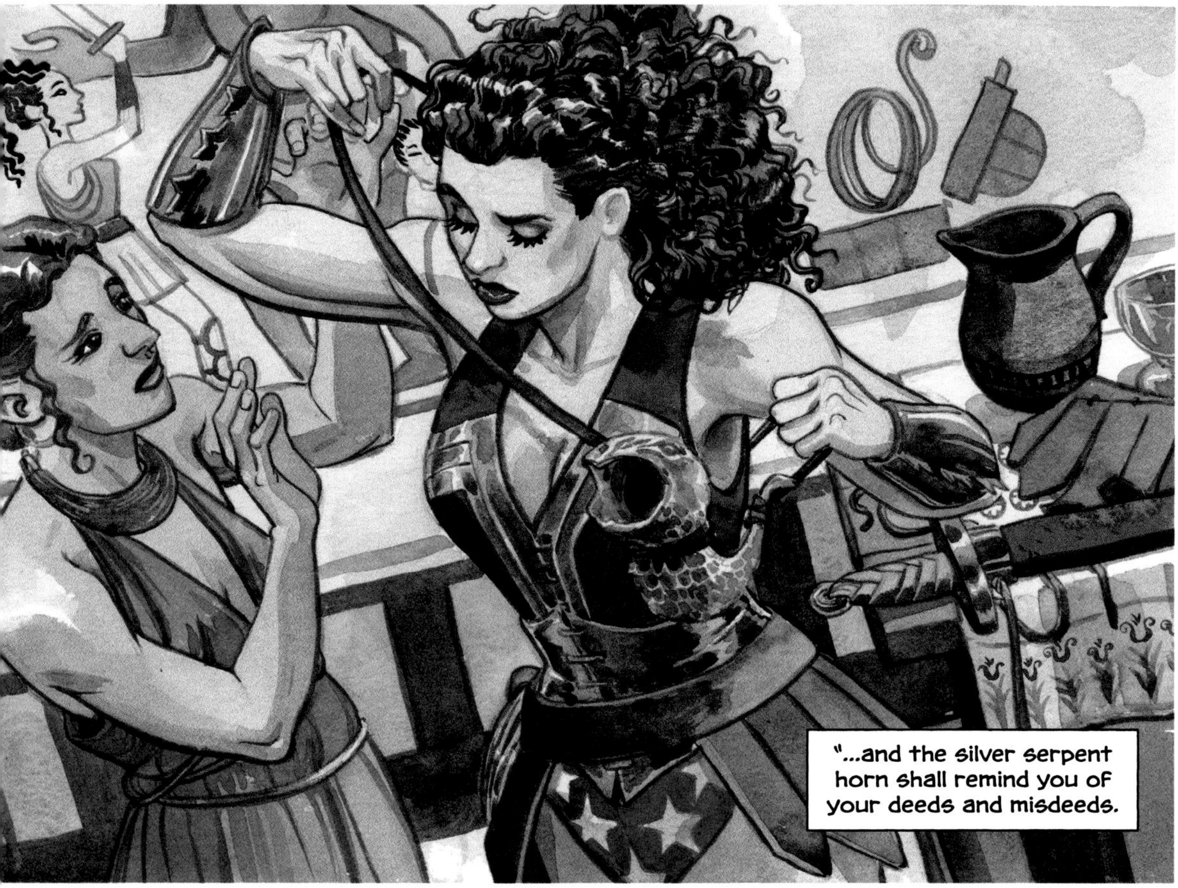
"...and the silver serpent horn shall remind you of your deeds and misdeeds.

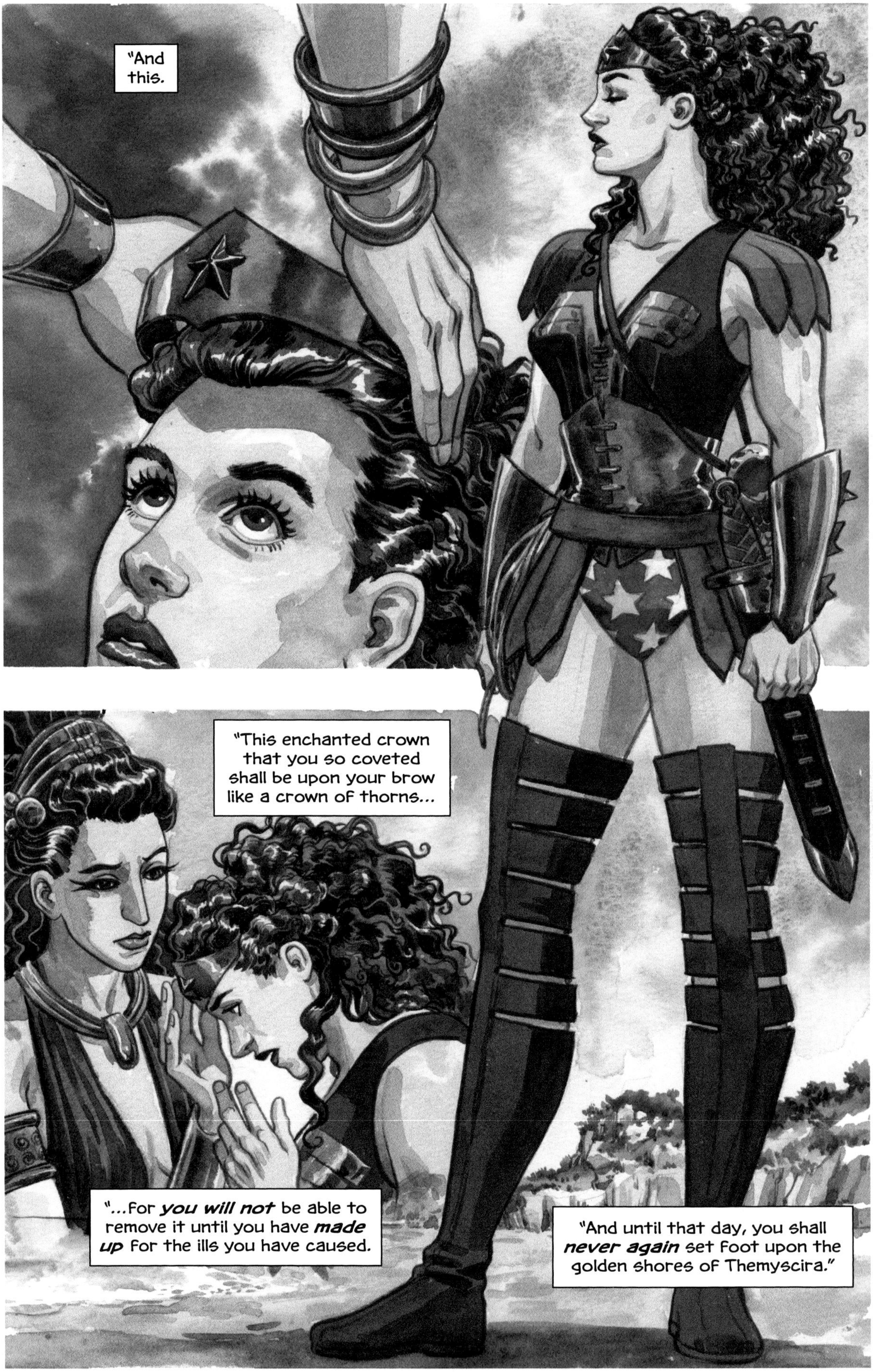
"And this.
"This enchanted crown that you so coveted shall be upon your brow like a crown of thorns...
"...for ***you will not*** be able to remove it until you have ***made up*** for the ills you have caused.
"And until that day, you shall ***never again*** set foot upon the golden shores of Themyscira."

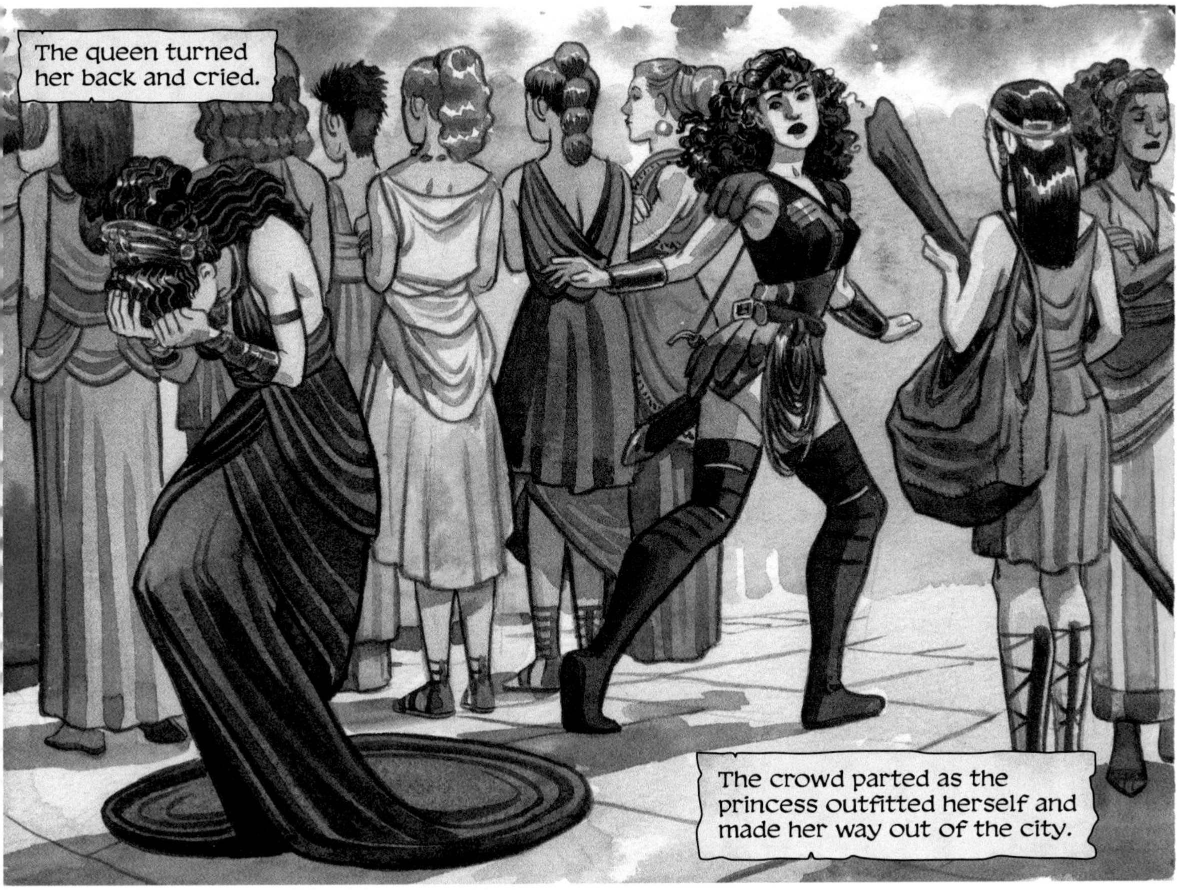
The queen turned her back and cried.
The crowd parted as the princess outfitted herself and made her way out of the city.

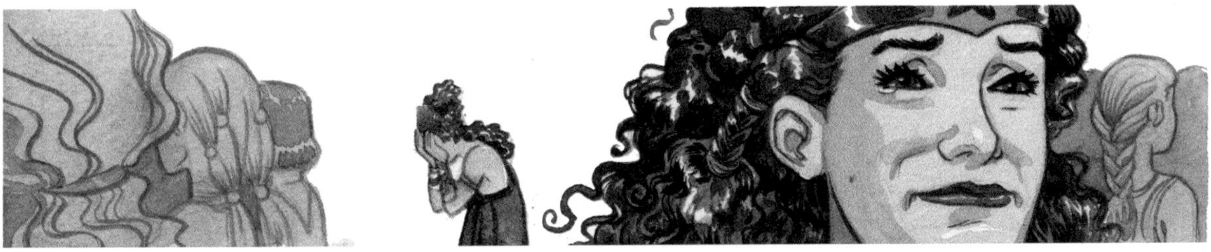

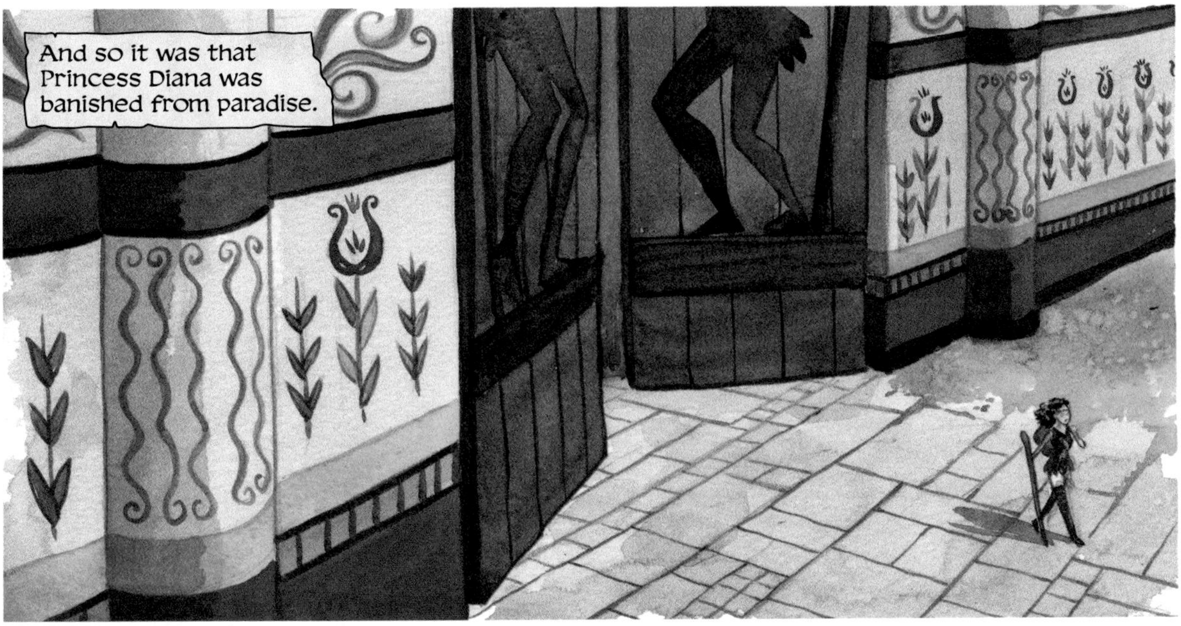
And so it was that Princess Diana was banished from paradise.

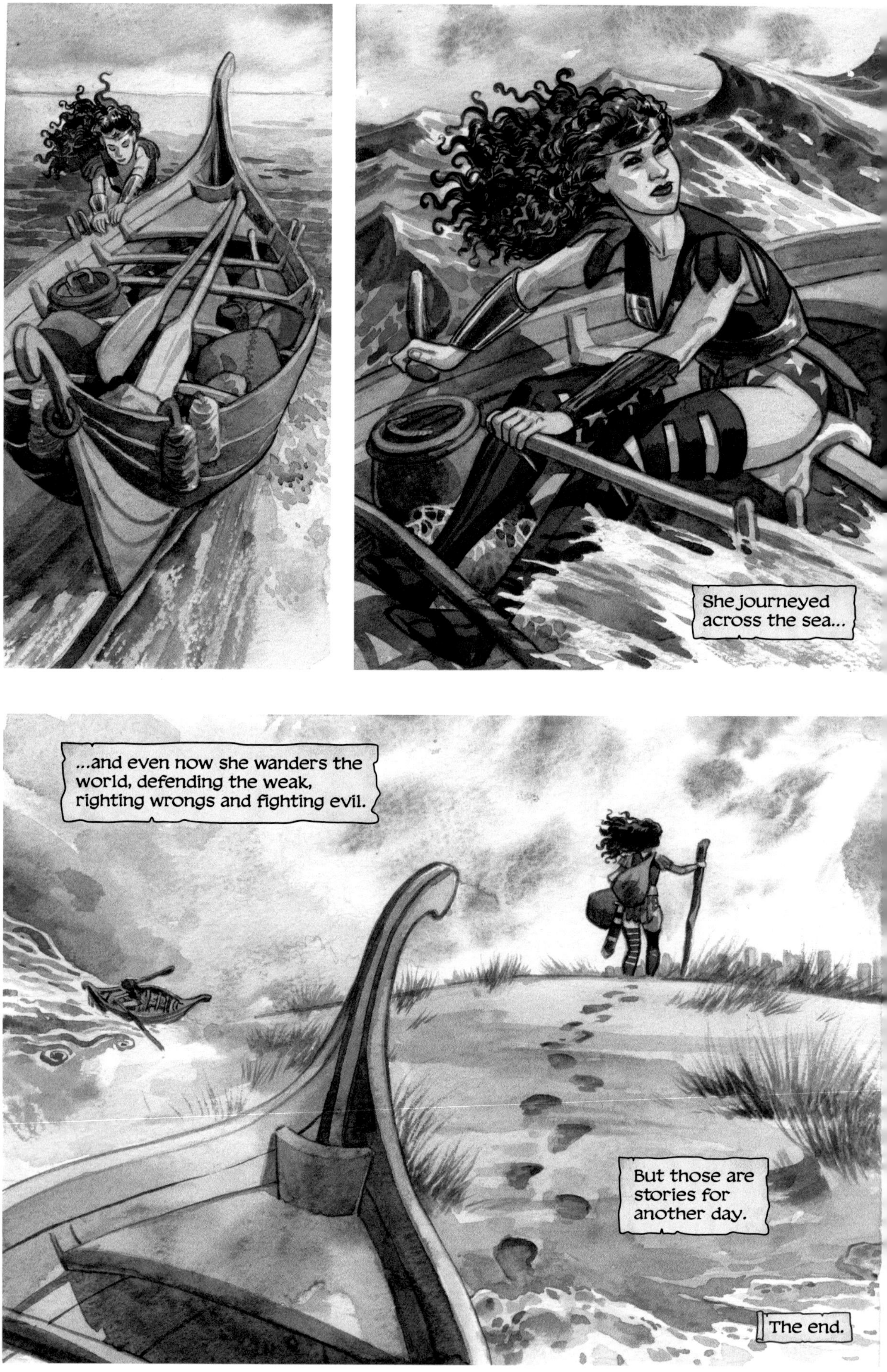
She journeyed across the sea...
...and even now she wanders the world, defending the weak, righting wrongs and fighting evil.
But those are stories for another day.
The end.

SKETCHBOOK

The following pages represent a behind-the-scenes look at my character design and painting process. So much happens in my mind while working on the page. There's a lot of improv that enters into my process, but it's all based on building blocks like these.

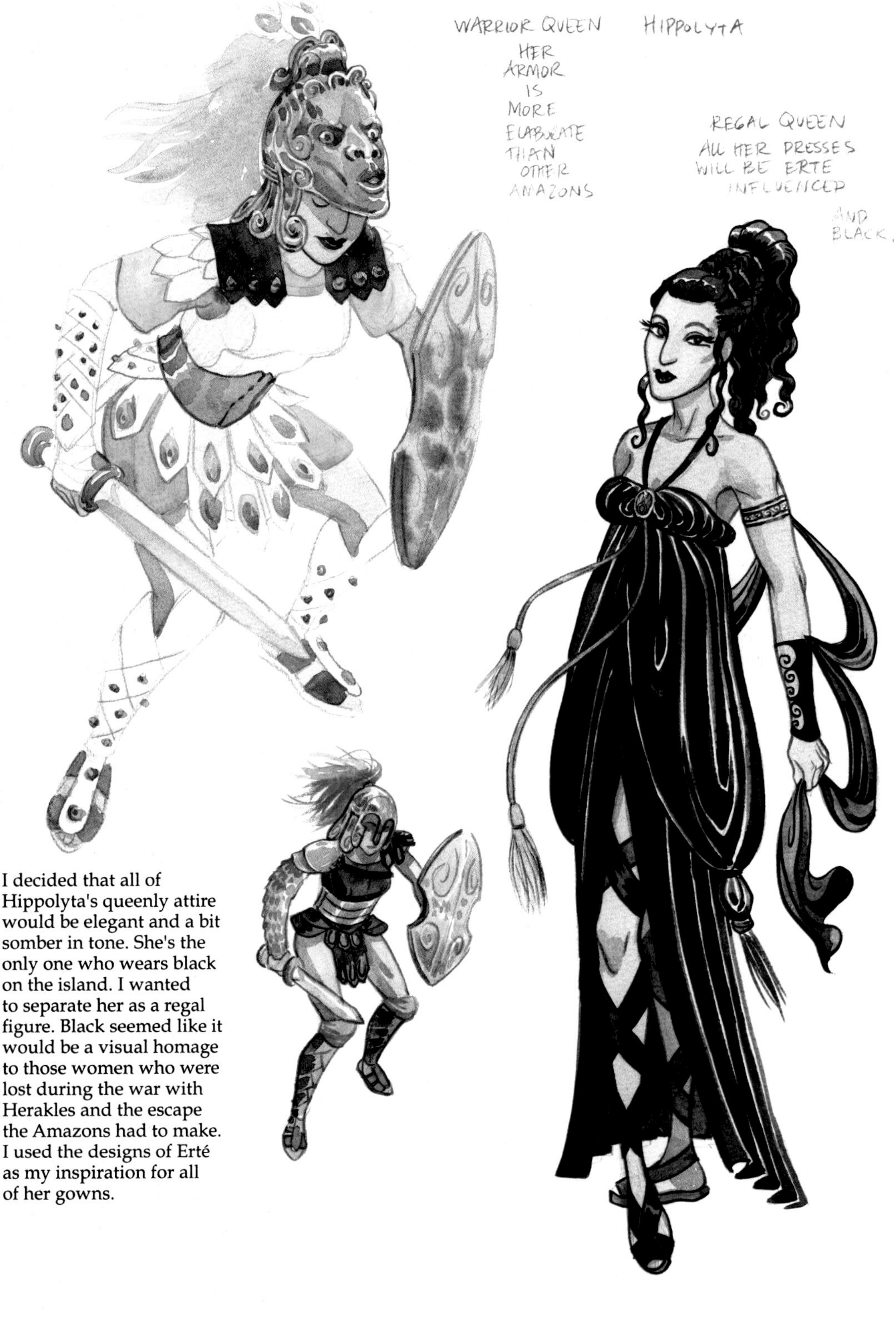

WARRIOR QUEEN
HER ARMOR IS MORE ELABORATE THAN OTHER AMAZONS
HIPPOLYTA
REGAL QUEEN
ALL HER DRESSES WILL BE ERTE INFLUENCED
AND BLACK.

I decided that all of Hippolyta's queenly attire would be elegant and a bit somber in tone. She's the only one who wears black on the island. I wanted to separate her as a regal figure. Black seemed like it would be a visual homage to those women who were lost during the war with Herakles and the escape the Amazons had to make. I used the designs of Erté as my inspiration for all of her gowns.

CREATING THE BOOK COVER

I teach comic book storytelling one day a week. One thing I always tell my students is "When I ask for thumbnail cover designs, make sure every cover is one you'd want to illustrate. If you have to send in five designs but you only have four that you really like and one that you just cranked out to get it done, even though you really don't like it much, guess what happens? Inevitably the art director will choose the one you hate. It just happens that way."

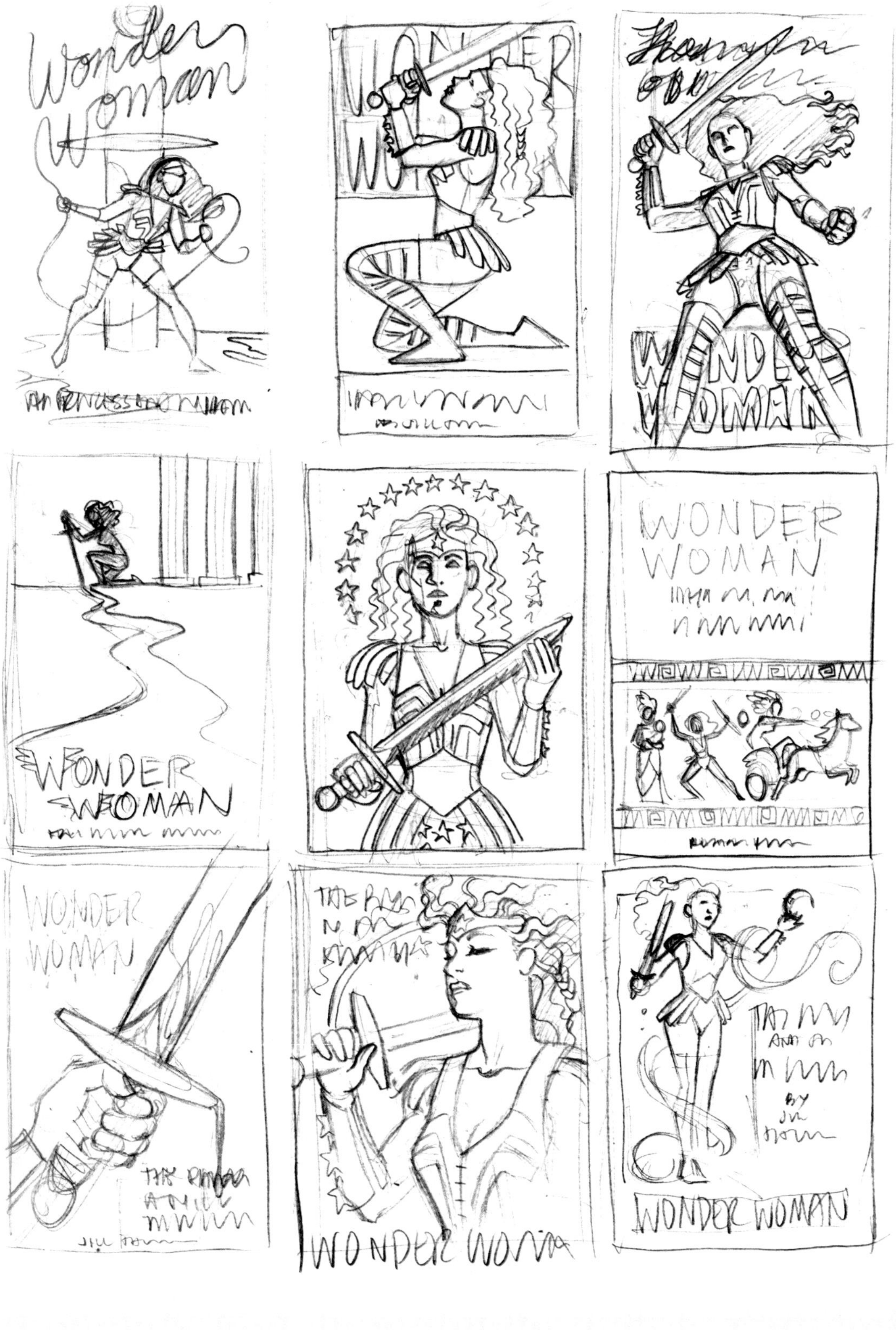

Wonder Woman
WONDER WOMAN
WONDER WOMAN
WONDER WOMAN
WONDER WOMAN
BY
WONDER WOMAN

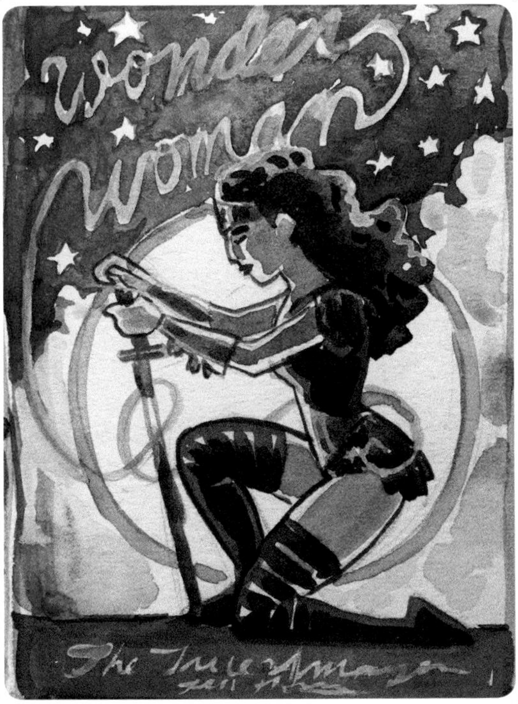
Wonder
Woman
The True Amazon

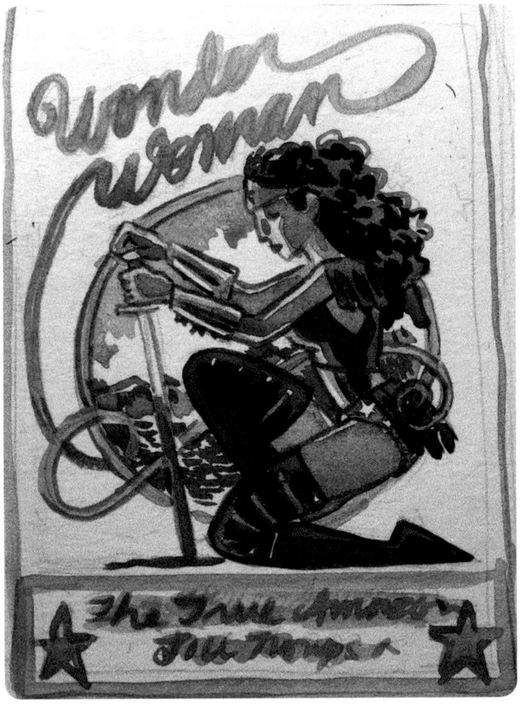
Wonder
Woman
The True Amazon

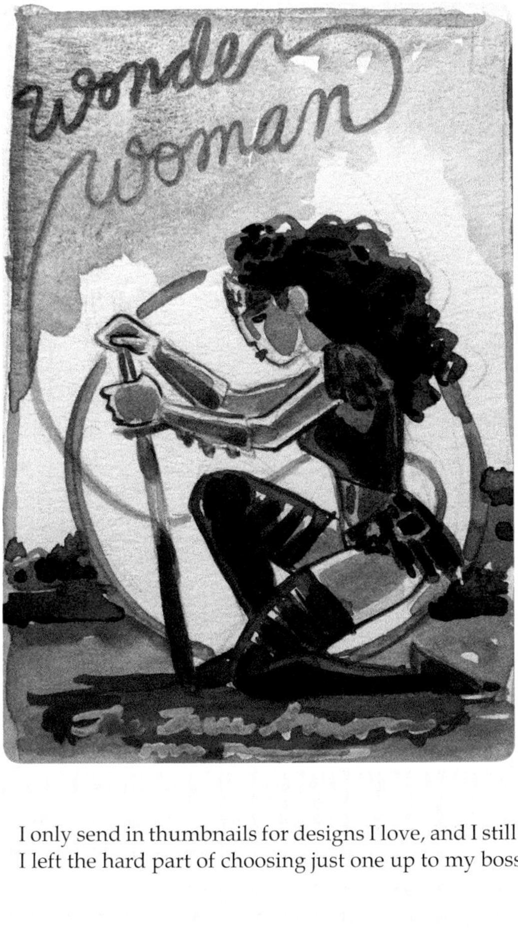
Wonder
Woman

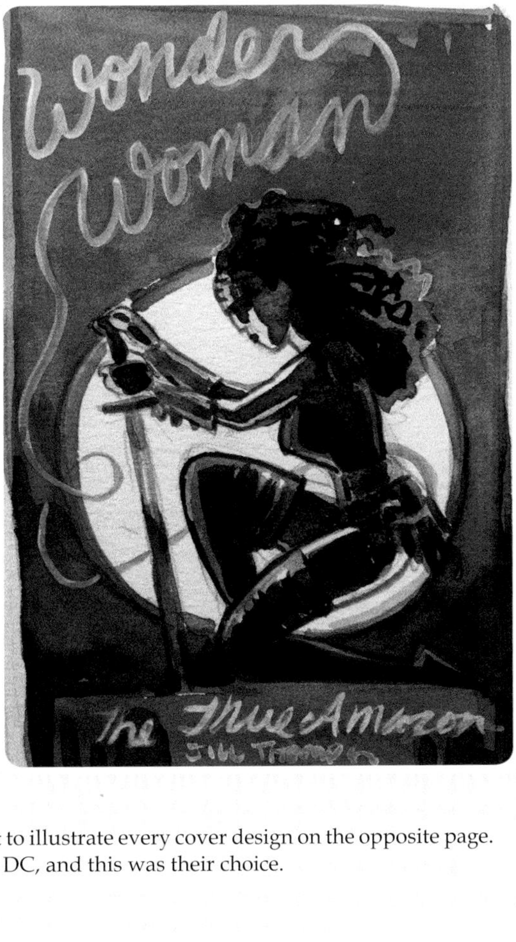
Wonder
Woman
The True Amazon

I only send in thumbnails for designs I love, and I still want to illustrate every cover design on the opposite page. I left the hard part of choosing just one up to my bosses at DC, and this was their choice.

FROM PENCILS TO COLOR

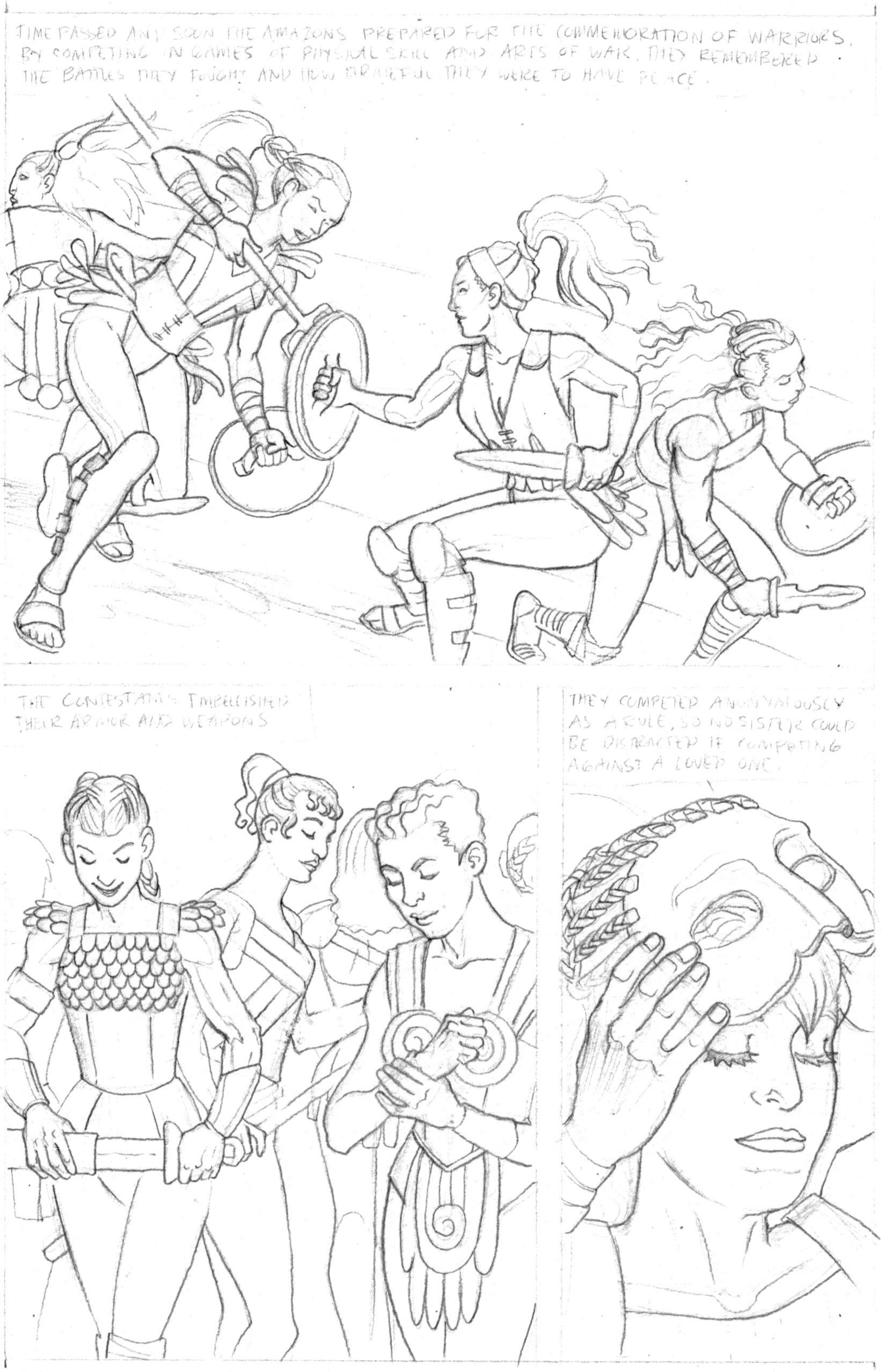

TIME PASSED AND SOON THE AMAZONS PREPARED FOR THE COMMEMORATION OF WARRIORS. BY COMPETING IN GAMES OF PHYSICAL SKILL AND ARTS OF WAR, THEY REMEMBERED THE BATTLES THEY FOUGHT AND HOW GRATEFUL THEY WERE TO HAVE PEACE.
THE CONTESTANTS EMBELLISHED THEIR ARMOR AND WEAPONS
THEY COMPETED ANONYMOUSLY AS A RULE, SO NO SISTER COULD BE DISTRACTED IF COMPETING AGAINST A LOVED ONE.

FROM PENCILS TO COLOR

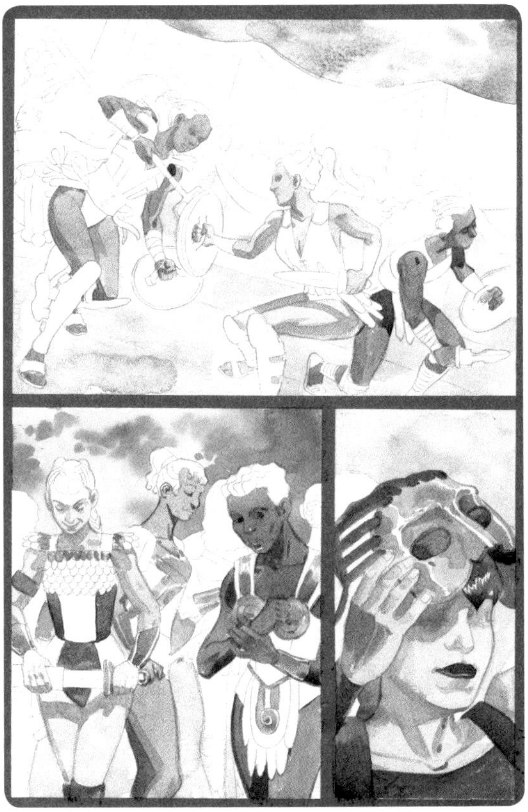

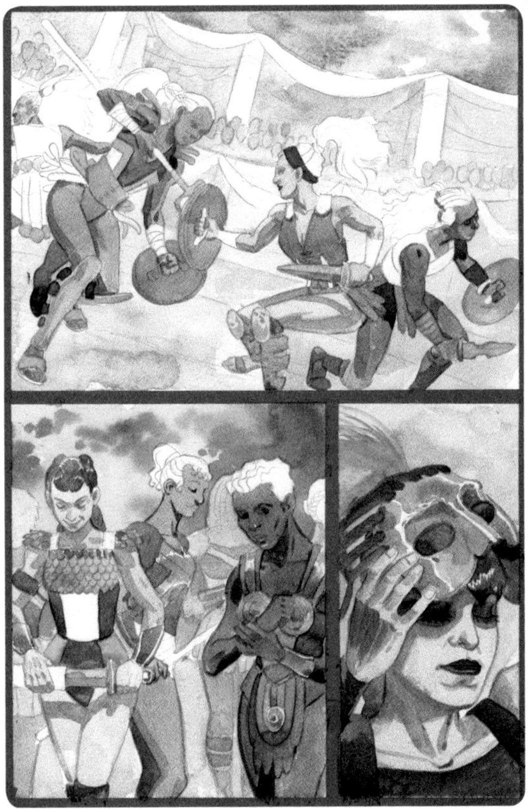

People always ask me how I create a comics page. It's definitely a labor of love. After I settle on the thumbnail design, I lightly sketch out the page and physically block in all the lettering. This tells me approximately how much space the lettering will take up before letterer Jason Arthur even starts to work on it. It also allows me control over how the reader digests the dialogue and acting on the page. Coupled with the art, lettering placement helps to create dramatic pauses, drama, humor, etc. The next step is to scan the pages. Then I go back and erase the lettering and darken the pencils just enough that I can paint from them. After that, I cut painter's tape and tape off all the gutters and panel borders to keep a crisp edge. The final step is the painting itself, and that part can take from 10 to 14 hours. There is no India ink on these pages; anything that looks like inking is actually a darker watercolor line based on the color of the item it surrounds. Green on foliage, brown on a horse or table, etc. As Mike Mignola once said, "You draw comics with paint more than you paint comics in a traditional painterly manner." And he was right on the money. I like how this looks for the comics medium. For other types of painting, I paint in a more traditional manner. But I find this serves my comics storytelling in the best possible way.

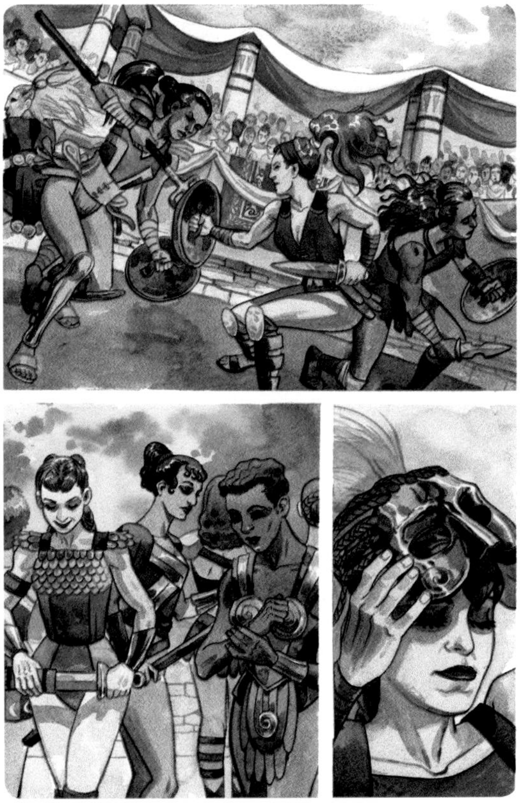

FROM PENCILS TO COLOR

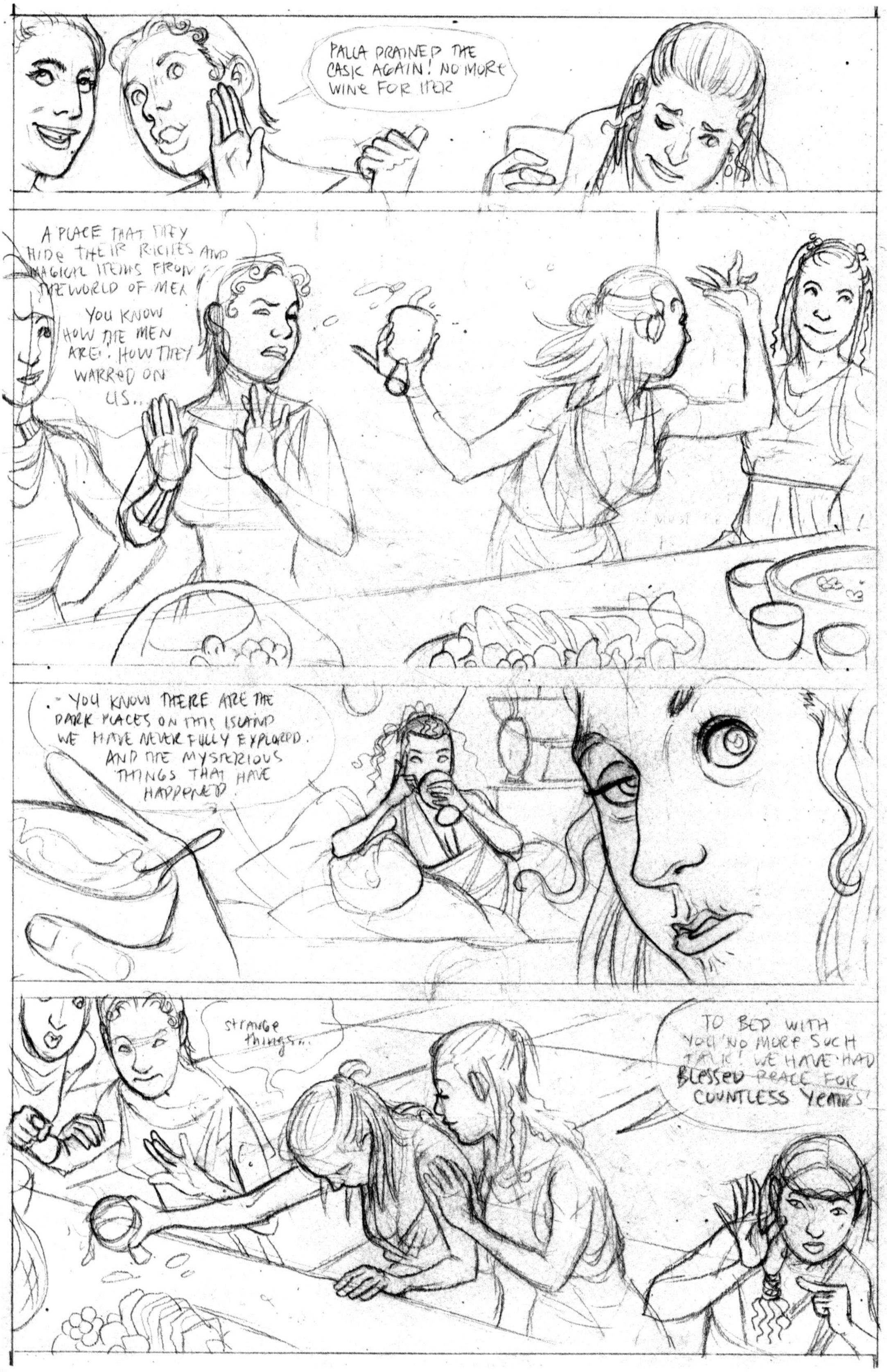
PALLA DRAINED THE CASK AGAIN! NO MORE WINE FOR HER
A PLACE THAT THEY HIDE THEIR RICHES AND MAGICAL ITEMS FROM THE WORLD OF MEN
YOU KNOW HOW THE MEN ARE! HOW THEY WARRED ON US...
...YOU KNOW THERE ARE THE DARK PLACES ON THIS ISLAND WE HAVE NEVER FULLY EXPLORED. AND THE MYSTERIOUS THINGS THAT HAVE HAPPENED!
strange things...
TO BED WITH YOU! NO MORE SUCH TALK! WE HAVE HAD BLESSED PEACE FOR COUNTLESS YEARS!

FROM PENCILS TO COLOR

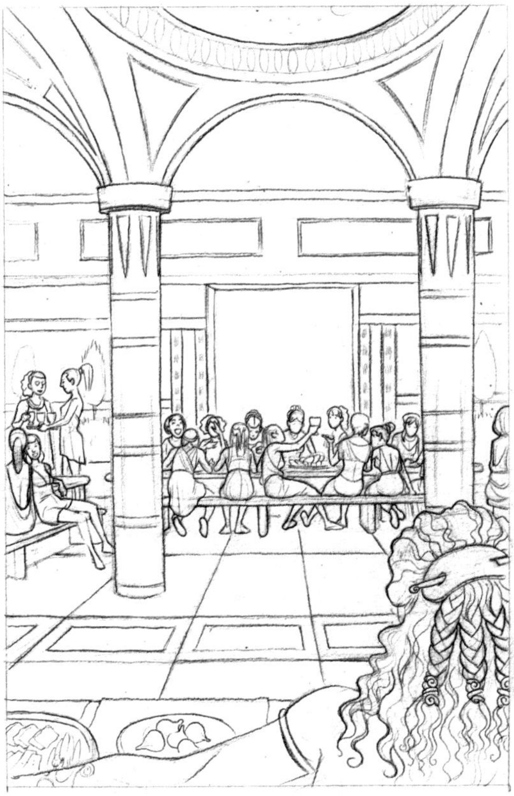

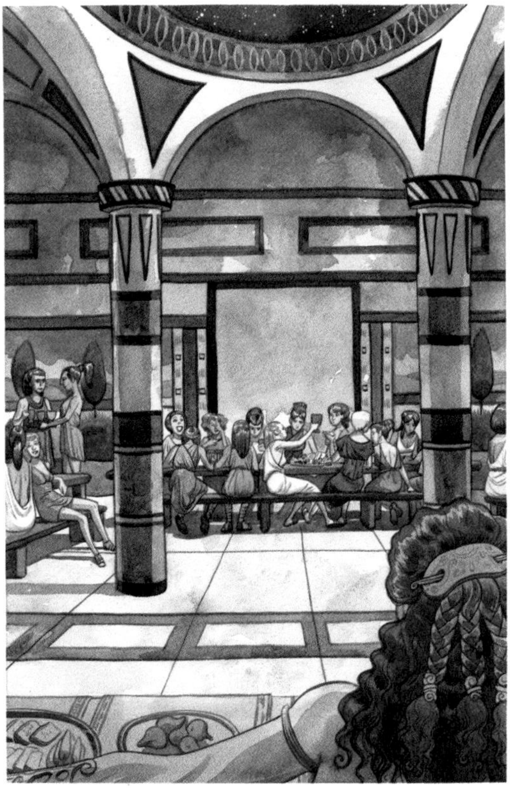

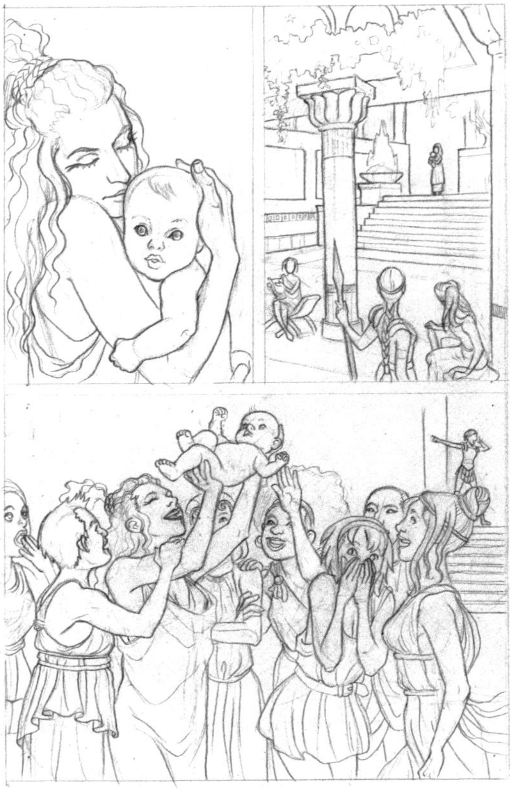

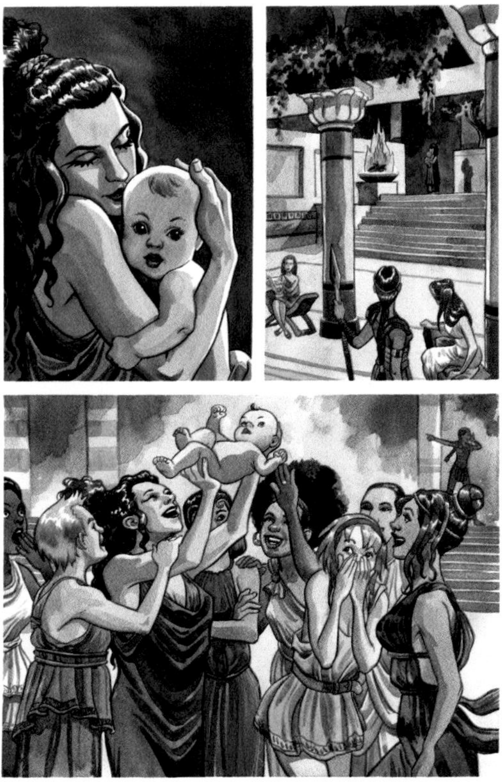

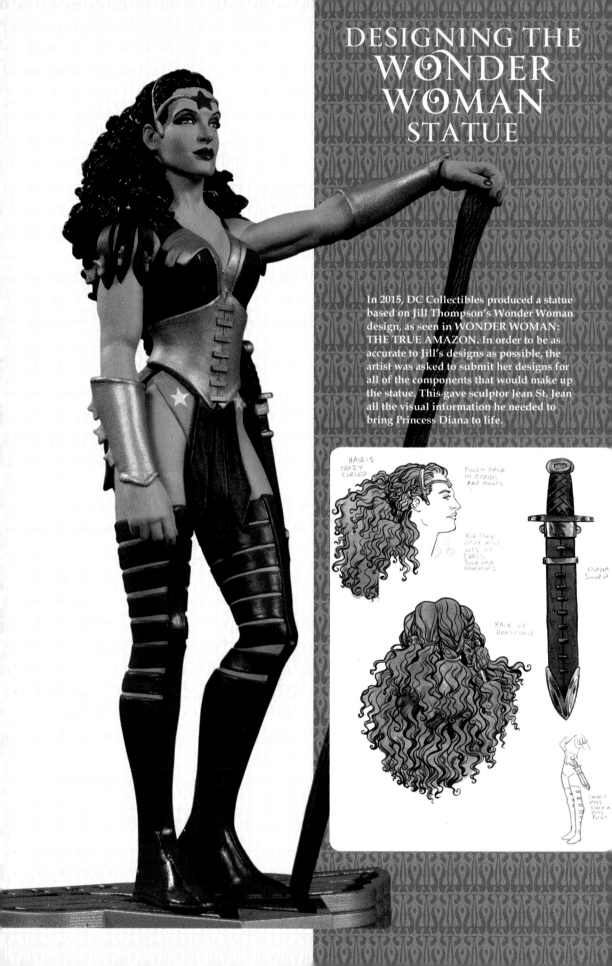

DESIGNING THE WONDER WOMAN STATUE

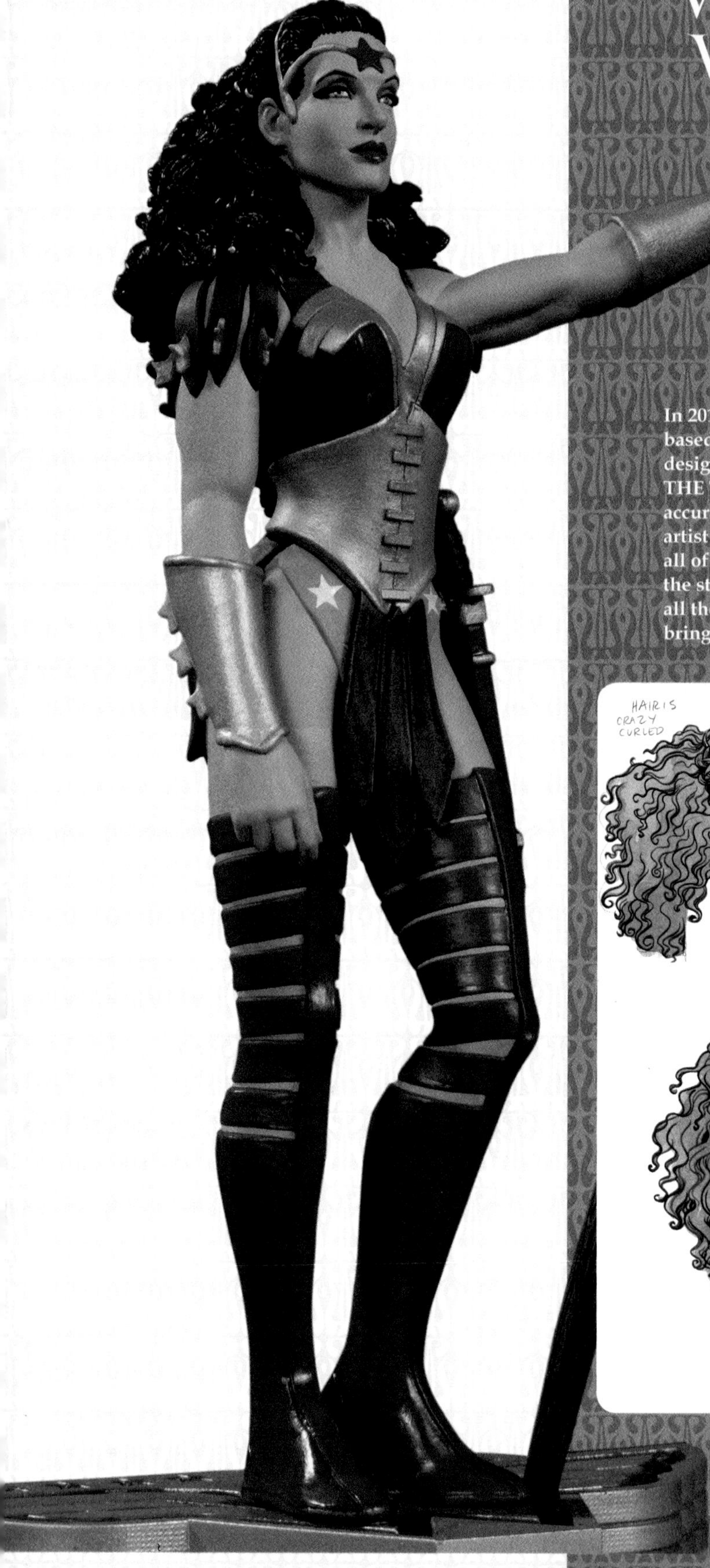

In 2015, DC Collectibles produced a statue based on Jill Thompson's Wonder Woman design, as seen in WONDER WOMAN: THE TRUE AMAZON. In order to be as accurate to Jill's designs as possible, the artist was asked to submit her designs for all of the components that would make up the statue. This gave sculptor Jean St. Jean all the visual information he needed to bring Princess Diana to life.

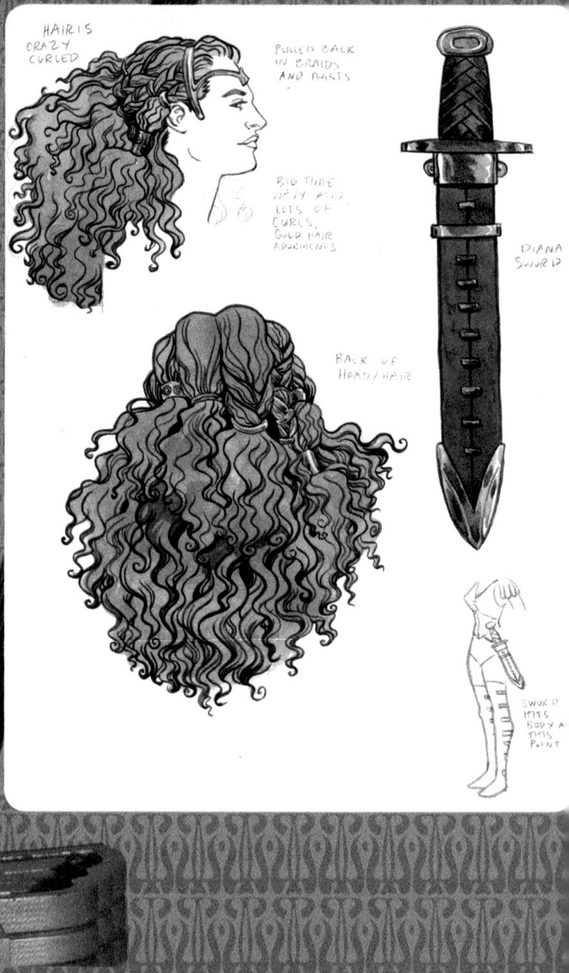
HAIR IS CRAZY CURLED
PULLED BACK IN BRAIDS AND TWISTS
BIG TIME WAVY AND LOTS OF CURLS, GOLD HAIR ADORNMENTS
DIANA SWORD
BACK OF HEAD / HAIR
SWORD HITS BODY A THIS POINT

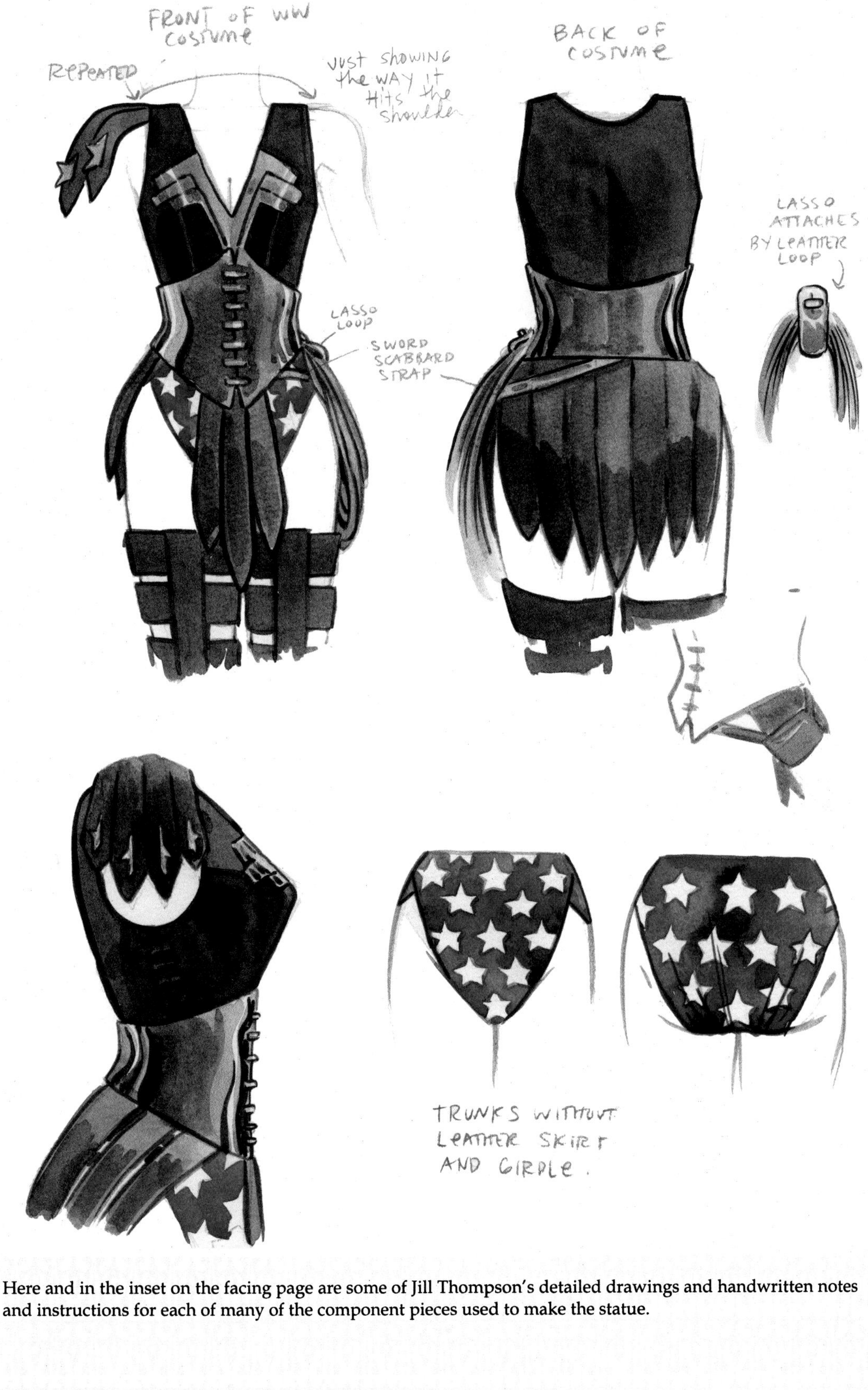
FRONT OF WW COSTUME
REPEATED
JUST SHOWING the WAY it Hits the shoulder
BACK OF COSTUME
LASSO ATTACHES BY LEATHER LOOP
LASSO LOOP
SWORD SCABBARD STRAP
TRUNKS WITHOUT LEATHER SKIRT AND GIRDLE.

Here and in the inset on the facing page are some of Jill Thompson's detailed drawings and handwritten notes and instructions for each of many of the component pieces used to make the statue.

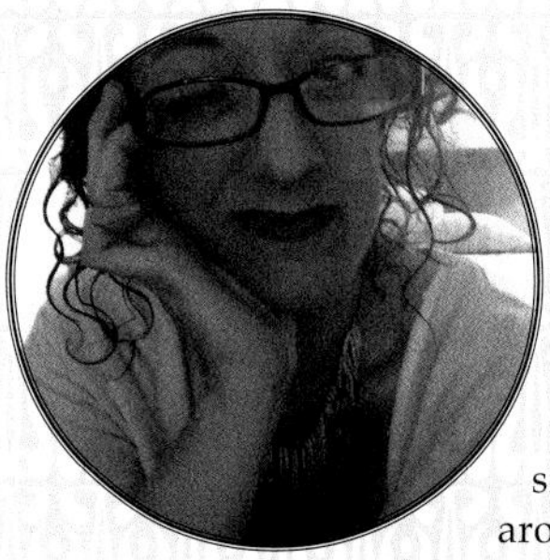

JILL THOMPSON

is a graduate of The American Academy of Art in Chicago. She has been working professionally as a comic book creator since she was a teenager and her work has been published around the world. She is the creator of The Scary Godmother, which has graced comics, stage and screen, as well as the graphic novel series for younger readers, *Magic Trixie*. Jill considers herself fortunate to have collaborated on comics such as WONDER WOMAN, SANDMAN, THE INVISIBLES, FINALS, *Beasts of Burden*, and many, many more.

Jill is the proud recipient of 7 Eisner Awards. She loves creating comics and has no plans of stopping anytime soon.

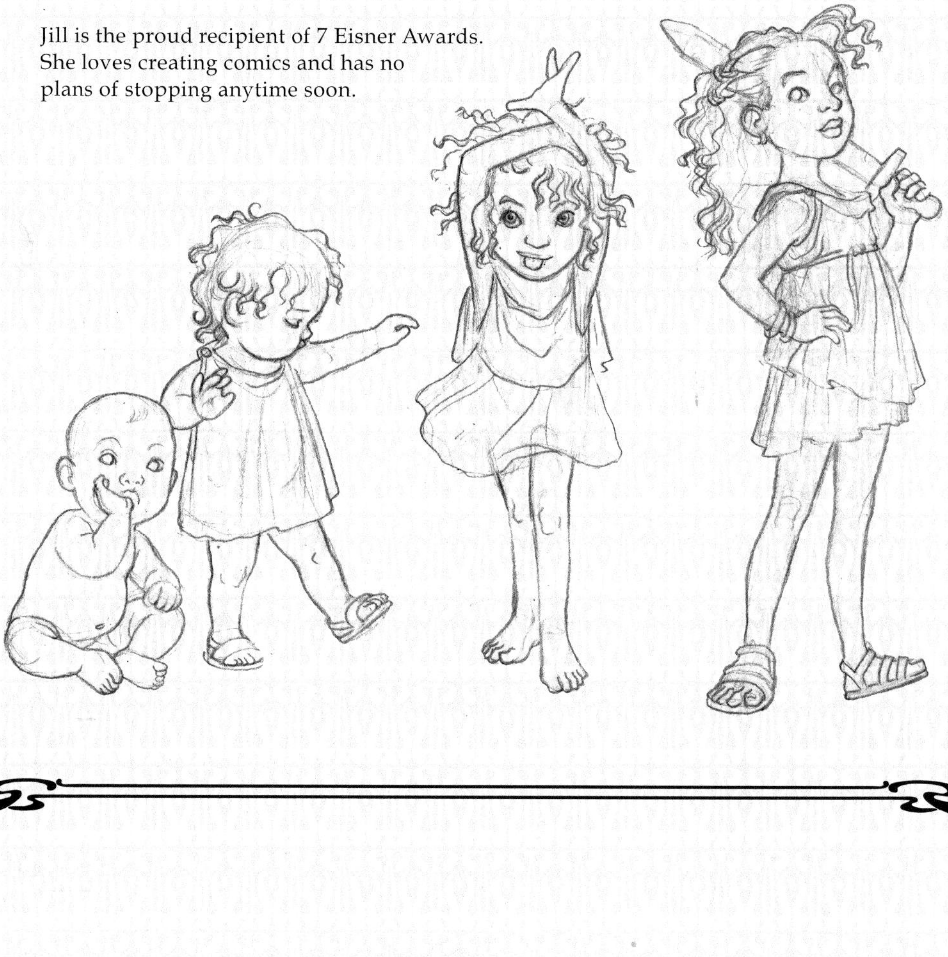

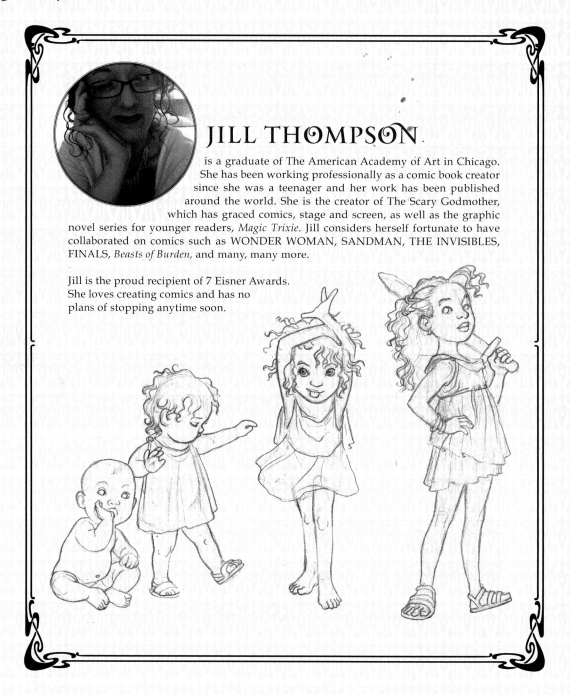